'This exciting collection offers an perspective on teaching and learning those who teach in universities – and significantly from the many new insights it provides.'

Chris James, Professor of Educational Leadership and Management, University of Bath

'An important addition to the growing literature exploring interactions between the social and physical dimensions of learning in higher education. The authors are experienced teachers who have located their own practical experiences within conceptual ideas about space and learning, and the resulting case studies powerfully convey this integration of theory and practice.'

Paul Temple, Honorary Associate Professor, Centre for Higher Education Studies, UCL Institute of Education

'In a busy world, where control and even surveillance are not far away, the matter of learning space becomes critical if higher education is to fulfil its responsibilities. *Reframing Space for Learning* takes these considerations seriously and opens windows into spacious forms of teaching. Through accessible chapters, the voices of students, diagrams and photographs, multiple spaces are not just depicted, but are here created. This lively and optimistic text demonstrates that new kinds of education are possible in universities. On the evidence here, the university still harbours spaces, and of many kinds.'

Ronald Barnett, Emeritus Professor of Higher Education, UCL Institute of Education

Reframing Space for Learning

Reframing Space for Learning
Excellence and Innovation in University Teaching

Edited by Tim Bilham, Claire Hamshire, Mary Hartog with Martina A. Doolan

IOE Press

First published in 2019 by the UCL Institute of Education Press, 20 Bedford Way, London WC1H 0AL

www.ucl-ioe-press.com

©2019 Tim Bilham, Claire Hamshire, Mary Hartog and Martina A. Doolan

British Library Cataloguing in Publication Data:
A catalogue record for this publication is available from the British Library

ISBNs
978-1-78277-246-0 (paperback)
978-1-78277-296-5 (PDF eBook)
978-1-78277-297-2 (ePub eBook)
978-1-78277-298-9 (Kindle eBook)

All rights reserved. No part of this publication may be reproduced, stored in a retrieval system, or transmitted in any form or by any means, electronic, mechanical, photocopying, recording or otherwise, without the prior permission of the copyright owner.

Every effort has been made to trace copyright holders and to obtain their permission for the use of copyright material. The publisher apologizes for any errors or omissions and would be grateful if notified of any corrections that should be incorporated in future reprints or editions of this book.

The opinions expressed in this publication are those of the contributors and do not necessarily reflect the views of the UCL Institute of Education.

Typeset by Quadrant Infotech (India) Pvt Ltd
Printed and bound by CPI Group (UK) Ltd, Croydon, CR0 4YY

Cover: © Jacob Lund/Shutterstock.com

Contents

List of illustrations — x

List of abbreviations — xiii

About the contributors — xv

Acknowledgements — xxv

How to use this book — xxvi

Foreword — xxviii
Becky Huxley-Binns

Introduction: Reframing spaces for learning — xxx
Tim Bilham

PART 1 PLACES OF LEARNING, SPACES FOR LEARNING

1. Beyond the walls: Learning and the importance of place — 2
   Tim Bilham

2. Authentic learning through place-based education — 12
   Derek France, Alice Mauchline, Brian Whalley, Martina A. Doolan and Tim Bilham

3. *Crossin' the Bridge*: Learning in community places — 29
   Tess Maginess and Tim Bilham

4. Moveable feasts: Unusual learning in unexpected spaces — 41
   Alison James

5. Creative learning spaces: Facilitating student-led learning — 53
   Carrie Winstanley and Kirsten Hardie

6. Making learning spaces: Working with architects and estates — 67
   Ingrid Murphy, Gareth Thomson, Kevin Singh and Tim Bilham

PART 2 SPACES FOR THE SELF

7. Borderland spaces: Moving towards self-authorship — 88
   Jennifer Hill, Helen Walkington and Pauline Kneale

8. Space for the self: Creating my academic identity — 102
   Mary Hartog

9. Creating space for the self: Thinking differently — 113
   Celia Hunt

10. Space for belonging: Induction and beyond — 124
    Ruth Matheson and Mark Sutcliffe

11. Spaces for performance: Becoming a professional — 137
    Laura Ritchie and Ben Hall

12. Recognizing the interior and relational spaces of workplace learning — 147
    Ruth Helyer, Philip Frame and Mary Hartog

PART 3 SOCIAL AND COLLABORATIVE SPACES

13. Live projects: Collaborative learning in and with authentic spaces — 161
    Jane Anderson

14. Collaborative and reflective spaces for developing professional practitioners — 174
    Claire Hamshire, Deborah O'Connor and Kirsten Jack

15. Reframing spaces for staff learning — 185
    Joy Jarvis and Rebecca Thomas

16. Towards a learning landscape: The potential for technologies to create social learning spaces — 199
    Peter Klappa, Simon Lancaster, Helena Gillespie, Claire Hamshire and Tim Bilham

17. Expanding the cross-cultural space: Providing international experiences in the digital global classroom — 209
    Natascha Radclyffe-Thomas, Catherine McDermott and Rachel Forsyth

18. Without walls: Using massive open online courses to extend collaborative learning spaces   224
Momna Hejmadi and Tim Bilham

PART 4 INTEGRATING SPACES

19. Thinking outside the box: Utilizing real-world space in teaching and learning   237
Clive Holtham and Angela Dove

Postscript: Teaching excellence and the NTFS   252
Sally Brown

Index   260

List of illustrations

Figures

2.1	Example data 'spikes' of sampling techniques and field sites using the Geospike app (Image: A.L. Mauchline, 2017; Creative Commons, CC BY-SA 3.0)	16
2.2	The context of use for KASPAR the robot (created by student group 2)	19
2.3	Scenario of parent, child and therapist: KASPAR the robot (created by student group 2)	19
2.4	An interface design to operate KASPAR the robot produced by a student group (created by student group 6)	20
2.5	Screenshot showing the introduction to the virtual clinic scenario (Image: G. Jones)	23
2.6	Participation in virtual clinics from students (n = 17), two tutors and one facilitator (Image: G. Jones)	25
4.1	Curvy bench on campus, University of Winchester (Image: A. James)	47
4.2	Balloon activity, Play and Creativity Festival, University of Winchester (Image: R. Cheetham)	49
5.1	Exhibition information panel and exhibition curation by Nicole Dujardin, Sophie Walker and Elene Edisherashvili (Image: K. Hardie)	61
6.1	CSAD Heart Space and atrium (Image: I. Murphy)	71
6.2	Individual student workspace (Image: I. Murphy)	72
6.3	Breakout space (Image: I. Murphy)	73
6.4	AR interactive tool wall (Image: I. Murphy)	75
6.5	RFID interactive material library (Image: I. Murphy, J. Pigott and A. Taylor, 2017)	76

List of illustrations

6.6	Final pre-production plan of proposed working-space development (Image: ADP Architecture Ltd)	78
6.7	The Den at BCU North Campus (Image: Emphasis Photography)	82
12.1	The articulation cycle (Frame, 2009)	151
13.1	Hoarding installations being used by the community (Image: J. Anderson)	168
15.1	'Going out' picnic baskets displayed in the exhibition (Image: R. Thomas)	190
15.2	The metaphor for learning processes (Image: J. Cooper)	192
15.3	A student response in their visual diary to a learning process card (Image: R. Thomas)	194
18.1	Average number of course comments posted per cohort by active learner type (Image: G. Upton)	227
18.2	Profile of social learner categories (self-identification based on comment posts) (Image: G. Upton)	228
18.3	Example of a wordcloud for cancer sufferers (Image: G. Upton)	229
19.1	Rational and intuitive qualities of management (Holtham, 2011)	238
19.2	Pizza box artefacts awaiting external examiner (Image: C. Holtham)	242
19.3	Inside a pizza box (Image: C. Holtham)	242
19.4	Components of the learning approach showing the four learning activities (Image: C. Holtham and A. Dove, 2019)	249

Tables

7.1	Higher education spaces and their potential borderland roles (Adapted from Hill *et al.*, 2016)	91
19.1	Six spectra relating to the intuitive and rational qualities needed by twenty-first-century managers	238

List of illustrations

19.2	Summary of how element delivers to the book themes: reflective journal	241
19.3	Summary of how element delivers to the book themes: artefact	243
19.4	Summary of how element delivers to the book themes: public exhibition	244
19.5	Summary of how element delivers to the book themes: external visits	248
19.6	Demonstration of how far each student output element contributes to the six intuitive qualities	249

List of abbreviations

ANTF	Association of National Teaching Fellows
AR	augmented reality
ASKE	attitudes, skills, knowledge and emotions
BCU	Birmingham City University
BCUR	UK British conference of undergraduate research
CDIO	conceive design implement and operate
cMOOC	connectivist massive open online course
CoP	community of practice
CSAD	Cardiff School of Art and Design
EPQ	Extended Project Qualification
FL	FutureLearn
GPS	global positioning system
HCI	human computer interaction
HE	higher education
HEA	Higher Education Academy (now Advance HE)
HEI	higher education institution
HRI	human robotic interaction
IFNTF	International Federation for National Teaching Fellows
IT	information technology
JISC	Joint Information Systems Committee
LCF	London College of Fashion
MA	Master of Arts
MMU	Manchester Metropolitan University
MOOC	massive open online course
NHS	National Health Service
NMC	UK Nursing and Midwifery Council
NSS	National Student Survey
NTF	National Teaching Fellow
NTFS	National Teaching Fellowship Scheme
OB	outward bound
PBL	problem-based learning
QAA	Quality Assurance Agency
R&D	research and development
REF	Research Excellence Framework
SEDA	Staff and Educational Developers Association
SEM	sport and exercise medicine

List of abbreviations

SME	small or medium-sized enterprise
STEM	science, technology, engineering, mathematics
TEF	Teaching Excellence Framework
UAL	University of the Arts London
UCAS	Universities and Colleges Admissions Service
UEA	University of East Anglia
VLE	virtual learning environment
WBL	work-based learning
xMOOC	eXtended massive open online course

About the contributors

Jane Anderson (NTF 2014) is an architect, Professor of Architecture and Programme Lead for Undergraduate Architecture at Oxford Brookes University where she runs OB1 LIVE, a programme of student community live projects. Jane co-founded the Live Projects Network, an online resource to connect live project activity across the globe (https://liveprojectsnetwork.org).

Tim Bilham (NTF 2007) is an independent consultant, specializing in mentoring applicants and institutions for NTF and other teaching excellence awards. With degrees in mathematics, engineering science and sustainable development, his research is on the health impacts of flooding and flood threat. Tim edited the first NTF book, *For the Love of Learning: Innovations from outstanding university teachers* (2013).

Sally Brown (NTF 2008) is an independent consultant and Emerita Professor at Leeds Beckett University. She is also Visiting Professor at the University of Plymouth, the University of South Wales and at Liverpool John Moores. She is Principal Fellow of the Higher Education Academy (HEA) and Staff and Educational Development Association Senior Fellow.

Martina A. Doolan (NTF 2007) has worked at the University of Hertfordshire since 1997 as blended learning teacher and Teaching Fellow. Embracing a socially constructivist approach to learning and teaching, she actively researches collaborative learning environments.

Angela Dove is Visiting Lecturer at Cass Business School, City, University of London. Over a period of 12 years, she has researched and developed art-based and reflective approaches and successfully incorporated them into mainstream teaching (Executive, MSc, MBA and BSc). Initially a designer in theatre and for the BBC, she founded a consultancy on co-creating knowledge spaces that works with government, research and development (R&D) organizations and universities.

About the contributors

Rachel Forsyth is Associate Head of the Centre for Excellence in Learning and Teaching at Manchester Metropolitan University (MMU) and Principal Fellow of the HEA. Her research interests centre on curriculum design and assessment management.

Philip Frame (NTF 2001) received his BA in Social Anthropology from the University of Sussex and his MSc in Organizational Development and PhD in Management from Sheffield Hallam University. He is Emeritus Associate Professor at Middlesex University Business School and Senior Teaching Fellow.

Derek France (NTF 2008) is Professor of Pedagogy in Geographical Sciences at the University of Chester. His research interests focus on the enhancement of student learning and academic practice issues of fieldwork, mobile learning and technology-enhanced learning through the NTF scheme project on enhancing fieldwork learning (www.enhancingfieldwork.org.uk).

Helena Gillespie is Academic Director of Widening Participation at the University of East Anglia (UEA). She has contributed to the strategic development of online learning for the university, including the development of UEA's relationship with FutureLearn. Helena is an experienced online and face-to-face educator.

Ben Hall is Head of Music at the University of Chichester and has developed one of the largest music programmes in the UK. His piano and organ repertoire includes premieres by composers Sir Lennox Berkeley, Ronald Stephenson, Richard Rodney Bennett and Edward Smaldone, and broadcasts and recitals across Europe, the UK, China and the USA.

Claire Hamshire (NTF 2012) has worked at MMU since 2003, initially as Senior Lecturer in Physiotherapy and now as Professor and Faculty Head of Education. Her research interests include student engagement, technology-enhanced learning, learning transitions and first-generation students' experiences of higher education.

About the contributors

Kirsten Hardie (NTF 2004) is Associate Professor at the Arts University Bournemouth, a museum consultant, event organizer and exhibition curator. Her pedagogic research includes object-based learning and student–staff partnership. Kirsten is Founding Co-President of the International Federation National Teaching Fellows (IFNTF), Secretary at Graphic Design Educators' Network and Former Chair at the Association of National Teaching Fellows (ANTF).

Mary Hartog (NTF 2006) is Director of Leadership and Organization Practice at Middlesex University Business School. Mary works with organizations to develop their talent and leadership and enhance business growth, through bespoke practice-based qualifications, using action learning and team coaching as key development tools. Her scholarship of teaching and learning has a focus on reflective practice.

Momna Hejmadi (NTF 2015) is Courses Director in the Department of Biology and Biochemistry at the University of Bath. She has researched and taught cancer genetics, receiving several awards in recognition of her teaching excellence. A keen advocate of global learning for all, she developed a successful, free online course 'Inside Cancer' and authored a free e-book on cancer biology.

Ruth Helyer (NTF 2013) is Professor of Work-Based Learning at Leeds Trinity University where she leads an innovative programme of higher education with employed students, working closely with businesses across many sectors. She is the editor of *The Work-based Learning Student Handbook* (2015).

Jennifer Hill (NTF 2011) is Associate Professor in Teaching and Learning at the University of the West of England, Bristol. Jenny teaches and researches in geography and higher education pedagogy focusing on participatory pedagogies, learning spaces, graduate attributes, assessment and feedback, and the teaching–research dialectic. With over 80 published journal papers, chapters and books, she is a member of the editorial boards

About the contributors

for *Higher Education Pedagogies* and *Journal of Geography in Higher Education*.

Clive Holtham (NTF 2003) is Professor of Information Management at Cass Business School, City, University of London. Clive is responsible for a significant strand of work on creativity, initially technology-orientated, now focusing on educational and arts-based approaches. He teaches, researches and consults on spaces for the creation and sharing of knowledge.

Celia Hunt (NTF 2004) is Emerita Reader in Continuing Education (Creative Writing) at the University of Sussex. She is the author of *Therapeutic Dimensions of Autobiography in Creative Writing* (2000), *Writing: Self and reflexivity* (with Fiona Sampson, 2006) and *Transformative Learning through Creative Life Writing* (2013).

Becky Huxley-Binns (NTF 2012) is Pro-Vice-Chancellor in Education at the University of Hull. She was previously Vice-Provost at the University of Law, and before that, Chair in Legal Education at Nottingham Trent University. She was Chair of the ANTF from 2018 until 2019.

Kirsten Jack (NTF 2014) is Reader at MMU. She is committed to excellence in learning and teaching and has a keen interest in pedagogical research, specifically the use of the arts to support nurses' self-awareness development.

Alison James (NTF 2014) is Professor of Learning and Teaching at the University of Winchester, Principal Fellow of the HEA and an accredited LEGO® SERIOUS PLAY® facilitator. She co-authored, with Professor Stephen Brookfield, *Engaging Imagination: Helping students become creative and reflective thinkers* (2014) and her interests include creative, alternative and playful pedagogies.

About the contributors

Joy Jarvis (NTF 2013) is Professor of Educational Practice at the School of Education, University of Hertfordshire, and has a particular interest in creating contexts to facilitate staff learning about teaching. She has learnt a great deal about educational practice and the value of working across disciplines from colleagues in the School of Creative Arts.

Peter Klappa (NTF 2014) originally trained as a secondary school teacher in Biology and Chemistry at the Ludwig-Maximilians Universitaet in Munich, Germany. After completing his PhD in Cell Biology and four years into postdoctoral researching at the Georg-August University in Goettingen, Peter moved to the University of Kent in Canterbury in 1995, where he worked as an EMBO Fellow and, later on, as a Wellcome Trust Fellow in the School of Biosciences. Peter was appointed as lecturer in 1998, and is currently Reader in Biochemistry and Master of Rutherford College at the University of Kent.

Pauline Kneale (NTF 2002) is Professor of Pedagogy and Enterprise and Director of the Pedagogic Research Institute and Observatory at the University of Plymouth. Her recent work includes an edited volume on teaching at Master's level, projects on inclusive assessment and student engagement, and HEA-funded projects 'Evaluating teaching development in higher education: Towards impact assessment' and 'Learner Analytics'.

Simon Lancaster (NTF 2013) is the former pedagogical innovation ambassador at the UEA. In 2013 he was recognized by the Royal Society of Chemistry Higher Education Award for 'blurring the boundaries between the internet and the lecture theatre'. He is the author and facilitator of *The Chemistry Vignettes*, a popular series of open educational resources.

Catherine McDermott (NTF 2015) won the Sir Misha Black Award in 2016 for outstanding services to design education and for her work helping to establish a new generation of international curators in the emerging creative economies of Africa, Asia and South America. She is currently Professor at the School of Design, Kingston University, and Secretary of ICOM UK.

About the contributors

Tess Maginess (NTF 2013) is Senior Lecturer in Literature at Queen's University Belfast, where much of her work is with older learners. Recent publications include *Enhancing the Wellbeing and Wisdom of Older Learners: A co-research paradigm* (2016). She has contributed several articles on innovative pedagogy and participative research to international peer-reviewed journals.

Ruth Matheson (NTF 2012) is Head of Learning, Teaching and Student Experience in the Faculty of Life Sciences and Education at the University of South Wales. Her research interests focus on students as partners, belonging, problem-based learning, creativity and innovative pedagogies. She is the co-editor of and contributor to *Transition In, Through and Out of Higher Education: International case studies and best practice* (2018).

Alice Mauchline is Senior Research Fellow and a bioscientist at the University of Reading. She has research interests in agricultural ecology and policy evaluation. Her pedagogic research focuses on improving the student fieldwork experience and the integration of citizen science approaches into teaching.

Ingrid Murphy (NTF 2015) is the academic lead for transdisciplinarity at Cardiff School of Art & Design, Cardiff Metropolitan University, where she also leads the FabCre8 research group. Ingrid co-developed and teaches on the school's Artist, Designer: Maker course. A practicing ceramic artist, Ingrid combines traditional craft skills with emergent digital technologies.

Deborah O'Connor is Senior Lecturer and Educational Lead in the Department of Health Professions at MMU. Deborah is also a specialist neurological physiotherapist, with extensive experience in the field of stroke rehabilitation. Research interests include the use of technology as a pedagogical tool to support student engagement.

About the contributors

Natascha Radclyffe-Thomas (NTF 2016) is Course Leader for BA (Hons) Fashion Marketing at the London College of Fashion. Her international teaching experiences informed her EdD on cross-cultural pedagogies. In 2017 Natascha was recognized as a University of the Arts London senior teaching scholar for her teaching and pedagogic research initiatives, including e-learning and internationalizing the curriculum.

Laura Ritchie (NTF 2012) is Professor of Learning and Teaching at the University of Chichester and leads the Music with Teaching (Pedagogy) and MA Performance degrees. She uses music as a voice for connection across disciplines and writes about learning. Laura has authored two books: *Fostering Self-efficacy in Higher Education Students* and *California Dreaming*.

Kevin Singh (NTF 2015) is Professor and Head of the Birmingham School of Architecture and Design at Birmingham City University. He is a member of the Royal Institute of British Architects Education Committee, chairs RIBA validation panels, and is a founding director of Space* Studio, an architecture and interior design SME practice.

Mark Sutcliffe is Senior Lecturer in Strategic Management and Postgraduate Programme Director at Cardiff School of Management, Cardiff Metropolitan University. He was awarded a university student-led teaching fellowship in 2015. Mark's research interests focus on ways to enhance student belonging, especially at the postgraduate level, and developing creative and innovative approaches to teaching, learning and assessment.

Rebecca Thomas is an academic developer at UEA, using play, participatory making and other unconventional methods to foster a curiosity-driven approach to teaching with academic staff. A practising artist, she is also a regular contributor to the web journals *Creative Academic, imagineED* and *The Creative Post*.

About the contributors

Gareth Thomson (NTF 2016) is Reader in Mechanical Engineering and Design at Aston University. He is heavily involved in active learning within the engineering education field and is an active member of international partnerships, including 'Conceive, Design, Implement & Operate' (CDIO) and the European Society for Engineering Education (SEFI).

Helen Walkington (NTF 2009) is Professor of Higher Education at Oxford Brookes University where she teaches geography, conducts research in higher education pedagogy and has embedded Get Published!, a university-wide student experience project. Helen is an experienced presenter and has given conference keynote speeches nationally and internationally on the research–teaching nexus.

Brian Whalley (NTF 2008) is Emeritus Professor of Geomorphology at Queen's University Belfast and Visiting Professor at the University of Sheffield. He has had a long interest in cognition and pedagogy, especially by promoting and enhancing the student learning experience through fieldwork and the use of technology-enhanced learning.

Carrie Winstanley (NTF 2008) has taught in schools and higher education for 25 years and is Professor of Pedagogy at Roehampton University, London, where she works with students and with academic staff. Carrie is committed to encouraging children and adults to embrace visits to and learning in different spaces as a key part of their education.

Contributors to case study projects

Gabrielle Hass currently lectures on the BA (Hons) Graphic Design Course at the Arts University Bournemouth. Following a career in publishing and advertising, Gabrielle now works in higher education while living in Malaysia. She holds a Master's Research degree in design from Curtin University of Technology, Australia.

About the contributors

Adrian Huang is Lecturer on BA Fashion Media and Industries at LASALLE College of the Arts, Singapore, with a background in designing, producing and retailing fashion apparel and developing fashion training programmes for adult learners. His MA Arts Pedagogy explores the development of creative processes in design education and fashion entrepreneurship.

Rob Jackson is Professor of Molecular Microbiology in the School of Biological Sciences at the University of Reading. His research interests relate to environmental microbiology, which he uses to underpin teaching via an undergraduate field course to study microbes living in extreme environments in Iceland and Colombia.

Anais Lacouture (1987–2017) was an experienced international fashion business consultant and an enthusiastic and inspiring teacher working at RMIT University Vietnam. An early career teacher, with a strong reputation as a dedicated, energetic and creative educator, she practised her belief that education should be informed by life experience and self-development.

Julian Park (NTF 2008) is Professor of Agricultural Systems at the University of Reading and Principal Fellow of the HEA. His interests span both agriculture and enhancing the student experience across the bioscience discipline.

Anne Peirson-Smith is Assistant Professor in the Department of English, City University of Hong Kong, an internship and projects co-coordinator and a BA programme leader. With a professional background in public relations (PR) and branding, her research explores fashion communication and marketing, the creative industries, popular culture, PR and branding.

Ana Roncha is Course Leader for MA Strategic Fashion Marketing and a former postdoctoral research fellow in Enterprise, Collaborations

About the contributors

and Innovation at the London College of Fashion, with a background in brand management. Her research explores how innovation drives business development and value creation across SMEs and leads to increased competitive advantage in the fashion sector.

Mick Walters teaches Robotics and Artificial Intelligence at the University of Hertfordshire. He researches robot appearance and behaviour to facilitate interaction with people. He has worked on EU-funded projects researching companion and domestic service robots and the AURORA project, which helped develop a new version of KASPAR, a robot used for therapy for children with autism.

Acknowledgements

We must thank all the contributors to this book for their willingness to provide several iterations of their work as the focus of the book emerged and was re-imagined both after our writing retreat at Lewes and subsequently. We thank them for their patience, enthusiasm and inspirational ideas. Thanks are also due to case study authors for allowing their work to be woven together and to those who helped with the weaving. Many case study projects involved other colleagues, and we recognize here their contribution to these fascinating and valuable stories.

Grateful thanks are due to the Association of National Teaching Fellows (ANTF) for their support and collegiality and to those who were not selected for this volume; we hope they have found alternative opportunities to publish. Their work was just as influential. Special thanks go to Kirsten Hardie, Chair of the ANTF (2012–15) who provided funding for our Lewes and Birmingham events and supported the activity with such enthusiasm, to Martina A. Doolan who was part of the team that conceived the idea at Lewes and reviewed the original submissions and early drafts of chapters and to Sally Brown, ANTF chair (2015–18) who has encouraged us to the finish line.

Thanks are also due to our respective institutions who have supported the individual authors and editors in giving them the funds and time needed to make such valuable contributions to the dissemination of excellence in learning and teaching.

We would like to acknowledge the confidence and support of our publisher, UCL IOE Press, in championing the importance of learning and teaching in our universities and, in particular, Pat Gordon-Smith for her patience and wise counsel in bringing this particular book to its audience.

We thank our respective families and friends who have given us space through the long and often solitary process of writing and editing. And finally we acknowledge all the many students across our institutions without whose involvement this work would not have been possible.

Tim Bilham
Claire Hamshire
Mary Hartog

How to use this book

Reframing Space for Learning consists of a collection of essays and case studies around broad themes of spaces and places that facilitate and support authentic learning, space for the self and social and collaborative learning. Although grouped under these broad headings, many essays clearly cover multiple themes. This table provides a guide to some of the sub-themes that emerge across chapters.

If you are interested in a particular area you may find this table useful in identifying chapters and case studies of interest. We are also sure that you will draw out your own sub-themes and make your own connections as you engage with the text.

Topics and sub-themes	Chapters
action learning	2, 8, 10
active learning	2, 4
authentic learning	1, 2, 6, 13, 14, 19
becoming	11, 14
belonging	1, 7, 10
blended learning	2, 16
borderland spaces	7
citizenship	17
collaborative and social spaces, collaborative learning	3, 13, 14, 15, 16, 17, 18, 19
communities of practice	2, 14
connectivist pedagogy	18
constructivist pedagogy, situated learning	1, 2, 18, 19
creativity, creative writing	4, 9, 17
cultural space	5, 17
curation, learning through…	4, 5, 17, 19
design education	5, 6, 13, 17
dialogic spaces	15
disruptive spaces	15, 19
experiential learning	2, 5, 13
field studies	2
filmmaking	3
free writing	9
identity	10, 11, 19
intentionality	9

Topics and sub-themes	Chapters
interdisciplinary learning	13
interior space	4, 8, 12
internationalization, international students	10, 17, 18
knowledge co-production	16, 17, 18
learning design, co-design, participatory design	6, 16
liminal spaces	4, 5, 7
live projects	6, 13, 19
living theory	8
maker spaces	6, 19
museums, galleries	5, 19
online learning, distance learning	1, 2, 14, 16, 17, 18
participatory learning and design, co-design	3, 6
performance space	11
place-based pedagogies	1, 2
play	4, 15
practice spaces	7, 14
problem-based learning, project-based learning	2, 6, 13
professional development, lifelong learning	6, 8, 11, 14
public engagement, outreach	18
real, learning from the	12
reflection, reflexivity	8, 9, 11, 12, 14, 19
relational spaces	2, 12, 15
self-esteem, self-efficacy, self-concept, resilience	11, 12
sense of place, place attachment	1, 3
sense of self, self-authorship, self-awareness	7, 8, 9, 12
social capital, cultural capital	1, 3, 7
social learners	18
social media	16
staff development	6, 15
student-centred learning	5,
students as researchers, conference space	7, 8, 9, 17
transition	1, 5, 10
virtual spaces, digital spaces	2, 14, 16, 17, 18
voice, student voice, writing voice	8, 9, 19
vulnerable places	13
work-based learning	12

Foreword

Becky Huxley-Binns
Chair of the Association of National Teaching Fellows

It is with the greatest of pleasure that I welcome the second book written by UK National Teaching Fellows. To be awarded a National Teaching Fellowship is an exceptional honour, recognizing as it does the teaching excellence that resides in our universities. It is also a great privilege since it enables entry into a vibrant and energizing learning community that offers a locus for professional engagement with peers who share a love of learning and a commitment to foregrounding the student experience. This book demonstrates the power of that community of practice and showcases the outstanding teaching and learning that is provided by some of the best teachers in the United Kingdom.

I am writing this foreword while travelling home from a very rewarding but thought-provoking conference on higher education. The coach of the train I am on is too cold from the air conditioning, too crowded and very noisy, and I am sure my laptop is not at a height or an angle of which any occupational health professional would approve. Yet, I am in a happy bubble. I am carving out some space and time to reflect on the examples of student learning spaces I have heard about over the past couple of days: from students dancing on tables during their lunch break in a performing arts programme, to commuter lounges on university campuses designed specifically for local students to hang out between taught sessions, to online discussion boards for peer-to-peer feedback in the digital space. This excellent book takes these sorts of examples further, and challenges us to think in new ways about the educational, social, affective, physical, virtual, temporal, creative, fluid, collaborative spaces and places in which learning takes place. What strikes me is that this book reveals the rich diversity of learning experiences which all have a significant impact on our environment.

Reframing Space for Learning is very timely. Universities increasingly understand the connection between the learning environment and the learning experience, and that connection is mutual and reciprocal. Learners bring their characteristics, personalities and expectations into the spaces, and the dynamics and constructs of that space create and impact on the student learning. A key theme across this book is the need for universities to create and adapt such spaces in collaboration with students.

As our lives as academics seem to get busier and as we face increasing challenges, the spaces we inhabit matter more and more. We need space and time to think – to learn and meet and debate. We need spaces to be alone and spaces to be together. This book not only deals with the rich variety of student-learning spaces but recognizes and celebrates the importance of spaces for those who teach and support student learning. Colleagues, we must take care of our own spaces, as well as ourselves.

Introduction: Reframing spaces for learning

Tim Bilham

Reframing Space for Learning is a collection of essays and case studies based around the broad themes of creating space for learning. These include physical spaces for learning both inside and outside the academy, technological and virtual learning spaces, and educational, personal and reflective spaces. This book illustrates how spaces for learning are reframed, re-imagined and extended, providing exemplars of innovative pedagogies situated in various subject disciplines and learning contexts within higher education (HE). It explores spaces that bridge traditional environments and practices that optimize unique, unusual and relevant locations. In doing so it identifies current and emerging examples of teaching excellence inside, outside and beyond 'the classroom'.

Reframing Space for Learning is the second book compiled and written by UK National Teaching Fellows (NTFs). It is intentionally a book about practice, about learning and teaching practice, which explores the often-neglected importance of learning spaces and places in university teaching. Each chapter provides sufficient theory and context to locate the practical examples, thereby enabling readers to consider how they might translate them to their own situations. By taking a practical approach, we are also seeking to influence teaching colleagues who themselves may influence, within their own institutions and at a policy level, the dialogue about the appropriateness of our spaces for teaching, thus responding to Boddington and Boys's call for action (2011).

The authors come from many disciplines: the creative arts, fashion, music, engineering, architecture, computer science, biosciences, health, chemistry, geography, management and education, as well as lifelong learning and professional development. Their students are undergraduates, postgraduates, doctoral students, professionals, carers, even patients and, in the case of massive open online courses (MOOCs), participants who just want to learn. The authors work in many different organizational cultures and in many different ways, but what unites them is an unswerving commitment to excellence in supporting their students and in disseminating their expertise and experience to other HE teachers. In doing so, they have transcended their own discipline by writing in ways that enable others to see

Introduction

opportunities for their own practice. We hope that this will inspire others to explore, innovate, take risks and evaluate their own teaching and learning practice to enhance the experience for all students.

Learning Spaces

At a broad institutional level, and with a few notable exceptions (Boddington and Boys, 2011; Savin-Baden, 2008; Temple and Barnett, 2007; Temple and Fillippakou, 2007; Oblinger, 2006) learning spaces in HE have not previously attracted much attention since teaching and learning are often considered as taking place independently of the spaces in which it is located (Temple, 2011). In planning this book we recognized that much teaching in HE is still framed by the university's physical architecture and that these structures, together with institutional agendas for efficiency have hitherto encouraged predominantly didactic and instructional teaching approaches. Diana Oblinger (2006) uses the term 'built pedagogy' to describe the way space can determine how we teach. Yet, changes in our understanding of learning, in our students' demographics, attitudes and expectations, and changes in how we use technologies for learning have outstripped, in many institutions, the capabilities of our predominantly campus-based learning spaces (Oblinger, 2006).

Learning is both a spatial and a social experience. The relationship between the learner and their situated environment is well recognized as crucial to the learning process (Lave and Wenger, 1991), as is the relationship of the learner within a community of learners, peers or practice. Space is more than simply physical or virtual; it encompasses the relational and liminal spaces of these learning communities, and the personal and reflective spaces of the self. It embraces the curriculum and pedagogical spaces and recognizes that location and place are also social constructs where student identity, as well as connectedness and belonging to their university, have the potential to impact on their learning, commitment and engagement. The use of a different place and space can position, shape, shift and lift learning and teaching expectations and experiences: a change of space can change and liberate learning: 'Spaces are themselves agents for change. Changed spaces will change practice' (JISC, 2006). This book explores the practices of colleagues in HE and how they have adapted, refined and changed their teaching practices to reflect the spaces they find themselves in, or in which they choose to engage with their students.

This book uniquely explores space as both a 'learning place' – situated in a learning context that might be physical, virtual, in work or in the field – and as a 'belonging space' where all learners, students and staff find a place to learn, engage and develop individually and collectively, formally and informally, socially and experientially, to improve the educational experience. There are of course many excellent texts on learning spaces, especially physical and technological spaces, but *Reframing Space for Learning* is the first to explore, through examples of excellent and innovative practice, both the importance of place and of belonging to that place, in terms of teaching and learning.

These learning spaces draw out a number of key pedagogic themes such as belonging, collaboration and authentic learning. They include spaces for individual learners and spaces in which communities of learners are engaged in learning their practice and learning together.

How this book evolved

In the summer of 2014, a group of around 30 NTFs gathered in a hotel in Lewes, Sussex, for a writing retreat, generously funded by the Association of National Teaching Fellows (ANTF). We were eager to build on the success of the first NTF book *For the Love of Learning: Innovations from outstanding university teachers* (Bilham, 2013). Facilitated by Clive Holtham and members of the editorial team, we worked around tables or in the garden; sometimes in topic groups, sometimes across disciplines, we shared, explored and re-imagined. We used our working spaces flexibly and imaginatively, culminating ultimately, in using cardboard hexagons to explore and collect our ideas for a book. What emerged were themes around the self, around collaboration and belonging, technology, place and space. At that point we imagined our overarching theme would be about change, including a focus on policy and practice, which seemed appropriate with the imminent introduction of the UK's Teaching Excellence Framework (TEF). We consulted externally and were encouraged to ensure that the book reflected the implicit and explicit strengths of our NTF community, that of practice excellence and innovation. The following spring we held a follow-up event alongside the ANTF symposium in Birmingham. By this stage, our focus around place and space was becoming sharper and we invited further contributions from the NTF community that spoke to innovative pedagogy and practice around these themes. Once the major chapter contributions were received, the editors reviewed the structure. Having identified some important gaps, we put out a further call for a series of focused case studies of good practice that addressed key issues and complemented existing contributions. In this way the book has evolved incrementally and creatively. It has been redesigned, refined and occasionally re-imagined.

Introduction

We received many sparkling contributions, truly representing the remarkable and innovative work that is a feature of the professional practice of National Teaching Fellows. It is regretful that we cannot include them all. Eventually we settled upon 19 chapters containing 31 case studies.

In exploring these learning spaces you will travel on a journey that takes you to London's Oxford Street and South Armagh, the Churchill War Museum and the Priest's House Museum in Dorset, the Hunterian Museum and the London Metropolitan Archive. Together, we go on a detective tour in Lime Grove and join sports medicine doctors in a virtual clinic. We journey to Iceland, Vietnam, Hong Kong, China, Singapore, Ireland and Zimbabwe and we join staff on a picnic!

We see students at play with balloons, making baskets in Africa, creating cubes to represent their origins, expectations and aspirations, creating community installations in urban spaces and playing fields and learning in a robot house. We see them in audition and induction, in rehearsal and in moments of transition and in performance. We see them assuming professional roles at academic conferences, in workplaces, on their placement years and in caring roles. We follow students into many different places, into work, into cafés, libraries and museums, into the laboratory, into 'bandit country' on the borders and into cultures unfamiliar to them. And we note their anxieties at being in unfamiliar surroundings, the loneliness and frustrations of finding their 'own voice' and their collective endeavours and enthusiasms. In all these instances, the spaces they inhabit are critical to their learning and their experiences. There are many places where we learn, formal and informal, structured and unstructured, social and personal, and to illustrate we propose an ecology of space and place for learning that feature in this book:

- unusual places
- environmental places
- virtual places
- community spaces
- campus spaces
- workplaces
- urban places
- artistic places
- aesthetic places
- conversational spaces
- dialogic spaces
- cognitive spaces

Tim Bilham

- transitional spaces
- belonging spaces.

You will find examples of all of these somewhere on your journey through these chapters. You will also find many examples of NTFs working and writing together, and with other colleagues within and outside their own institutions. Such collaborations in scholarship are a powerful feature of the NTF community.

Influences

In creating and compiling this book, we acknowledge the influence of many other writers, most notably Anne Boddington and Jos Boys (2011) and their inspiring text *Re-Shaping Learning: A critical reader,* the formative work of Maggi Savin-Baden (2008) *Learning Spaces: Creating opportunities for knowledge creation in academic life* and the influential work of Ronald Barnett (2011), most notably his framework and taxonomy for learning spaces. Many of their influences can be seen permeating this book. Indeed, many chapter authors and some case study contributors have drawn specifically from Barnett's work (ibid.), positioning their practice within one, or more, of the domains of learning spaces that he describes in *Configuring Learning Spaces: Noticing the invisible.*

Barnett classifies learning spaces in three broad domains:

1. material and physical spaces, including on- and off-campus spaces such as lecture halls and classrooms, museums and art galleries, community halls and workplaces, field and virtual environments
2. educational spaces, including curriculum spaces in which knowledge and skills are ordered and structured through disciplinary consensus and pedagogical spaces that determine how the relational spaces between students and tutors are conceived and practised. It is here that the boundaries of knowledge are defined, and the limits and opportunities of a 'freedom to learn' determined
3. interior spaces, which for the student includes the psychic and ontological space of the individual and is where the student's very being lies. It is where the formation of self, and personal and professional identity comes into play. The capacity of this learning space is determined by the willingness of the student to engage and their ability to recognize the risks in opening themselves up to learning. Thus, risk should be balanced to manage the security and anxiety of students, and safe learning spaces created that support and enable student learning.

Introduction

The borders of these domains are permeable and the spaces they encompass merge with one another to create transitional and non-hierarchical spaces.

The idea of learning space, says Barnett (ibid.), is an idea of its time. It is a response to the current uncertainties where much is in a state of flux, including the identity of self. The appeal for student learning is clear, especially as students think of themselves as lifelong learners, engaged in processes of continuous personal and professional development that require a rebranding of themselves in response to the demands of a global economy and a volatile and uncertain world. According to Barnett (ibid.), the values that inform and shape learning spaces are concerned with knowing, doing and being. These learning spaces, although contested, offer opportunities for improvement and development for being and knowing in the world. They may be fraught with anxieties for students, be full of hope and offer opportunity, be sites of liberation and autonomy in learning and they may also be found wanting and empty. For our learners, knowledge and deep understanding need to be balanced with the development of identity and becoming.

Savin-Baden (2008) engaged us with the importance of finding space within academic life for the self. She promotes the need for writing spaces, dialogic spaces and reflective spaces, of recognizing the utility of boundary and liminal spaces and of the importance of developing identity in new teaching places and digital spaces. In talking about the need for finding spaces to write, she calls for support for staff and students to also find their 'writing voice'. She talks about the temporal qualities of space, and about creating time as well as space. Of course when we talk of creating space for something, we actually often mean creating time. All of these concepts are to be found as influences in the chapters in this book.

Importantly in our context she asserts that creativity and innovation can be stifled by the pressure to complete our routine institutional responsibilities and she aspires for spaces where creativity is enabled and ideas can grow – for 'spaces where being with our thoughts offers opportunities to rearrange them in spaces where the values of being are more central than the values of doing' (ibid.: 8). In short, she is calling for space for good scholarship; space for scholarship in our teaching and research, in our disciplines and within the practice of learning and teaching. The collaborations evident in this book where NTFs have engaged in practice and scholarship with colleagues and students demonstrates the importance of dialogic spaces for crafting excellence.

Finally, Boddington and Boys (2011) provided an invaluable method of thinking and talking about spaces for learning, about the contemporary discourse on space and learning and a solid theoretical underpinning of how learning spaces should be conceptualized, designed and reframed. They stress the importance of recognizing the socio-spatial practices of education and the need for collaboration between those who design the physical and digital spaces and those who design the learning – students or teachers – in order to create spaces for learning that establish optimal conditions for it. They call for a sharing of perspectives and methodologies. We trust that the practical and creative examples provided throughout this volume contribute to this shared understanding and inspire others to experiment and innovate.

How is this book structured?

We have modified Barnett's (2011) classification of learning spaces to reflect the individual contributions we received and to recognize our prime focus upon presenting examples of practice. This has resulted in the book being structured in four parts: the first three being fundamentally centred around physical spaces and places, interior and personal spaces and social and collaborative spaces for learning. The fourth part provides an example of how these themes are integrated into practice. In doing so, we recognize that we immediately set ourselves up for criticism and suggestions of alternative classifications and we also acknowledge Barnett's cautioning that it is not possible to neatly represent spaces in linear form, or as Venn diagrams as they are 'more like clouds ... fuzzy, inchoate and fluid' (ibid.: 169). Readers will quickly spot that many chapters and cases unsurprisingly fall between and run across our inadequate classifications. As a result we have tried to identify connections and draw parallels within the chapters and we attempt to summarize overall the emerging themes and issues in the section 'How to use this book'.

Part 1 is 'Places of Learning, Spaces for Learning'. In Chapter 1, Tim Bilham opens with an exploration of place and of the importance of creating a sense of place for learning. In doing so he introduces ideas of authentic learning, place-based education, belonging and situated learning, and identifies the educational and societal changes that act as drivers for reconceptualizing our ideas of learning spaces and that are foundations for subsequent chapters. In Chapter 2, we explore further the ideas of place-based education through our first three case studies. Derek France, Alice Mauchline and Brian Whalley, working collaboratively with colleagues from the universities of Reading and Akureyri, Iceland, report on active learning through fieldwork in authentic environmental places. They describe the associated use of technological spaces that are also considered in later chapters. Martina A. Doolan takes her students into a research and development (R&D) facility, in the form of a real house where students experience humanoid robots supporting children on the autistic spectrum. This allows Martina to explore the relational spaces between tutor and learner in diminishing the polarization between research and teaching. In the final example, Tim Bilham demonstrates the effective use of virtual learning to simulate places that might be inaccessible to students, or to create virtual examples of situations that occur infrequently. In Chapter 3, Tess Maginess 'crosses a bridge' between two cultures in supporting rural communities and uses participatory filmmaking in raising awareness of sensitive issues around mental health. In Chapter 4, Alison James explores how curriculum space is reframed, and how campus spaces are reappraised and used in novel and unusual ways. She describes a detective tour and a caravan conference, which permit a sharpened awareness of the spaces around us, demonstrating unconventional spaces that are legitimate learning locations.

The use of novel places for learning is further exemplified in Chapter 5, which stresses the importance of student-led learning in creative learning spaces. Carrie Winstanley explores the liminal and transitional spaces that can cause anxiety in our students by sharing her work in using museum spaces and reflecting upon the role of the tutor. Kirsten Hardie extends these ideas and describes collaborative and cross-disciplinary learning in which students transformed museum and gallery spaces to create an exhibition space for Valentine's Day cards and an accompanying tea party. By Chapter 6, we are considering how academic teachers might influence the physical fabric of new and refurbished buildings, mindful of the proposition that 'learning spaces ought themselves to learn' (Ellis and Goodyear, 2016: 193) and challenging the orthodoxy of 'future proofing' buildings, which is a flawed concept unless we know the future! Three NTFs had a unique opportunity to work with architects and their estates' teams to create learning spaces that were equipped to provide for the special circumstances they faced in delivering their subject. Ingrid Murphy creates a maker space for her Artist, Designer: Maker students, which demonstrates the benefits of flexibility and how architectural spaces change teaching practice in profound ways. Gareth Thomson faced the need for his engineering programme to comply with professional and global requirements to provide creative spaces for students to experience authentic engineering practice. He concludes by providing valuable advice for those in similar situations. Kevin Singh, himself an architect, describes his collaboration with students as ultimate users of two spaces, one social and the other the library.

Tim Bilham

In opening Part 2, 'Spaces for the Self', Jenny Hill, Helen Walkington and Pauline Kneale introduce us in Chapter 7 to the concept of borderland spaces, with examples of how the traditional uses of physical and virtual spaces can be relatively easily replaced by innovative, student-centred and constructivist teaching techniques. Their study demonstrates the empowering result of involving undergraduate students as legitimate participants in professional academic conferences. We continue this theme with two chapters that talk about the need for creating space for the self that are both presented in the form of personal stories. In Chapter 8, Celia Hunt contrasts the internal space of the learner and the external space necessary for enabling the generation of space for the self. She illustrates this through describing her module for doctoral students on creative life writing and the personal experiences of one of her students. In Chapter 9, Mary Hartog describes her own experiences, and influences, as she developed her own academic identity and the particular importance of interior space, reflective spaces and having a sense of self.

The importance of transitional spaces and belonging are convincingly demonstrated in Ruth Matheson and Mark Sutcliffe's Chapter 10. Reflecting upon their experiences of teaching cross-cultural postgraduate students, they evidence the effectiveness of practical and integrated interventions during student induction and confirm again the importance of developing a sense of belonging in our students. This chapter also introduces the idea of identity, which is explored further in subsequent chapters. In Chapter 11, Laura Ritchie and Ben Hall neatly consider the student journey to becoming a professional through a series of metaphorical spaces – audition, rehearsal and performance – that are clearly relevant for their music students, but translate equally well to other career and learning pathways. Chapter 12 explores learning from work from the perspective of the interior space of the self. Ruth Helyer, Philip Frame and Mary Hartog reflect upon the relational, reflective, curriculum and pedagogic spaces that are characteristic of work-based learning illustrated through two case examples, differentiated by the types of learner: Philip Frame considers learning from part-time work, while Mary Hartog describes a doctoral student's learning journey, where work is the field of study as well as its location.

Part 3, 'Social and Collaborative Spaces', is opened by another architect, Jane Anderson, who delves into the benefits of utilizing live projects, demonstrating the impact resulting from facilitating collaborative learning in authentic places and illustrating this with examples of working in community spaces that are frequently disconnected from education and other practices. She also extends our consideration of the temporal characteristics of space and stresses the importance of considering ethical aspects of our interventions in places that are sometimes vulnerable. We have been cautious to avoid the assumption that any technology and use of virtual spaces in teaching and learning necessarily means they are innovative, as a result of their ubiquitousness, networking, mobile capabilities and the ability to personalize learning through their use (Sharples *et al.*, 2005). We acknowledge the typically conservative use of technology in HE that merely reproduces traditional classroom learning on a virtual platform and that universities have some work to do to fully exploit the use of technology in teaching and learning. Chapter 14 by Claire Hamshire, Deborah O'Connor and Kirsten Jack provides a bridge between authentic and virtual spaces, demonstrating how commonly available mobile technologies can be utilized very effectively in developing professional skills, collaborative learning and reflection and how clinical spaces are used effectively for creating trust and collaboration between professional practitioners.

The creation of reflective spaces for student learning is given considerable attention in the literature but less so for staff learning and development (Savin-Baden, 2008). We rectify this in Chapter 15 in which Joy Jarvis and Rebecca Thomas stress the need for dialogic space for staff (also called for by Savin-Baden) and relational spaces. They provide this through social gatherings – a staff picnic – and through the use of illustrations as a metaphor for learning processes that prompt discussion and engagement. Technological spaces are considered further in Chapter 16, where Peter Klappa reports on the benefits of using live-streams in undergraduate learning, and Simon Lancaster and Helena Gillespie demonstrate that sometimes unintended benefits arise from teaching initiatives, in their case resulting in students co-authoring content.

The final two chapters in Part 3 extend our notion of learning spaces to global contexts reaching out to learners in ways previously unimaginable. Chapter 17 explores cross-cultural spaces, with three cases drawn from the creative industries and which use technology to create digital global classrooms. Rachel Forsyth deals with the contested concept of internationalization before Natascha Radclyffe-Thomas describes her multi-country collaboration that uses social media in co-creating learning, and Catherine Thomas illustrates her work in Africa and China. In Chapter 18 Momna Hejmadi convincingly demonstrates the tremendous reach of the MOOC space, creating as she did a truly global and collaborative learning space that attracted an amazingly diverse and large group of global learners and resulted in many unexpected, yet positive outcomes and impacting upon teaching and learning in surprising ways.

Tim Bilham

We conclude our journey in Part 4 with a case study that integrates many of the ideas previously discussed. In Chapter 19, Clive Holtham and Angela Dove think outside the box (Clive's pizza box artefacts have inspired many subsequent ideas) and outside traditional teaching spaces to envisage a demand for maker spaces and in evaluating a learning intervention that disrupted conventional ideas by taking their management students into unfamiliar surroundings. They integrate ideas of unusual physical space, interior space and collaborative learning in a module designed to develop their students' intuitive skills, which also serves as an insightful way of bringing together many of the themes that run through the book.

Who is this book for?

This book will be valuable to university teachers and learning support staff, course and programme leaders, staff developers, quality assurance staff and all those keen to inspire excellence and innovation in teaching and learning. This includes early career staff on initial training courses or seeking professional recognition, as well as their mentors and managers. We hope that it might also inspire others to seek recognition of their excellence in teaching practice in their own context, discipline or country. While the chapters and case studies are from UK National Teaching Fellows the application of these ideas has a universal and global reach. It will provide an invaluable insight for estates' staff, architects and those determining the configuration of our future learning and teaching spaces in demonstrating what academic teachers and students value and what affordances they require in the spaces in which they work, study and learn.

The contributions in this book extend our notions of excellence beyond the metrics-based approaches of the TEF in the UK, providing authentic examples from teaching practice of excellence in teaching and learning.

Rationale for chapters and case studies

The chapters for *Reframing Space for Learning* have been selected after satisfying several key criteria. They are innovative and demonstrate currency and excellence in their field. They are located within a diverse range of discipline-based research and pedagogical research areas and provide an evidential basis for effectiveness. They offer illustrative practical examples for teaching in HE that can be translated across and beyond their own discipline. They have all been authored by NTFs (some with colleagues), who have been recognized as demonstrating excellence by their peers and by their students. Of course they only represent a fraction of the excellent work that goes on inside and outside the community of NTFs, but we hope to give a flavour of what is happening, what is possible and stimulate an ongoing debate on the impact and importance of learning spaces within our higher education institutions.

Conclusion

Reframing Space for Learning does not address one single discipline and its associated theory. Rather, each chapter individually draws upon current theories of learning, reflective practice and belonging that locate their own work and its application. Overall the book draws out and collates the common themes, including theories of constructivist learning, sense of place and critical pedagogies.

In collaborating in the writing of the book, NTFs are recognizing a new 'research space', a pan-disciplinary research area that is evolving, located in the field of practice-based research, appropriate for future learning and teaching, and arguably becoming more important in teaching and learning than a discipline of singularity. Academic disciplines are 'slices into the world; learning spaces are educational vehicles for traversing the world' (Barnett, 2011: 176). We hope that the examples given in this book go some way to illustrate how we are helping our students to do just that.

References

Barnett, R. (2011) 'Configuring learning spaces: Noticing the invisible'. In Boddington, A. and Boys, J. (eds) *Re-shaping learning: A critical reader: The future of learning spaces in post-compulsory education*. Rotterdam: Sense Publishers, 167–78.

Bilham, T. (ed.) (2013) *For the Love of Learning: Innovations from outstanding university teachers*. Basingstoke: Palgrave Macmillan.

Boddington, A. and Boys, J. (2011) 'Reshaping learning – an introduction'. In Boddington, A. and Boys, J. (eds) *Re-Shaping Learning: A critical reader: The future of learning spaces in post-compulsory education*. Rotterdam: Sense Publishers, xi–xxii.

Ellis, R.A. and Goodyear, P. (2016) 'Context and implications document for models of learning space: Integrating research on space, place and learning in higher education'. *Review of Education*, 4 (2), 192–4.

JISC (Joint Information Systems Committee) (2006) *Designing Spaces for Effective Learning: A guide to 21st-century-learning space design*. Bristol: Joint Information Systems Committee. Online. https://tinyurl.com/yysabygu (accessed 24 February 2019).

Lave, J. and Wenger, E. (1991) *Situated Learning: Legitimate peripheral participation*. Cambridge: Cambridge University Press.

Oblinger, D.G. (2006) 'Space as a change agent'. In Oblinger, D.G. (ed.) *Learning Spaces*. Washington, DC: EDUCAUSE, 1.1–1.4.

Savin-Baden, M. (2008) *Learning Spaces: Creating opportunities for knowledge creation in academic life*. Maidenhead: Open University Press.

Sharples, M., Taylor, J. and Vavoula, G. (2005) 'Towards a theory of mobile learning'. *Proceedings of mLearn*, 1 (1), 1–9.

Temple, P. (2011) 'Learning spaces as social capital'. In Boddington, A. and Boys, J. (eds) *Re-Shaping Learning: A critical reader: The future of learning spaces in post-compulsory education*. Rotterdam: Sense Publishers, 137–46.

Temple, P. and Barnett, R. (2007) 'Higher education space: Future directions'. *Planning for Higher Education*, 36 (1), 5–15.

Temple, P. and Fillippakou, O. (2007) *Learning Spaces for the 21st Century: A review of the literature*. York: Higher Education Academy.

Part One

Places of learning, spaces for learning

Chapter 1
Beyond the walls: Learning and the importance of place
Tim Bilham

> *The love of learning, the sequestered nooks,*
> *And all the sweet serenity of books*
>
> Henry Wadsworth Longfellow, 'Morituri Salutamus', 1875

Universities are described as places of learning, where knowledge is created and where students go to gain that knowledge. But our educational spaces, originally embodied by cloistered architectures, designed for dedicated scholarship and careful reflection by students, have increasingly become diverse, distributed and developmental (Ellis *et al.*, 2018; Oblinger, 2006).

Places of learning are no longer sequestered, no longer cloistered, no longer hidden away. Rather they are social spaces, where peer and community learning are nurtured and encouraged (Matthews *et al.*, 2011; Chism, 2006). These are places where informal and serendipitous contacts are facilitated (Temple, 2011), technologies permeate learning landscapes and experiential learning in authentic places develops skills and competencies that prepare students for employment (Ellis and Goodyear, 2018). Thus the places in which we learn, the locations in which we teach, have become transformed, re-imagined and 're-placed'. They have evolved to accommodate societal and educational change as our understanding of learning has been refined, as the expectations of our students have increased, as technologies have become ubiquitous (Oblinger, 2006), as the importance of informal and lifelong learning have been recognized, and situated and part-time study has become more commonplace. This is truly anytime anywhere education.

But place of learning has another important aspect. Just as place, socially conceived, invokes potent emotions of attachment and meaning (Altman and Low, 1992) so the place where we study is imbued with powerful characteristics of attachment, identity and belonging and, after graduation, loyalty and nostalgia; university fundraising campaigns capitalize upon this characteristic regularly. For university to have meaning beyond spaces to which students travel to access, or receive, knowledge, we should think beyond the physical spatiality of the material and consider the importance of establishing a 'feeling of place' (Tuan, 1977: 14). In applying this to learning spaces Boddington and Boys (2011) propose that space should be viewed in terms of its 'occupation' or as a socio-spatial practice. Put another way, learning is both socially and physically situated (Goodyear and Ellis, 2007), and acquired, not through a fixed curriculum, but through social systems (Wenger, 1998).

This chapter explores the importance of 'place' or of having a 'sense of place' for learning in university education. It considers both the benefits of explicitly using place as location, as part of our pedagogy, and the power of place in creating a feeling of belonging. It does this by drawing upon concepts of place, identity and the social construction of knowledge. In these ways it aims to provide a perspective from which to view other chapters in this volume, many of which consider place as authentic learning locations (particularly in Chapters 2–5, 13 and 17) and others that emphasize the power of place to elicit feelings of belonging and attachment (in Chapters 10, 11 and 15).

Place as location

Place is important to learning because the location positions education in authentic settings, emphasizing in our teaching 'real-world' and 'hands-on' experiential learning (Sobel, 2004). Authentic learning is considered to take place when the learning place and associated scenarios experienced by students are typical of the places and practices that students are expected to experience once qualified. It has grown from the idea of the 'centrality' of practices to human activity, and is often fundamental to professional roles (Sheringham and Stewart, 2011).

Consequently, teaching in authentic places promotes applied learning in both physical and social contexts: in workplaces and in the community, in studios and outdoors, on the streets and within professional or virtual networks. These approaches, known as place-based pedagogies, are invariably cross-disciplinary and intercultural, and primarily designed to motivate students through scientific and social connections to their surroundings (Gruenewald and Smith, 2014). A focus upon disciplinary standards and achievements is often a secondary objective (Smith and Sobel, 2010). Frequently, although not invariably, such pedagogies focus upon local environments and communities.

Place-based pedagogies
Place-based education (Sobel, 2004), or situated learning (Lave and Wenger, 1991), already common in universities, is translated to undergraduate, postgraduate and professional studies through field trips, laboratory

work, museum education and practice-based learning. Such place-based pedagogies seek to return learning to physical, environmental and cultural spaces as a way of situating learning in contexts that are meaningful and relevant (Grunewald, 2008; Orr, 1992). Places such as communities, cities, workplaces and field sites are often used to underpin disciplines such as sociology, archaeology, architecture, fine art, history, music, environmental sciences, health and geography.

Place as social construct

The concept of place has a different connotation as a social construct (Tuan, 1977) and in locations where people and communities have deep affective relationships (Altman and Low, 1992) infused with personal meaning, and hence strong identity and feelings of belonging (Massey and Jess, 1995). In his seminal work, *Space and Place*, Tuan (1977) conceives of space and place as co-dependent, with space being without social connections through human involvement. Distinctly, place is space imbued with meaning, significance and belonging (ibid.).

Attachment to place, which has its origins in environmental psychology, was first used to refer to the phenomenon of human–place bonding (Altman and Low, 1992): emotional links and memories associated with place attachment generally have positive affective bonds (Brown and Perkins, 1992). In a different conceptualization, sense of place is commonly seen as incorporating two main components: place attachment, reflecting the strength of attraction to place, and place meaning, explaining the reasons for such attraction. Because of the power of the emotional attachment to the place of learning, the value of this to our teaching should not be underestimated.

Ideas of place and sense of place are used commonly within many disciplines, for example architecture, ecology, sociology, psychology and health and education. In learning and teaching, sense of place is explored in terms of childhood development (Wilson, 1997), situated pedagogy (Kitchens, 2009), critical pedagogy (Gruenewald, 2008), place-based education (Gruenewald and Smith, 2014; Sobel, 2004) and higher education (HE) (Williams and Arnott, 2016; Orr, 1992). The significance of having a sense of place in virtual worlds was identified by Joshua Meyrowitz (1986) who observed that virtual places within virtual communities would be likely to develop a sense of being placeless. Rovai (2002) contends that a sense of community in the virtual space is crucial to engagement. In contrast, a separation of place, because learners are geographically distributed, tends to reduce this sense of community, giving rise to feelings of disconnection.

Social constructivist learning theories recognize that both situation and community enhance learning (Lave and Wenger, 1991) and that it is at its most influential among the learning of professionals through communities of practice (Wenger, 1998). In situated learning theory, situations are not necessarily physical places, but are a construct of the learner's experience in the social environment (Kolb and Kolb, 2005). Situated learning theory enriches the learning space by constantly reminding us that the learning space extends beyond the tutor, the student and the classroom, indeed 'education springs from the interactions and experiences of people and places; from experiences of belonging, dwelling, ownership and responsibility in relation to interactions between university, people and society' (Nørgård and Bengtsen, 2016: 5).

Belonging

Much work on belonging in HE has focused upon retention, particularly among first-year students (Hoffman *et al.*, 2002), although there is some evidence for an association between a sense of belonging and student engagement and success. In an Australian study among part-time students, a sense of belonging to their institution was found to be a particularly strong indicator of engagement for first-year university students (Krause *et al.*, 2005). A HEFCE (Higher Education Funding Council for England) study on student engagement found 'a compelling case that belonging is critical to student retention and success' (Thomas, 2012: 10). Thomas describes belonging at both an individual and social level, individually through a connectedness to the institution and socially through a sense of belonging to a community, and to the institution as socially constructed (Massey and Jess, 1995). The notion of belonging is fundamental to Wenger's (1998) conception of communities of practice, and the social construction of knowledge within groups of learners.

Impact of place upon learning

At this point we should acknowledge that such plurality of place concepts is complex and contested (Hayden, 1997), and although the concepts are pervasive and used in many disciplines (Altman and Low, 1992) their application to learning in universities is not well researched. University spaces and places impact in complex ways on the institution's academic endeavours (Temple, 2011), but there is limited evidence on exactly how the physical campus influences the quality of the learner experience (Jamieson, 2003) or academic effectiveness (Temple and Barnett, 2007). Temple (2011) argues that one mechanism may be through the transformation of physical capital into social capital via locational capital. In other words, as university spaces accrete meaning for their students and staff, they contribute to the creation of social capital that has been shown to support student learning through reciprocity, authenticity and commitment (Barnett, 2007).

Transition to university

Learning spaces are seen as moments of transition between states of learning encompassing boundaries and thresholds (Boddington and Boys, 2011; Meyer and Land, 2006; Lave and Wenger, 1991). First-year undergraduates are the group most likely to experience geographical relocation and dislocation from home. Many scholars (Relph, 1976; Feldman, 1990) see home as a central reference point uniquely providing predictability and familiarity. The importance of home is emphasized by the well-being people experience associated with home and the distress caused by its absence or remoteness (Easthorpe, 2004). Chow and Healey (2008) found that over their first five transitional months, first-year undergraduates' sense of place and place identity did evolve but that location, in itself, was insufficient to create a sense of place and develop attachments. Consequently the need for social engagement is essential to successful transition and to improving retention (Krause *et al.*, 2005; see also Chapter 10 in this volume).

Part-time, work-based and distance students

The importance of belonging to an institution is also important for part-time learners. Kember and Leung (2004) show that coping strategies are significantly associated with an institutional sense of belonging, and that this sense of belonging is stronger if accompanied by regular study routines, strong social support and high levels of self-determination. Part-time students notably report the need for personal self-sacrifice in order to find the time to study following the views of Casey (2001) who sees the self as intimately part of place.

Distance education programmes experience a 10–20 per cent higher rate of dropout than traditional face-to-face courses (Rovai, 2002). Physical separation from the university and its community can give rise to disconnection that, rather than being focused within first-year transitions, can persist throughout the typically longer study periods of these courses. The need to develop a sense of belonging and a sense of place in distance and online programmes thus becomes of crucial importance.

Lessons for institutions

Diana Oblinger (2006) identifies three societal and educational changes that are drivers for these recent and radical departures from traditional approaches to learning and teaching:

- changes in our student learners
- changes in our understanding of learning
- changes in the uses of technologies for learning.

Our current students have different expectations, attitudes and skills compared to their predecessors. Their ready access to knowledge through the internet and the increased costs of enrolment in HE result in current students reporting low satisfaction with conventional teaching methods (Dziuban *et al.*, 2005). Some are driven by concepts of value and student debt, others by an instrumental focus upon outcomes and employability, most by their routine use of social media and preference for highly connected social communication, thereby often resulting in them favouring experiential and active learning.

Additionally many students work part-time, alongside their study, or have external responsibilities that put pressures and constraints upon their time. At the same time, our knowledge of what constitutes effective learning has seen teachers valuing informal learning, immediacy in terms of support, development of skills that include integrating writing with searching for information online and with research, being a reflective learner and additionally learning in authentic locations (Oblinger, 2006). And technology is an enabler of all this; students use their online peer networks and the internet as their information sources, they dislocate their learning from the timetable by studying recorded sessions and they gain knowledge wherever they can and not only from their own university.

Learning spaces can have a positive impact upon learning, bringing learners together, encouraging experimentation, collaboration and risk-taking (Oblinger, 2006). Brooks (2011) found that achievement of learning outcomes was significantly improved in student cohorts that experienced learning in an active learning classroom, including technology-enhanced learning, over a traditional classroom. Kahu and Nelson (2018) contend that belonging, well-being and self-efficacy are critical in mediating the interactions between institutional characteristics and student success and engagement. According to Kuh *et al.* (2010), the buildings and campus landscape present messages that influence students' feelings of well-being, belonging and identity. They go on to claim that this aids learning, although in general there is a paucity of empirical research on how spaces affect learning activities (Yeoman, 2018).

The emergence of the constructivist paradigm in universities has led to a focus upon learning rather than teaching. This is underpinned by a move towards student-centred learning and a consideration of the relationship between the learner and the spaces that they inhabit – 'their places' (Brown and Long, 2006). From this perspective, the entire campus, and all its external and extra-mural locations, become part of a potential learning space at any time.

However, space can also carry an 'unspoken message of silence and disconnectedness' with the place (Oblinger, 2006: 1.1) resulting from a tendency for universities to separate the people in HE from the places they inhabit through a preoccupation with the provision of physical workspaces for students and staff, but ignoring the importance of universities as experiential places of being and belonging (Nørgård and Bengtsen, 2016).

At a wider institutional level, Nørgård and Bengtsen (ibid.) promote academic citizenship as a prerequisite for the fuller integration of universities with society. They recognize the concept of service that universities are expected to provide to society (Macfarlane, 2007) and the moral responsibility that this places upon students: the idea of a 'public student' (Barnett, 2015: 23). Similar ideas are borne out in teaching that involves 'service learning', community engagement and 'live' projects (see also Chapters 3 and 13 in this volume).

Conclusion

Place is a powerful concept to use in considering contemporary learning and teaching in universities. When student learning can take place anywhere and at any time, it is critical to understand the affordances that 'place' brings to learning (Goodyear, 2008). Where we study, with whom we study and how we connect to those places and people are fundamental to successful learning and teaching. Using location to provide authentic experiential learning and recognizing the importance of belonging to a place, in improving student well-being and student experiences, are considerations that need to be central to learning space design and refurbishment. Furthermore, as universities identify and utilize alternative locations for learning outside the campus – for instance workplaces, galleries, field sites, virtual environments and informal networks – creating a sense of place in these settings provides unique challenges for educators.

References

Altman, I. and Low, S.M. (eds) (1992) *Place Attachment*. New York: Plenum Press.

Barnett, R. (2007) *A Will to Learn: Being a student in an age of uncertainty*. Maidenhead: Open University Press.

Barnett, R. (2015) 'In search of a public: Higher education in a global age'. In Filippakou, O. and Williams, G. (eds) *Higher Education as a Public Good: Critical perspectives on theory, policy and practice*. New York: Peter Lang, 15–28.

Boddington, A. and Boys, J. (2011) 'Reshaping learning – an introduction'. In Boddington, A. and Boys, J. (eds) *Re-Shaping Learning: A critical reader: The future of learning spaces in post-compulsory education*. Rotterdam: Sense Publishers, xi–xxii.

Brooks, D.C. (2011) 'Space matters: The impact of formal learning environments on student learning'. *British Journal of Educational Technology*, 42 (5), 719–26.

Brown, B.B. and Perkins, D.D. (1992) 'Disruptions in place attachment'. In Altman, I. and Low, S.M. (eds) *Place Attachment*. New York: Plenum Press, 279–304.

Brown, M. and Long, P. (2006) 'Trends in learning space design'. In Oblinger, D.G. (ed.) *Learning Spaces*. Washington, DC: EDUCAUSE, 9.1–9.11.

Casey, E.S. (2001) 'Body, self, and landscape: A geophilosophical inquiry into the place-world'. In Adams, P.C., Hoelscher, S. and Till, K.E. (eds) *Textures of Place: Exploring humanist geographies*. Minneapolis: University of Minnesota Press, 403–25.

Chism, N.V.N. (2006) 'Challenging traditional assumptions and rethinking learning spaces'. In Oblinger, D.G. (ed.) *Learning Spaces*. Washington, DC: EDUCAUSE, 2.1–2.12.

Chow, K. and Healey, M. (2008) 'Place attachment and place identity: First-year undergraduates making the transition from home to university'. *Journal of Environmental Psychology*, 28 (4), 362–72.

Dziuban, C., Moskal, P. and Hartman, J. (2005) 'Higher education, blended learning and the generations: Knowledge is power – no more'. In Bourne, J. and Moore, J.C. (eds) *Elements of Quality Online Education: Engaging communities*. Needham, MA: Sloan Center for Online Education, 85–100.

Easthope, H. (2004) 'A place called home'. *Housing, Theory and Society*, 21 (3), 128–38.

Ellis, R.A. and Goodyear, P. (eds) (2018) *Spaces of Teaching and Learning: Integrating perspectives on research and practice*. Singapore: Springer.

Ellis, R.A., Goodyear, P. and Marmot, A. (2018) 'Spaces of teaching and learning: An orientation'. In Ellis, R.A. and Goodyear, P. (eds) *Spaces of Teaching and Learning: Integrating perspectives on research and practice*. Singapore: Springer, 1–11.

Feldman, R.M. (1990) 'Settlement-identity: Psychological bonds with home places in a mobile society'. *Environment and Behavior*, 22 (2), 183–229.

Goodyear, P. (2008) 'Flexible learning and the architecture of learning places'. In Spector, J.M., Merrill, M.D., van Merriënboer, J. and Driscoll, M.P. (eds) *Handbook of Research on Educational Communications and Technology*. 3rd ed. New York: Lawrence Erlbaum Associates, 251–7.

Goodyear, P. and Ellis, R. (2007) 'Students' interpretations of learning tasks: Implications for educational design'. In *Proceedings of the ASCILITE 2007 Conference*, Singapore, 339–46.

Gruenewald, D.A. (2008) 'The best of both worlds: A critical pedagogy of place'. *Environmental Education Research*, 14 (3), 308–24.

Gruenewald, D.A. and Smith, G.A. (eds) (2014) *Place-Based Education in the Global Age: Local diversity*. New York: Psychology Press.

Hayden, D. (1997) *The Power of Place: Urban landscapes as public history*. Cambridge, MA: MIT Press.

Hoffman, M., Richmond, J., Morrow, J. and Salomone, K. (2002) 'Investigating "sense of belonging" in first-year college students'. *Journal of College Student Retention: Research, Theory and Practice*, 4 (3), 227–56.

Jamieson, P. (2003) 'Designing more effective on-campus teaching and learning spaces: A role for academic developers'. *International Journal for Academic Development*, 8 (1–2), 119–33.

Kahu, E.R. and Nelson, K. (2018) 'Student engagement in the educational interface: Understanding the mechanisms of student success'. *Higher Education Research and Development*, 37 (1), 58–71.

Kember, D. and Leung, D.Y.P. (2004) 'Relationship between the employment of coping mechanisms and a sense of belonging for part-time students'. *Educational Psychology*, 24 (3), 345–57.

Kitchens, J. (2009) 'Situated pedagogy and the Situationist International: Countering a pedagogy of placelessness'. *Educational Studies*, 45 (3), 240–61.

Kolb, A.Y. and Kolb, D.A. (2005) 'Learning styles and learning spaces: Enhancing experiential learning in higher education'. *Academy of Management Learning and Education*, 4 (2), 193–212.

Krause, K.-L., Hartley, R., James, R. and McInnis, C. (2005) *The First Year Experience in Australian Universities: Findings from a decade of national studies*. Canberra: Department of Education, Science and Training. Online. https://tinyurl.com/yx95a39t (accessed 24 February 2019).

Kuh, G.D., Kinzie, J., Schuh, J.H., Whitt, E.J. and Associates (2010) *Student Success in College: Creating conditions that matter*. Rev. ed. San Francisco: Jossey-Bass.

Lave, J. and Wenger, E. (1991) *Situated Learning: Legitimate peripheral participation*. Cambridge: Cambridge University Press.

Macfarlane, B. (2007) *The Academic Citizen: The virtue of service in university life*. London: Routledge.

Massey, D. and Jess, P. (eds) (1995) *A Place in the World? Places, cultures and globalization*. Oxford: Oxford University Press.

Matthews, K.E., Andrews, V. and Adams, P. (2011) 'Social learning spaces and student engagement'. *Higher Education Research and Development*, 30 (2), 105–20.

Meyer, J.H.F. and Land, R. (eds) (2006) *Overcoming Barriers to Student Understanding: Threshold concepts and troublesome knowledge*. London: Routledge.

Meyrowitz, J. (1986) *No Sense of Place: The impact of electronic media on social behavior*. New York: Oxford University Press.

Nørgård, R.T. and Bengtsen, S.S.E. (2016) 'Academic citizenship beyond the campus: A call for the placeful university'. *Higher Education Research and Development*, 35 (1), 4–16.

Oblinger, D.G. (2006) 'Space as a change agent'. In Oblinger, D.G. (ed.) *Learning Spaces*. Washington, DC: EDUCAUSE, 1.1–1.4.

Orr, D.W. (1992) *Ecological Literacy: Education and the transition to a postmodern world*. Albany: State University of New York Press.

Relph, E. (1976) *Place and Placelessness*. London: Pion.

Rovai, A. (2002) 'Building a sense of community at a distance'. *International Review of Research in Open and Distance Learning*, 3 (1), 1–16. Online. www.irrodl.org/index.php/irrodl/article/view/79/153 (accessed 19 February 2019).

Sheringham, S. and Stewart, S. (2011) 'Fragile constructions: Processes for reshaping learning spaces'. In Boddington, A. and Boys, J. (eds) *Re-Shaping Learning: A critical reader: The future of learning spaces in post-compulsory education*. Rotterdam: Sense Publishers, 105–18.

Smith, G.A. and Sobel, D. (2010) *Place- and Community-Based Education in Schools*. New York: Routledge.

Sobel, D. (2004) 'Place-based education: Connecting classroom and community'. *Nature and Listening*, 4, 1–7.

Temple, P. (2011) 'Learning spaces as social capital'. In Boddington, A. and Boys, J. (eds) *Re-Shaping Learning: A critical reader: The future of learning spaces in post-compulsory education*. Rotterdam: Sense Publishers, 137–46.

Temple, P. and Barnett, R. (2007) 'Higher education space: Future directions'. *Planning for Higher Education*, 36 (1), 5–15.

Thomas, L. (2012) *Building Student Engagement and Belonging in Higher Education at a Time of Change: Final report from the what works? student retention and success programme*. London: Paul Hamlyn Foundation.

Tuan, Y.-F. (1977) *Space and Place: The perspective of experience*. Minneapolis: University of Minnesota Press.

Wenger, E. (1998) *Communities of Practice: Learning, meaning, and identity*. Cambridge: Cambridge University Press.

Williams, D. and Arnott, N.J. (2016) 'Achieving a sense of place: A qualitative case study of "place making" on an undergraduate nursing satellite campus'. Paper presented at the 6th International Nurse Education Conference (NETNEP), Brisbane, 3–6 April 2016.

Wilson, R. (1997) 'A sense of place'. *Early Childhood Education Journal*, 24 (3), 191–4.

Yeoman, P. (2018) 'The material correspondence of learning'. In Ellis, R.A. and Goodyear, P. (eds) *Spaces of Teaching and Learning: Integrating perspectives on research and practice*. Singapore: Springer, 81–103.

Chapter 2

Authentic learning through place-based education

Derek France, Alice Mauchline, Brian Whalley, Martina A. Doolan and Tim Bilham

This chapter continues our exploration of the importance of space and place in facilitating the creation of authentic learning opportunities.

Authentic learning is rooted in learning that is both situated and experiential (Herrington and Herrington, 2006), seeking to provide authentic contexts for active learning and authentic activities that reflect the 'real-life' practice for which students are preparing. Authentic learning requires the application of relevant knowledge and technical and interpersonal skills to the solution of real problems. As such, it lies on one end of the continuum from deductive and prescriptive learning to inductive and investigative learning (Renzulli *et al.*, 2004). Lombardi (2007) argues that authentic learning experiences enable our learners to appreciate the subtle, unwritten and interpersonal knowledge that communities of practice unconsciously utilize on a daily basis. As such, learning becomes social, concrete and requiring judgement 'just as it is in the actual workplace' (ibid.: 2). Consequently, authentic learning is closely associated with both problems and places.

Place-based education

Place-based education creates authentic learning experiences and places them beyond the walls of the classroom. David Sobel (2004) defines place-based education as an approach that uses aspects of a local environment, including cultural and historical information, in addition to the natural and built environments, as the integrating context for learning.

In fact, place-based education is both an old and a new pedagogy (Gruenewald and Smith, 2014). John Dewey (1938) contended that truly authentic learning required the involvement of students in real-world activities, solving real-world problems. A survey of the literature reveals that many place-based learning projects originate from within the science disciplines (Sobel, 2004) or are environmentally based, thus drawing in aspects of the social sciences (Resor, 2010). They are usually multidisciplinary and interdisciplinary and frequently deploy problem-based and active learning approaches in striving to create authenticity. Students become active, participatory and collaborative learners co-creating knowledge through learning communities and professional communities of practice (Wenger, 1998) and reflecting the pedagogic spaces outlined by Barnett (2011). Problem-based learning (PBL) is a common methodology along with, for instance, role play, case studies and participation in actual and virtual communities of practice that are employed to ensure authenticity in learning (Lombardi, 2007).

In exploring authentic learning on university courses, Stein *et al.* (2004), using a perspective of legitimate, peripheral participation (Lave and Wenger, 1991), see authentic learning as requiring participation within communities of practice (CoP). They propose that academic input is through facilitation and mentorship, which allows students to participate in the CoP, engaging in real-world activities and using the real language of that community without full participation, thus providing students with the space to make sense of the community.

Why is authenticity important in learning?

We are living in a world of immense social and technological change, affecting the ways we work, the ways we communicate and the ways we live. Implicit in this is an unprecedented level of uncertainty and rapid change. Our students need to be knowledgeable about a wider range of concepts and are required to be able to apply them to a wider range of contexts than at any time before. As teachers we need to enable this learning and that requires a fundamental examination of universities' reliance upon decontextualized and abstract forms of learning (Herrington *et al.*, 2010).

What characterizes authentic learning?

Authentic learning requires students to engage in realistic tasks that provide complex activities and that are necessarily collaborative in some form. Many of our HE colleagues provide these without labelling them as authentic, but in doing so, HE teachers must take risks and be prepared to offer high levels of support, guidance and resources. Herrington and Herrington (2006) inextricably link the move towards authentic learning, assessments and tasks with moves from instructivist to constructivist approaches: from bounded sequential learning designs to open and flexible contents, from support provided solely by the tutor to the creation of communities of learners and from standardized tests and academic exercises to assessment via production of authentic artefacts and completion of authentic tasks. In terms of space they see a parallel shift, from learning fixed in institutions to distributed and contextual learning, and objective, predetermined knowledge replaced by knowledge built by, and shared within, the community.

This chapter explores three specific examples of place-based education in university teaching. We start with the classic idea of learning in the field, in this instance augmented by innovative use of technology and international collaboration. We then consider the use of 'laboratory' spaces creatively designed to simulate living in an authentic house, and finally the creation of a virtual space that simulates a real place that may be inaccessible to most learners.

Bounded and unbounded spaces to promote active learning
For this project Alice Mauchline, Brian Whalley and Derek France worked with Julian Park (NTF 2008) and Rob Jackson, University of Reading

Fieldwork provides time and spaces where a range of skills can be integrated (Fuller *et al.*, 2006; Kent *et al.*, 1997) and practised through active learning with tasks designed specifically for students undertaking fieldwork and other types of 'out-of-classroom' experiences. As far as possible these tasks should be authentic and also incorporate cognitive domains. Indeed, Herrington and Herrington (2006: 2) argue that 'cognitive authenticity rather than physical authenticity' is most important in authentic learning design and that 'authenticity goes beyond mere relevance'. Consequently our tasks involve problem-solving and enquiry-based learning: fieldwork tasks are invariably based upon PBL in the context of authentic problems and questions.

Student fieldwork is a component of many undergraduate degree programmes. In science-based disciplines, such as archaeology, geography, geology, ecology and biological sciences, it invariably plays an important role and can be a (near) unique selling point for some applicants. More than half of the respondents in a survey of bioscience lecturers stated that the fieldwork component of their degree course was important for it to remain competitive against other degree programmes: 'One of the things we find in recruiting students is that the array of field courses we offer is actually a major selling point' (Mauchline *et al.*, 2013). At its best, fieldwork provides active and participatory involvement; at its most pedestrian merely a 'Cook's Tour'. In avoiding this, and to promote active learning, authentic tasks are valuable ways of engaging students in fieldwork as well as developing their competencies, skills and transferrable attributes (Whalley, 2013). By aligning the tasks (what is asked of students) and the activities (what students actually do) within a learning scheme, tutors have a structure within which scaffolding for student learning can be provided.

Students undertaking fieldwork projects experience, and utilize, multiple learning spaces, that may be out of the classroom (laboratory, library or café) or in the field (exploration site, and/or virtual exploration using tablets and smartphones and appropriate applications) that, for instance, extend and enhance data gathering, analysis and research. It is especially important that tutors use their imagination in planning student activities and relate them to the curriculum space within modules and programmes (Barnett, 2011). Traditional (non-active) approaches such as 'We always do it this way' are, we suggest, no longer tenable.

As many field courses are often residential and last several days they provide an opportunity to enhance social skills and problem- or enquiry-based learning will invariably employ group work. Thus, collaboration can extend into several learning spaces from the initial project planning, before going into the field, through laboratory or library work and post-fieldwork data analysis in reporting and publicly presenting findings. The innovative use of technology, in our case using iPads to facilitate the collaborative activities, extends the fieldwork learning spaces and is found to promote active learning (Whalley *et al.*, 2018). Asking students to undertake authentic tasks within the domains and learning outcomes as well as delivering subject-directed competencies and attributes needs careful thought. The following example shows both student collaboration and innovative use of mobile technologies combining to extend the learning spaces, both the relational space and the material space (Barnett, 2011).

Final-year undergraduates from the University of Reading, UK, and the University of Akureyri, Iceland, collaborated on a joint microbiology field-based module. Previously, students were often provided with microbial samples to work with in the lab without a real appreciation of the environment from which they were taken. Consequently this field-based module was developed to provide final-year students with an environmental understanding of microbial extremophiles and to help the students develop field-sampling skills (Jackson, 2012). A class set of iPads was used to support and engage the students in their fieldwork learning and to facilitate collaboration and communication between the students and staff in the large multi-national team (34 students and 10 staff). The students worked collaboratively, through a group work app, *Geospike*, to record field notes of the environmental conditions (weather, physical details of the site, habitat type) and the exact sample site location. Student groups attached representative photos of the local environment and of any specific field methods employed, as illustrated in Figure 2.1.

Back in the laboratory, the students (n = 23) accessed the group Geospike account and GPS Log mobile apps to produce maps at suitable scales for inclusion in their presentations and field reports. Student feedback on this was overwhelmingly positive:

> It brings together several useful applications in one place e.g. GPS, photo, video, internet, so we don't need 3 or 4 pieces of equipment.

> We can record GPS location and bring all the manuals/protocols/photos with you easy to find and fast to obtain info. Durable iPads survive rain, mud and rips/crumpling of paper sheets.

The shared Geospike map provided the student group with a permanent record of the field locations and environmental conditions from which their microbial samples were taken (France *et al.*, 2015) and the group was able to refer to the Geospike database for data on the field locations while conducting laboratory experiments on the various field samples. Data were thus passed through several learning spaces (France *et al.*, 2013).

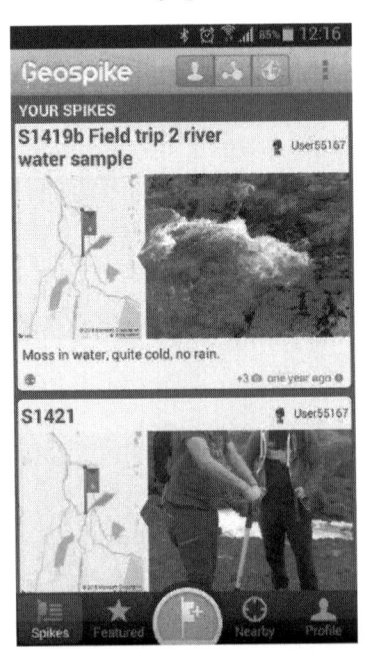

Figure 2.1: Example data 'spikes' of sampling techniques and field sites using the Geospike app
Image: A.L. Mauchline, 2017 (Creative Commons, CC BY-SA 3.0)

Collective use of tablet technology provided an innovative and efficient way of recording group field site data with the Geospike and GPS Log apps (see the map in France *et al.*, 2015: 50), which facilitated sharing and display during, and after, the fieldwork (Mauchline *et al.*, 2015). This enabled student groups to co-create a novel dataset of potentially important microbial extremophile samples with a visual and geo-tagged record of the field sampling techniques. The use of the technology on fieldwork not only exemplifies active practice for students but also shows how they might use it in research and employment.

Reality spaces: Utilizing real-world research and development spaces

For this project Martina A. Doolan worked with Mick Walters and the research team at the Robot House, University of Hertfordshire

This case study illustrates how students experience a real research and development (R&D) facility – the Robot House at the University of Hertfordshire – as a learning space within a Master's in computer science programme.

Designing the learning space

The Robot House is a three-bedroom semi-detached house occupied by a number of robots used for human–robot interaction (HRI) research in adaptive systems. HRI is defined as 'a field of study dedicated to understanding, designing, and evaluating robotic systems for use by or with humans. Interaction, by definition, requires communication between robots and humans' (Goodrich and Schultz, 2007: 204). Situated off campus in a residential area alongside other dwellings, the house is fully wired with sensors and cameras, but otherwise is a typical British semi-detached house providing an ecologically valid domestic environment for conducting HRI studies. Within these spaces, students are given the opportunity to engage in a rich R&D experience, developing their subject knowledge, research and analysis skills.

To develop a usable interface, computer scientists first need to understand the problem space for which they are designing. This includes understanding who are the users, how they will use the system and importantly the environment in which the system will be used. Students were tasked with conceptualizing the problem space by designing and analysing various models to understand essential or unnecessary attributes and functions. This iterative process begins with undertaking user and usage research, which is a key component in HRI and human–computer interaction (HCI). HCI is defined as 'a discipline concerned with the design, evaluation and implementation of interactive computing systems for human use and with the study of major phenomena surrounding them' (Hewett *et al.*, 1992). The user research was made authentic by providing access to PhD and postdoctoral researchers in our Adaptive Systems Research group – the resulting discourse between designers and users engaged and supported our students in more creative thinking and the use of design sketching. This is a unique opportunity as these spaces tend to be closed and are generally not accessible to students studying on taught programmes.

Incorporating the space within the curriculum

International students studying on the HCI programme at the University of Hertfordshire collaboratively design a user interface, based upon authentic research processes within HRI, as part of a group assessment project. The students choose from a range of projects, including a general-purpose domestic service robot Care-O-Bot (Fraunhofer Institute for Manufacturing Engineering and Automation, 2016) developed to provide elderly care in supporting a number of tasks around the home such as fetching and carrying (Reiser *et al.*, 2013), KASPAR, a child-sized robot used primarily by therapists and teachers for providing therapy for children with autism (Dautenhahn *et al.*, 2009), Baxter, a light industrial stationary robot designed to perform various pick and place tasks, either autonomously or co-operatively with human co-workers (see www.rethinkrobotics.com), and CHARLY (Companion Humanoid Autonomous Robot for Living with You) used as an avatar to provide a remote user with a presence at a location that may be many miles from the user's actual location (Walters *et al.*, 2012). This case study will focus upon KASPAR, exploring the affordances of the authentic physical location and the curriculum and relational spaces (Barnett, 2011) provided to students through their engagement with the project.

In addition to the material and environmental space of the Robot House, our design concept considered how we might optimize the curriculum and relational spaces experienced by our students. Barnett (2011) describes curriculum spaces as those that are intentionally opened up to student learning and the relational spaces as the, often resulting, pedagogical spaces between the tutor and students and within the students' community. By establishing the group project as part of an authentic 'real-world' task, we aimed to open our students' eyes to the practical and applied nature of their study, and, through encouraging student–researcher dialogue, to the way knowledge can be co-constructed within collaborative relationships.

Authentic learning through place-based education

Outcomes

Student outcomes include storyboarding the user relationships with KASPAR and demonstrating an understanding of the tasks of the therapist in operating KASPAR to support children on the autistic spectrum in developing their social interaction skills (Figures 2.2 and 2.3). Given that students do not have access to the therapist and the children, working within an authentic space setting offered by the Robot House enabled them to understand the challenges of bringing research to practical outcomes.

Figure 2.2: The context of use for KASPAR the robot (created by student group 2)

Figure 2.3: Scenario of parent, child and therapist: KASPAR the robot (created by student group 2)

Figure 2.4 shows an interface design completed by one student group to be used by a therapist when operating KASPAR. This was originally sketched and revised based on feedback from the tutor and peers in the class (relational space).

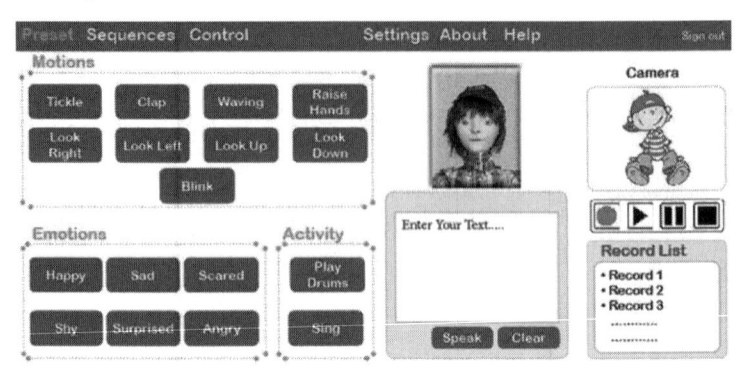

Figure 2.4: An interface design to operate KASPAR the robot produced by a student group (created by student group 6)

Evaluation

Our evaluation of the programme identified student benefits related to location in the physical, curriculum and relational spaces as follows:

> Access to the robots in the robotic laboratory supported my study greatly as it let me have hands on practical experience in robotics.

> Usually we spend the entire semester coming to class and listening to the teacher, in this class we give and can get feedback, can discuss ideas and make corrections to confusions and mistakes, we get a chance to have our say.

In this relational space, the students expressed how they were empowered to engage in lively discussions around the mini-project outputs, which were designed to be shared, nurture interactivity within and between student groups, and engage in dialogue with their peers and tutor. Within the relational space, students were keen to share their discovered knowledge:

> The mini-project activities are very helpful and provide us postgraduates with the opportunity to expand our knowledge and skills by presenting to the group as well as seeing what ideas and concepts other groups have come up with.

> Looking at other students' work presentations helped me understand better.

> It is a chance for the groups to assess their work as it progresses; by getting feedback thusly, they can correct any mistake.

With this in mind, the acquisition of knowledge and its application was encouraged through the assessment design and access to real research spaces, which included opportunities to meet with the PhD and postdoctoral researchers and exposure to state-of-the-art robots *in situ* in the Robot House and in the Robotic Laboratory based at the university. This supported students in ascertaining the requirements of the user interface, understanding the likely users and how the robot would be used. Additionally, access to authentic research infrastructure and processes immersed students in a more realistic research context, helping them to gain insights into the robot's environment necessary to develop a suitable interface design.

> Being in the Robot Laboratory helped me to be clearer and understand how to design better.

Observations

The concepts of research-informed learning, authentic assessment, active and collaborative learning are transferable and applicable to any discipline. Making explicit the links between research, learning and teaching in curriculum design promotes collaboration and interactivity and benefits student learning (Brew, 2006; Doolan and Walters, 2016). Pushing the boundaries of space by utilizing research spaces beyond those timetabled and not ordinarily accessible is valuable to student learning and raising student awareness that they are part of a research-informed learning culture through access to 'forbidden' research spaces has a positive impact on their student experience.

Acknowledgements

Thanks to Professor Kerstin Dautenhahn, the Adaptive Research Systems Group Lead, the staff and research students within the group and to the students who participated on the course and agreed to share their experiences.

Virtual clinics: Online learning spaces

For this project Tim Bilham worked collaboratively with clinical and educational-technology colleagues at the University of Bath. This case is discussed in Savin-Baden (2007) and a summary can also be found in Jones et al. (2006).

Our final case study also uses technology, but not as a way of extending the learning space of classical fieldwork, or of being the primary mechanism for delivering adaptive systems, but rather as a way of simulating places and locations that are normally inaccessible to most students.

Virtual clinics were conceived as a mechanism to bring authentic, practice-based learning opportunities to doctors studying an online postgraduate programme in sport and exercise medicine (SEM). The learners were remote, typically time-poor and unable to directly experience the location. Evaluation of the students' assessment results had identified the need for more direct clinical experience, a frequent challenge for online programmes.

Conceptualizing the learning space

The use of e-learning was critical to the delivery of the programme. All of our students were geographically distant, many of them working across the world. They were working full-time as clinicians, studying part-time and needed to access the course at times convenient for themselves, rather than at scheduled times.

The virtual clinics were situated within an MSc, for which we had universally adopted a constructivist approach (Lave and Wenger, 1991), recognizing that our students had much to offer through their extensive and collective professional experiences. Herrington *et al.* (2010) argue that single perspectives are inadequate and that complexity can enhance student learning. Instead of exposure to a single expert view, students are immersed in complex and contested perspectives and experiences, and provide differences of opinion that characterize all authentic settings (Sandberg and Wielinga, 1992). In this way, we had sought to avoid the criticism levelled at faculty who are content with converting courses to online formats without pedagogical change (Herrington *et al.*, 2010):

> Great being online approaching clinical problems together … everyone has different ways of looking at problems. (Student evaluation)

Designing the learning space

We extended the use of PBL by adapting a model originally proposed by Barrows and Tamblyn (1980), developing it to encourage epistemological competence (Savin-Baden, 2000). Learners saw the resulting co-creation of knowledge positively:

> Working in a group is beneficial, making you feel involved in a case.

Authentic learning through place-based education

It was interesting to get other people's thoughts and respond to them. (Focus group evaluation)

This concept of situated cognition, which contends that knowledge cannot be separated from its situational context (Choi and Hannafin, 1995), was used throughout with the design of deploying technology as a cognitive tool, rather than only as an alternative form of delivery (Herrington *et al.*, 2010), in which students learn with the technology. One example of a scenario provided through the virtual clinics placed each student as the team doctor to a junior (under 18) national sports team on tour at an international team championship, in unfamiliar surroundings and in an unfamiliar culture. The students had to use and manage a body of knowledge about sports physiology, psychology, nutrition, injury diagnosis and management, and ethics as applied to a sport's team doctor scenario. They were faced with the competing demands of coaches, team management and the welfare of the athletes, reflecting authentic and complex challenges found in real-world learning.

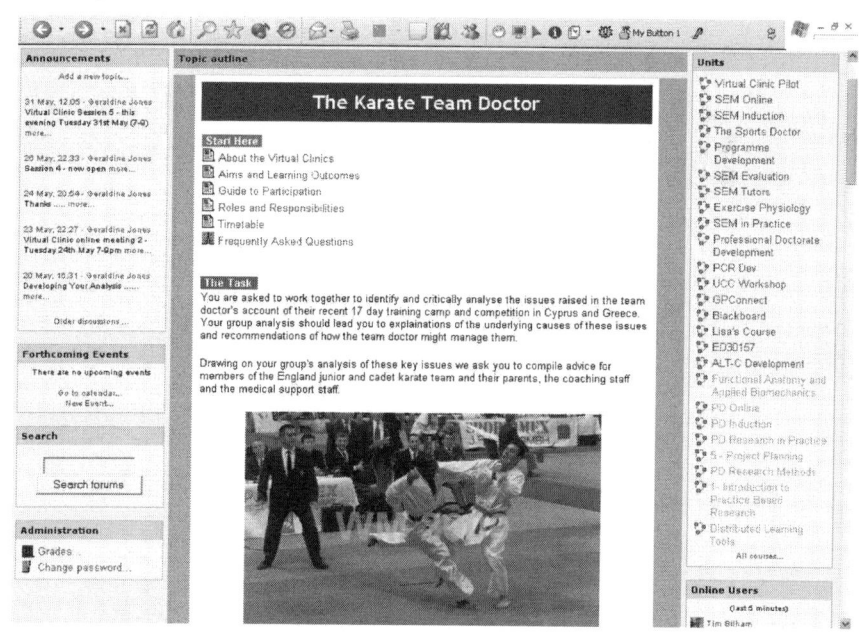

Figure 2.5: Screenshot showing the introduction to the virtual clinic scenario

Image: G. Jones

They engaged in asynchronous activities, e-tivities (Salmon, 2002) and online discussion. This allowed us to accommodate different time zones and different work schedules, but we also experimented with some synchronous and mediated discussions to facilitate immediacy and foster a group identity.

The clinical scenario (Figure 2.5) was developed based on the direct personal experience of one of the design team, a clinician tutor and elite sports doctor. The scenario was analysed and deconstructed into a range of learning issues and presented to students as a text narrative (Greenhalgh, 1999), together with a series of supporting resources utilizing a variety of media forms. Activities that scaffolded engagement with learning were designed and framed as e-tivities.

Evaluation

Our evaluation looked at participation, the appropriateness of the e-tivities and scaffolding for online PBL, the creation of communities of learners and the drivers of and barriers to student and tutor participation. The main benefits were:

- very high levels of participation, especially in synchronous events – about 100 posts and 2,500 accesses from 17 students over two hours (see Figure 2.6)
- scheduling and scaffolding meant that the group did not spend time self-managing
- those with little online experience were able to participate
- synchronous meetings seemed to create a 'virtual proximity', which enabled socialization
- the authentic nature of the scenario stimulated great interest.

Overall 70 per cent of students would recommend this form of learning to clinical colleagues.

> It is hard work working this way though particularly helpful.

> Quite fun. Need to be able to think clearly despite distractions – so a bit like life really!

Challenges identified included that:

- synchronous meetings seem to create expectations of high tutor involvement, and tutors naturally adopted a leadership, rather than a facilitative role, limiting the opportunities for the co-creation of knowledge
- synchronous meetings were only suitable for small groups (< 15) as it was difficult to keep track of posted comments.

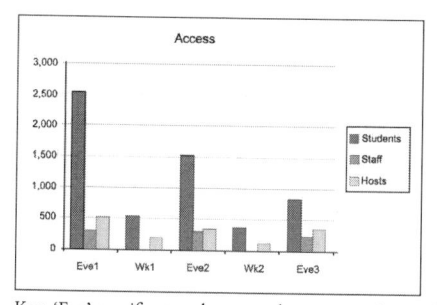

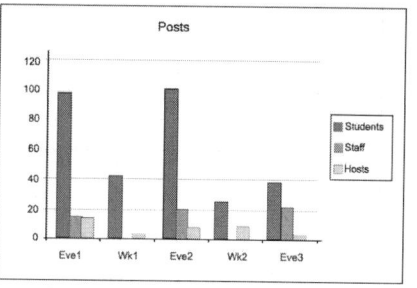

Authentic learning through place-based education

Key: 'Eve' specifies two-hour synchronous session; 'Wk' specifies asynchronous activity over seven days

Figure 2.6: Participation in virtual clinics from students (n = 17), two tutors and one facilitator.

Image: G. Jones

Virtual spaces are well suited to providing exposure to cases, places and contexts that are rare, occurring infrequently, inaccessible or occur in dangerous situations. Simulating these events provides students with experiences that might otherwise be denied them.

Lessons learnt

The examples in this chapter demonstrate that successful authentic learning is more than merely about relevance. It is about connecting students through communities of practice, moving them from the periphery towards the centre of this community by engaging them in the solving and analysis of credible problems and locating their learning in real or simulated situations. The philosophical shift from a behaviourist to a constructivist learning paradigm supports such initiatives, with authentic learning being principally based upon situated learning theory. The case studies presented here demonstrate that authentic learning can be located in any number of places – we illustrate a field location, a laboratory, an R&D facility and a virtual environment. Such places can be situated either on or off campus and are given authenticity through their context, cognitive challenges and legitimate participation from students. Each of our examples stretch the student experience beyond what is merely relevant, to provide and promote learning that requires student engagement in authentic problem-solving, moving the learners from observers to engaged and fully functioning participants and giving them access to areas of experience and communities of mature practice.

References

Barnett, R. (2011) 'Configuring learning spaces: Noticing the invisible'. In Boddington, A. and Boys, J. (eds) *Re-Shaping Learning: A critical reader: The future of learning spaces in post-compulsory education*. Rotterdam: Sense Publishers, 167–78.

Barrows, H.S. and Tamblyn, R.M. (1980) *Problem-Based Learning: An approach to medical education*. New York: Springer.

Brew, A. (2006) *Research and Teaching: Beyond the divide*. Basingstoke: Palgrave Macmillan.

Choi, J.-I. and Hannafin, M. (1995) 'Situated cognition and learning environments: Roles, structures, and implications for design'. *Educational Technology Research and Development*, 43 (2), 53–69.

Dautenhahn, K., Nehaniv, C.L., Walters, M.L., Robins, B., Kose-Bagci, H., Mirza, N.A. and Blow, M. (2009) 'KASPAR – a minimally expressive humanoid robot for human–robot interaction research'. *Applied Bionics and Biomechanics*, 6 (3–4), 369–97.

Dewey, J. (1938) *Experience and Education*. New York: Macmillan.

Doolan, M. and Walters, M. (2016) 'Repurposing the learning environment: Using robots to engage and support students in collaborative learning through assessment design'. In Novotná, J. and Jančařík, A. (eds) *Proceedings of the 15th European Conference on e-Learning (ECEL 2016), Charles University, Prague, Czech Republic, 27–28 October 2016*. Reading: Academic Conferences and Publishing International, 166–73.

France, D., Whalley, W.B. and Mauchline, A.L. (2013) 'Using mobile devices to enhance undergraduate field research'. *CUR Quarterly*, 34 (2), 38–42.

France, D., Whalley, W.B., Mauchline, A., Powell, V., Welsh, K., Lerczak, A., Park, J. and Bednarz, R. (2015) *Enhancing Fieldwork Learning Using Mobile Technologies* (Springer Briefs in Ecology). Cham: Springer.

Fraunhofer Institute for Manufacturing Engineering and Automation (2016) 'Care-O-bot 3®'. Online. www.care-o-bot.de/en/care-o-bot-3.html (accessed 8 April 2017).

Fuller, I., Edmondson, S., France, D., Higgitt, D. and Ratinen, I. (2006) 'International perspectives on the effectiveness of geography fieldwork for learning'. *Journal of Geography in Higher Education*, 30 (1), 89–101.

Goodrich, M.A. and Schultz, A.C. (2007) 'Human–robot interaction: A survey'. *Foundations and Trends in Human–Computer Interaction*, 1 (3), 203–75.

Greenhalgh, T. (1999) 'Narrative based medicine in an evidence based world'. *BMJ*, 318 (7179), 323–5.

Gruenewald, D.A. and Smith, G.A. (eds) (2014) *Place-Based Education in the Global Age: Local diversity*. New York: Psychology Press.

Herrington, A. and Herrington, J. (eds) (2006) *Authentic Learning Environments in Higher Education*. Hershey, PA: Information Science Publishing.

Herrington, J., Reeves, T.C. and Oliver, R. (2010) *A Guide to Authentic e-Learning*. New York: Routledge.

Hewett, T.T., Baecker, R., Card, S., Carey, T., Gasen, J., Mantei, M., Perlman, G., Strong, G. and Verplank, W. (1992) *ACM SIGCHI Curricula for Human–Computer Interaction*. New York: Association for Computing Machinery.

Jackson, R. (2012) 'Heading to the Arctic to teach students about the wonderful world of "extreme" microbes'. Engage in Teaching and Learning blog, 3 September. Online. http://tinyurl.com/pvkgac2 (accessed 5 January 2017).

Jones, G., Miller, S., England, M. and Bilham, T. (2006) 'Virtual clinics: Online places for problem-based learning'. ALT Online Newsletter, 4. Online. https://tinyurl.com/yxzzuow7 (accessed 24 February 2019).

Kent, M., Gilbertson, D.D. and Hunt, C.O. (1997) 'Fieldwork in geography teaching: A critical review of the literature and approaches'. *Journal of Geography in Higher Education*, 21 (3), 313–32.

Lave, J. and Wenger, E. (1991) *Situated Learning: Legitimate peripheral participation*. Cambridge: Cambridge University Press.

Lombardi, M.M. (2007) *Authentic Learning for the 21st Century: An overview* (EDUCAUSE Learning Initiative Paper 1). Washington, DC: EDUCAUSE.

Mauchline, A.L., Peacock, J. and Park, J.R. (2013) 'The future of bioscience fieldwork in UK higher education'. *Bioscience Education*, 21 (1), 7–19.

Mauchline, A.L., Jackson, R.W. and France, D. (2015) 'Case study: Technology-enhanced learning on an international fieldtrip'. In Brown, S. *Learning, Teaching and Assessment in Higher Education: Global perspectives*. London: Palgrave, 81–2.

Reiser, U., Jacobs, T., Arbeiter, G., Parlitz, C. and Dautenhahn, K. (2013) 'Care-O-bot® 3 – vision of a robot butler'. In Trappl, R. (ed.) *Your Virtual Butler: The making-of* (Lecture Notes in Artificial Intelligence 7407). Heidelberg: Springer, 97–116.

Renzulli, J.S., Gentry, M. and Reis, S.M. (2004) 'A time and a place for authentic learning'. *Educational Leadership*, 62 (1), 73–7.

Resor, C.W. (2010) 'Place-based education: What is its place in the social studies classroom?'. *The Social Studies*, 101 (5), 185–8.

Salmon, G. (2002) *E-tivities: The key to active online learning*. London: Kogan Page.

Sandberg, J. and Wielinga, B. (1992) 'Situated cognition: A paradigm shift?'. *Journal of Artificial Intelligence in Education*, 3 (2), 129–38.

Savin-Baden, M. (2000) *Problem-Based Learning in Higher Education: Untold stories*. Buckingham: Society for Research into Higher Education and Open University Press.

Savin-Baden, M. (2007) *A Practical Guide to Problem-Based Learning Online*. New York: Routledge.

Sobel, D. (2004) 'Place-based education: Connecting classroom and community'. *Nature and Listening*, 4, 1–7.

Stein, S.J., Isaacs, G. and Andrews, T. (2004) 'Incorporating authentic learning experiences within a university course'. *Studies in Higher Education*, 29 (2), 239–58.

Walters, M.L., Syrdal, D.S., Dautenhahn, K., Dumitriu, A., May, A., Christiansen, B. and Koay, K.L. (2012) 'My familiar robot companion: Preferences and perceptions of CHARLY, a Companion Humanoid Autonomous Robot for Living with You'. In Herrmann, G., Studley, M., Pearson, M., Conn, A., Melhuish, C., Witkowski, M., Kim, J.-H. and Vadakkepat, P. (eds) *Advances in Autonomous Robotics: Joint Proceedings of the 13th Annual TAROS Conference and the 15th Annual FIRA RoboWorld Congress, Bristol, UK,*

August 20–23, 2012 (Lecture Notes in Artificial Intelligence 7429). Heidelberg: Springer, 300–12.

Wenger, E. (1998) 'Communities of practice: Learning as a social system'. *Systems Thinker*, 9 (5), 2–3.

Whalley, B. (2013) 'Teaching with assessment, feedback and feed-forward: Using "preflights" to assist student achievement'. In Bilham, T. (ed.) *For the Love of Learning: Innovations from outstanding university teachers*. Basingstoke: Palgrave Macmillan, 97–102.

Whalley, W.B., Mauchline, A.L., France, D., Park, J. and Welsh, K. (2018) 'The iPad six years on: Progress and problems for enhancing mobile learning with special reference to fieldwork education'. In Crompton, H. and Traxler, J. (eds) *Mobile Learning in Higher Education: Challenges in context*. New York: Routledge, 8–18.

Chapter 3

Crossin' the Bridge: Learning in community places
Tess Maginess and Tim Bilham

This chapter widens our exploration of the importance of place in providing unique and sometimes transformative learning opportunities. Whereas the previous chapter is concerned with place as the site of *activity*, this chapter demonstrates the importance of place as the site of *community*, indeed places in which personal and community bonds with the place are what drives learner engagement and participation and ensures the success of the learning intervention.

This type of place-based learning relies less on the authenticity of place and more on learners' attachment to place through their community ties (Altman and Low, 1992; see also Chapter 1 in this volume). The chapter also introduces the notion of restorative environments in helping to improve individual and community well-being. At the individual level, Hartig (2004) contends that attachment to place contributes to personal identity and thus place attachment, place identity and restorative experiences are mutually influential. At the community level, place-based education contends that study of place, and study in places, increases learner engagement through intergenerational and experiential learning that impacts positively upon the well-being of communities (Gruenewald, 2003).

This chapter explores an adult learning intervention in Northern Ireland aimed at increasing awareness of mental health among an identified at-risk group of men living in rural communities. In doing so, it speaks to broader themes in higher education (HE) of democracy, politics and inclusion, made possible by the way place and space has been utilized and through the long extra-mural tradition of taking university education to community places.

Learning and social capital

There is powerful evidence of the impact of community learning, social capital and social support on mental and physical well-being. In a major systematic review of 23 relevant research studies, de Wit *et al.* (2018) explored how community-based initiatives can improve the health literacy of older adults and communities. They found that the two key determinants are collaborative learning and social support. In an inquiry into the future of lifelong learning, Field (2009: 5) found 'overwhelming' evidence that learning promotes well-being and that participation in learning enhances social capital. Merriam and Kee (2014) also demonstrated that such relationships between lifelong learning and community well-being are effectively mediated through social capital.

This appears to be particularly effective for older, isolated communities: one of the key findings in the review of the 'mental wealth of nations' (Beddington *et al.*, 2008) identified that learning that continued throughout life had a direct and significant effect upon mental health and well-being, particularly in older age groups. Furthermore, in a field research study, Golding (2011: 103) found that, for older men, learning is most effective when it is 'social, local, practical, situated and in groups' and that this was particularly true for men who were isolated. They found that such informal learning had 'benefits to their own wellbeing, the wellbeing of other men, and the wellbeing of their communities' (ibid.). The example we explore in this chapter features a group with just these sorts of characteristics: rural men, often isolated, exploring issues around their mental health, engaging in a practical and collaborative community-learning project, in a situated environment where attachment to their place and to their community is an essential reason for their participation.

The case study takes a narrative form of Tess Maginess' own story, written in the first person, interleaved with reflections and analysis. This allows Tess' own voice to demonstrate the sensitivity, flexibility and empathy that are necessary in these types of adult learning projects. As a result, we realize that these places are empowering environments and significantly we also hear learners' voices emerging through the work – voices that would otherwise be silent – in representing a group that is traditionally marginalized in HE.

Crossin' the Bridge
Tess Maginess

The making of a film called *Crossin' the Bridge* resulted from an adult learning project focused on increasing awareness of mental health and mental illness among rural men in Northern Ireland, instigated and funded by the Health Promotion Agency.

The context
The emotional and mental well-being of rural populations is recognized as a neglected area in promoting public health (LGA, 2017). In Northern Ireland 33 per cent of the population live in rural areas, compared to 18.5 per cent in England and Wales (MHF, 2016) and the prevalence of mental health problems in the population is 25 per cent higher than in England (MHF, 2016). Communities in Northern Ireland are strong: 72.3 per cent reporting feeling a sense of belonging to their community, compared to 62.8 per cent in the rest of the UK (Siegler, 2016).

Our partnership, approach and philosophy
The project is one in a series of collaborative partnerships for facilitating education in the community, which aim to create learning spaces beyond the campus that are unlike many conceptualizations of *intra muros* learning spaces (MacPhee, 2009). Delivered though the university's adult education Open Learning Programme, this partnership involved the School of Education at Queen's University, Belfast, the Nerve Centre, a creative digital learning and training organization based in Derry and Belfast, and Out and About, a pan-disability voluntary group from the Armagh area. These projects frequently deploy arts-based approaches, reflecting the literature on their effectiveness in education (Rolling, 2010; Rooney, 2004), and confirmed by our own experience. Additionally, the partners held a strong conviction that such research should be meaningful and relevant to communities and undertaken with them, rather than applied to them.

This links with recognized research models such as participatory action research that aims to address inequalities and offer greater empowerment to marginalized groups. Colom (2010) demonstrates that using arts-based models such as filmmaking enhances and deepens the collective character of the educational experience and enables participants to draw upon real-life experiences (Shaw, 2012) as well as to take ownership of the learning and research agenda. The project was carried out for the community to benefit and, contingent upon that, the participants were co-researchers. They were not, as is so often the case, merely 'subjects' to be interviewed, classified or asset stripped of valuable data for the academy.

The location and the participants
Armagh is a small cathedral city some 40 miles south-west of Belfast in Northern Ireland, with a large rural hinterland. The aim was to work with three voluntary groups involving men in the area. Gruenewald (2003) argues that place-based education is constructivist, experiential and contextual,

concerned as it is with nurturing and learning from places, regions and communities. As such, it is frequently associated with ecological, outdoor and rural education.

The first group was in South Armagh; Menaware, a grass-roots affiliation of men from the Crossmaglen area in South Armagh and others from Monaghan in Ireland – that is, men from each side of the Irish border. Even long after the end of 'the Troubles' (the colloquial name for the civil conflict in the latter part of the twentieth century), Crossmaglen is still often referred to as 'bandit country' and the people are understandably defensive. In a study assessing the mental health of a nationally represented population in Northern Ireland (n = 1,694) O'Reilly and Stevenson (2003) found that it was probable that the mental health of Northern Ireland's population had been significantly affected by the Troubles. The second group was the Bardic Theatre in Donaghmore, a village about 12 miles west of Armagh, and the third group was the Southern Education and Library Board Youth Service (Young Men at Risk) in Craigavon, a sprawling semi-rural/semi-suburban area, some 12 miles east of Armagh.

Each group was given the choice of what kind of art form they wanted to work with: the Crossmaglen participants chose film, which is the focus of this case study, the men in Donaghmore chose to write and stage a play and the Craigavon group chose to create a toolkit, incorporating some of the creative material produced by the other two groups.

The intervention

At the beginning of the Crossmaglen project we envisaged a set of talks about mental health and illness followed by workshops on filmmaking and a final project to bring together these two sets of skills and knowledge. But the men did not like this approach, rightly disrupting conventional pedagogies. Consequently we changed the format so that we had the 'talky stuff' in the mornings and the practical stuff in the afternoons.

In retrospect, the men were right to change the scheduling of the workshops. They found it easier to absorb the mental health information gradually and they were able to engage in the film earlier and imaginatively because the filmmaking workshops allowed them to articulate what they were learning into a film. The learning was, thus, more coherent and organic, aptly demonstrating 'learner voice' in action (Healey *et al.*, 2014: 46).

Our 'physical and material spaces' (Barnett, 2011: 168) were a community centre and a local hotel (proper food and the conversations between sessions being an important constituent in the 'manners' of hospitality among the people). These were natural spaces for the men, whereas a clinical or traditional classroom setting would have been perceived as artificial or too official. I encouraged the men to shape the project in terms of location and timetabling by working together during evenings and weekends, and sometimes in spurts of concentrated time, sometimes for a whole day.

As the project progressed, a whole series of other places and spaces also became 'locations' for learning. Such spaces promoted trust and further informal learning. As a film project, it was natural to go to many places in the community. Thus, the film was literally embedded in the community, and part of it. This powerfully highlights the particular potentiality of using learning media like filmmaking which 'decentre' the classroom (Rickert, 2007) and the use of information technology (IT) in expanding the geography of learning spaces to nourish learners (Scott et al., 2016). Especially relevant to this is the literature pointing to the potential of using IT to enact arts-based approaches, especially with non-traditional learners (Fiske, 1999; Maginess, 2017).

Narushima (2005) has found that the promotion of transformative learning opportunities enables community volunteering and promotes citizen participation, especially among older adults. The mental health workshops focused on the real experience of suffering mental ill health, about the prejudice and stigma, about the lives of carers, about what services and supports were actually available, about how people with mental illness could recover. Consequently these workshops required tutors with empathy, experience and sensitivity and I recruited them with considerable care. Most were male, many also rural. They included carers, men who had themselves suffered from mental ill health, professionals or people from the voluntary sector. All had a drive to give 'something back'.

The corresponding workshops on filmmaking were led by a tutor from the Nerve Centre. The learning style was always informal and participative. The curriculum was agreed, disputed and refashioned to meet what was relevant for the participant, and because the project was a film, they began to use what they were learning in the mental health workshops as the basis for their 'script'. The men came to understand that learning, from which many of them had felt alienated, was quite different from the instrumental models they had been accustomed to at school. They saw that education, and indeed research, could be created locally and that they were the ones guiding, constructing and deciding what it was, and that it could, after all, be great craic (fun).

Challenges

Community engagement projects of this type invariably face problems. The Crossmaglen project was made most difficult because of the sensitive nature of the target issue. Consequently we encountered considerable difficulty in finding voluntary groups involving men who were willing to work with us.

Golding (2008) and Parr (2007) have demonstrated that men are especially reluctant about talking through personal emotion and illness, and other research indicates that concern about stigma prevents many people from seeking mental health services, resulting in reduced self-esteem and social disapproval (Corrigan, 2004). As a consequence, men experiencing mental distress may often hide it or mask their pain by using alcohol or drugs. Of course, such reluctance is not only to be found in rural areas, though there may be a tendency to imply that poor attitudes are only to be found in the 'backwoods'. In rural areas, because family networks are still very important, there is still more than a vestigial sense that mental illness is shameful, and stigma attaches to the whole family over generations. Consequently, mental illness is underreported and often left untreated, with serious consequences for the person experiencing distress and their family and friends.

Living in a place or community is the reason groups may come together, but it is the social capital of the group in that place that promotes the well-being of both the individual and the community (Beddington *et al.*, 2008; Golding, 2011). In Crossmaglen, we tried various forms of promoting the project with different groups, but the solution came only with the involvement of the chairperson of Menaware. He understood the project benefits, was able to persuade the men to engage and acted as the bridge crosser, allowing me into the community. The chairperson 'sold' the project to the men on the basis that they would learn how to make a film about their area; that was the hook. The learning was seen as practical, hands-on and likely to be enjoyable, aspects especially important for non-traditional male learners (Golding, 2008).

Christopher *et al.* (2008) have shown that community-based participatory research approaches help to build trust through allowing the 'voices' of participants to be heard, through shared decision-making and ownership and through valuing and utilizing the expertise of participants. Nonetheless, even with the chairperson's support, I still needed to connect with the men in order to start building trust. To achieve this, I used my knowledge of rural dialect and the culture of farming and storytelling to 'cross the bridge' into the world of these men.

It proved difficult to get them to acknowledge that mental illness was really an issue in the local area. In the early sessions when they were asked about what it was like to live in Crossmaglen, the response was Crossmaglen was a fine place, a rural idyll. It was clear that the men recognized the positive affective benefits of their place (Altman and Low, 1992), including its restorative characteristics (Hartig, 2004), while denying or submerging the negative aspects of isolation, loneliness, poverty and deprivation found especially among older people (LGA, 2017). Trust had to be built very gradually, so that the men could 'deconstruct' their ideal, but defensive, picture of their community.

The border-crossing held many dangers. An over-concentration on the baleful realities of life for those living with mental illness and their families could have led to a kind of pathologization of non-traditional learners from marginal communities (Chambers and Lavery, 2012; Gutiérrez *et al.*, 2010).

As the project unfurled over several months, I frequently got lost as the locations changed. While this was a matter of considerable hilarity among the men, my lostness was also a sort of metaphor. I did not really know where I was heading with such an experimental project and though many community projects have this quality, *Crossin' the Bridge* was the most extensive and challenging. I was 'dislocated', but then, ironically, so were the men. We all had to find our way together over unknown territory in darkness and to cross all kinds of bridges and borders in this 'messy' research (Cook, 2009).

As an academic coming from just such a marginal area, I was also aware that there might be perception that the powerful 'Academy' was simply using this kind of research for its own benefit. So it was crucial to accord the participants ownership and to conduct research that would be of primary benefit to their community. In terms of the power relations, I gradually convinced the men that they had as much to teach me as I had to teach them, since their experiential knowledge was as valuable as anything I brought to them (Kolb and Kolb, 2005). Also, as a carer, I deliberated a good deal about crossing that border between the private and the professional. None of us ever broke that trust, though the men knew that there was, during the long course of the project, considerable turbulence in my own private world.

Outcomes

As the men considered the idea of a film, another dynamic came into play. They decided not to make a documentary, considering it potentially too personal, and worried that people would think them pretentious. Instead they selected what was natural to them, storytelling, dramatization and music. By making and performing a story about a person experiencing severe mental distress, they were able to solve the problem of personal revelation while, at the same time, producing an artistically formed artefact that would both celebrate as well as challenge their own community. Furthermore, they could incorporate their new knowledge of mental health and illness and of the support systems available. What emerged was a story of compassion and solidarity with a person in mental distress, which had more to do with friendship than either family attitudes or professional services.

As they grew in confidence, the men began to realize that they could do something they had never done before and 'sell' this to their local community, thus raising awareness more widely. Scenes were filmed in people's houses, on loughs (lakes) and other places suggested by the men. Despite the difficulty of the topic, they testified to their pride in seeing 'Cross' (Crossmaglen) revealed to the wider world as a special and beautiful place; their place. That connection to place, their shared pride and delight in it, even on a freezing February morning, where we spent hours trying to get what would result in only 30 seconds of film, grew also into a pride in and solidarity with one another – as ordinary and extraordinary men.

And nobody ran them out of Crossmaglen when the film was screened. Instead the community showed a real delight in seeing their own place on film and an admiration for the men who had the courage to make a story about people who had often been shunned and excluded from their own place.

Familiarity and security of place is paramount in enabling learning to flourish and be shared. Belenky (1996) uses the metaphor of 'homeplaces' to describe the importance of creating safe spaces for learning. There are striking similarities with the theorizing of these issues and the practice of taking learning into the community of men with mental health issues, creating a safe space that makes it possible for them to speak of their experience rather than taking them to the university building in Belfast, where they would have felt, literally, 'out of place'. At a deep level, the men enacted a 're-representation of culture' (Riecken *et al.*, 2006: 265) in which the marginalized communities offer not just a resistance to the hegemony, but their own alternative representation of their culture.

Lessons learnt

Community interventionist projects are challenging and time-consuming but they can be hugely rewarding and transformative for all participants. We offer the following lessons from this project categorized around participation, partnership, the need for flexibility, consideration of outcomes and resources.

Participation

- Ensure that education should be with and not 'to' marginalized communities and recognize that trust has to be built gradually and setbacks will occur. Do not be afraid of 'messy' research.
- Empower participants to lead the project.
- Trust and valorize the experiential learning of adult students and their particular talents; enable learners to choose their involvement (the natural writers, the natural cameramen). Challenge them, but do not underestimate them.

Partnership

- Use partnership approaches to ensure the project has the necessary range of expertise needed. Be prepared to go beyond the walls of the Academy for tutors.
- Use partnership approaches to create interagency 'buy in' and co-working (for example: statutory health providers, voluntary sector).

Flexibility

- Be flexible about timetabling, location and teaching/learning styles.
- Consider non-traditional learning spaces, especially for those alienated from conventional education.
- Consider using arts-based approaches because they really do work, especially with non-traditional learners and they are much more fun!

Outcomes

- Choose a topic that has real relevance for the community; ensure the benefits are primarily flowing to the participants and their community.
- Ideally, construct projects around tangible legacies or learning products (for example: film, plays).
- Cherish outcomes such as the development of solidarity and friendship among participants. This is vital community social capital and can be built readily through collaborative projects.

Resources

- Recognize that external funding will be necessary as funding for these kinds of labour-intensive project is not generally available in universities.
- Ensure that the project is affordable (ideally free) to participants to create genuine access and ensure that support mechanisms are in place to meet the individual needs of participants.

References

Altman, I. and Low, S.M. (eds) (1992) *Place Attachment*. New York: Plenum Press.

Barnett, R. (2011) 'Configuring learning spaces: Noticing the invisible'. In Boddington, A. and Boys, J. (eds) *Re-Shaping Learning: A critical reader: The future of learning spaces in post-compulsory education*. Rotterdam: Sense Publishers, 167–78.

Beddington, J., Cooper, C.L., Field, J., Goswami, U., Huppert, F.A., Jenkins, R., Jones, H.S., Kirkwood, T.B.L., Sahakian, B.J. and Thomas, S.M. (2008) 'The mental wealth of nations'. *Nature*, 455 (7216), 1057–60.

Belenky, M.F. (1996) 'Public homeplaces: Nurturing the development of people, families, and communities'. In Goldberger, N., Tarule, J., Clinchy, B., and Belenky, M. (eds) *Knowledge, Difference, and Power: Essays inspired by women's ways of knowing*. New York: Basic Books, 393–430.

Chambers, D.J. and Lavery, S. (2012) 'Service-learning: A valuable component of pre-service teacher education'. *Australian Journal of Teacher Education*, 37 (4), 128–37.

Christopher, S., Watts, V., McCormick, A.K.H.G. and Young, S. (2008) 'Building and maintaining trust in a community-based participatory research partnership'. *American Journal of Public Health*, 98 (8), 1398–1406.

Colom, A. (2010) 'Participatory video and empowerment'. Online https://tinyurl.com/yxdvymyt (accessed 24 February 2019).

Cook, T. (2009) 'The purpose of mess in action research: Building rigour through a messy turn'. *Educational Action Research*, 17 (2), 277–91.

Corrigan, P. (2004) 'How stigma interferes with mental health care'. *American Psychologist*, 59 (7), 614–25.

de Wit, L., Fenenga, C., Giammarchi, C., di Furia, L., Hutter, I., de Winter, A. and Meijering, L. (2018) 'Community-based initiatives improving critical health literacy: A systematic review and meta-synthesis of qualitative evidence'. *BMC Public Health*, 18, Article 40, 1–11. Online. https://tinyurl.com/yxwwfzbl (accessed 19 February 2019).

Field, J. (2009) *Well-Being and Happiness* (IFLL Thematic Paper 4). Leicester: National Institute of Adult Continuing Education.

Fiske, E.B. (ed.) (1999) *Champions of Change: The impact of the arts on learning*. Washington, DC: Arts Education Partnership and President's Committee on the Arts and Humanities. Online. https://tinyurl.com/y5ocnbca (accessed 24 February 2019).

Golding, B. (2008) 'Researching men's sheds in community contexts in Australia: What does it suggest about adult education for older men?'. *Journal of Adult and Continuing Education*, 14 (1), 17–33.

Golding, B.G. (2011) 'Social, local, and situated: Recent findings about the effectiveness of older men's informal learning in community contexts'. *Adult Education Quarterly*, 61 (2), 103–20.

Gruenewald, D.A. (2003) 'The best of both worlds: A critical pedagogy of place'. *Educational Researcher*, 32 (4), 3–12.

Gutiérrez, K.D., Ali, A. and Henríquez, C. (2010) 'Syncretism and hybridity: Schooling, language, and race and students from non-dominant communities'. In Apple, M.W., Ball, S.J. and Gandin, L.A. (eds) *The Routledge International Handbook of the Sociology of Education*. London: Routledge, 358–69.

Hartig, T. (2004) 'Restorative environments'. In Spielberger, C. (ed.) *Encyclopedia of Applied Psychology* (Vol. 3). Oxford: Elsevier, 273–9.

Healey, M., Flint, A. and Harrington, K. (2014) *Engagement through Partnership: Students as partners in learning and teaching in higher education*. York: Higher Education Academy.

Kolb, A.Y. and Kolb, D.A. (2005) 'Learning styles and learning spaces: Enhancing experiential learning in higher education'. *Academy of Management Learning and Education*, 4 (2), 193–212.

LGA (Local Government Association) and PHE (Public Health England) (2017) *Health and Wellbeing in Rural Areas*. London: Local Government Association. Online. https://tinyurl.com/yxzuvd4y (accessed 24 February 2019).

MacPhee, L. (2009) 'Learning spaces: A tutorial'. EDUCAUSE *Review*, 26 March. Online. https://tinyurl.com/y27h4dly (accessed 24 February 2019).

Maginess, T. (2017) '*Crossin' the Bridge*: A participatory approach to filmmaking'. *New Directions for Adult and Continuing Education*, 154, 39–48.

Merriam, S.B. and Kee, Y. (2014) 'Promoting community wellbeing: The case for lifelong learning for older adults'. *Adult Education Quarterly*, 64 (2), 128–44.

MHF (Mental Health Foundation) (2016) *Mental Health in Northern Ireland: Fundamental facts 2016*. London: Mental Health Foundation. Online. https://tinyurl.com/yynrmkt7 (accessed 24 February 2019).

Narushima, M. (2005) '"Payback time": Community volunteering among older adults as a transformative mechanism'. *Ageing and Society*, 25 (4), 567–84.

O'Reilly, D. and Stevenson, M. (2003) 'Mental health in Northern Ireland: Have "the Troubles" made it worse?'. *Journal of Epidemiology and Community Health*, 57 (7), 488–92.

Parr, H. (2007) 'Collaborative film-making as process, method and text in mental health research'. *Cultural Geographies*, 14 (1), 114–38.

Rickert, T. (2007) *Acts of Enjoyment: Rhetoric, Žižek, and the return of the subject*. Pittsburgh, PA: University of Pittsburgh Press.

Riecken, T., Conibear, F., Michel, C., Lyall, J., Scott, T., Tanaka, M., Stewart, S., Riecken, J. and Strong-Wilson, T. (2006) 'Resistance through re-presenting culture: Aboriginal student filmmakers and a participatory action research project on health and wellness'. *Canadian Journal of Education*, 29 (1), 265–86.

Rolling, J.H. (2010) 'A paradigm analysis of arts-based research and implications for education'. *Studies in Art Education*, 51 (2), 102–14.

Rooney, R. (2004) *Arts-Based Teaching and Learning: Review of the literature*. Washington, DC: VSA Arts.

Scott, K.S., Sorokti, K.H. and Merrell, J.D. (2016) 'Learning "beyond the classroom" within an enterprise social network system'. *The Internet and Higher Education*, 29, 75–90.

Shaw, J. (2012) 'Using Participatory Video for Action Research: Negotiating the space between social process and research product.' Milton Keynes: Open University. Online. https://tinyurl.com/y2bwbj3j (accessed 24 February 2019).

Siegler, V. (2016) *Social Capital across the UK: 2011 to 2012*, London: Office for National Statistics.

Chapter 4
Moveable feasts: Unusual learning in unexpected spaces
Alison James

The stories of practice that populate this chapter all relate to a form of academic, professional development, both inside and outside any formal curriculum. They relate to physical, metaphorical, real, imaginative or virtual space and concern our identity as teachers, as well as our teaching practices. This space can be, as Savin-Baden (2008: 69) describes, pre-liminal or supraliminal, with the ability to 'disturb our position, perspective and views of the world'. They have much to do with how people construct spaces for learning (both physically and in their expectations), what they consider to be appropriate or inappropriate spaces for learning, and why. They reflect how space can influence how individuals experience things, something for which it is not always possible to legislate. The impact may be intellectual (prompting a new grasp of a concept or subject) or emotional, intuitive, visceral (affecting how you feel about yourself, your subject, your milieu). A sense of belonging in a space might encourage learning, while disconnecting from it may result in different kinds of awareness of insight.

Inside out, outside in

The impact of space and the environment on learning has been widely discussed since the 2010s (Savin-Baden, 2008; Boys, 2011; Boddington and Boys, 2011; Keppell *et al.*, 2011). Publications have explored the reconfiguration of classrooms and lecture theatres and other traditional fora, with a design explosion in the range of furniture and accoutrements now available to decorate physical space. The sources also remind us that space and place is not simply a matter of funky chairs or orange beanbags. Physical space is often territory, which is fought for, contested, or interpreted differently by those who want it. Barnett (2011), in his three-tier taxonomy of learning spaces, notes that they can be material and physical, educational or interior. However, estates staff and teaching teams may have conflicting views as to which of these categories should dominate.

This chapter explores all three categories of space, while agreeing with Barnett that the boundaries between them are permeable. It does, however, have a particular focus on the interior experience of space, as the individual encounters their immediate environment. The different stories of spatial navigation that follow combine elements of the material and educational with the ontological. They include awareness of space through walking or moving, of sensory triggers (taste, texture, sound, smell and surface) and realizations provoked by space. Some are structured, others free and improvised, but all illustrate Barnett's view of space and spaces as distinct concepts.

Investigating space

Engagement with different kinds of space/s is illustrated by a so-called Big Data Walkshop, hosted by the London School of Economics (LSE) in 2016. Its purpose, in support of PhD research, was to explore what big data is, where to find it, and what sites might be data-rich or data-poor. I was attracted to participating on two counts; one, I felt I needed to find out what big data was, and two, it was just around the corner from my office. I felt I could easily 'nip out' for staff development and then return to the day job without too much inconvenience. We met as a disparate group of strangers, were briefed on the proposition and then wandered out on the streets of London's Covent Garden. We then spent half an hour scrutinizing elements of the urban landscape for signs of big data – hidden in electric cables, street signs, marks on walls or the roadway. Spotting clues and signs in the dense, urban landscape was an illuminating and enjoyable way of grappling with a new and challenging concept. As strangers engaged in collective enquiry, it was also interesting to see how we established co-operation and points of connection for a very brief moment in time. It opened our eyes, as well, to things we normally overlook, which can be harnessed to provide rich learning opportunities.

The caravan conference

In 2014 at the London College of Fashion (LCF) I co-ordinated a so-called 'caravan conference', which moved between six campus sites in East, West and Central London instead of taking place in a fixed conference centre. Its theme was flexible and sustainable learning, so changes of format in sessions were especially welcomed. It was also important to break down notions of territory and ensure that staff at all six of the college sites felt involved. Bringing events to the various sites to encourage involvement forced us all to re-evaluate what we felt to be appropriate or good conference venues and opened our eyes to possibilities in our local surroundings.

The conference ran over four days and, in addition to indoor workshops on anything from sustainable fabrics to virtual learning, there were numerous outdoor events. These included:

- a campus wildlife walk, with beekeeping and bird watching
- a visit to the College Dye Garden to learn about natural dyeing and dye cultivation through plant growing
- learning walks (These took many forms. One was a drawing and data gathering activity around Oxford Street, while another was a tour of East End street art in and around Brick Lane. A third, the Detective Tour, is discussed below.)
- additionally, and outside the conference, the cultural and historical studies department at LCF ran Visual Culture Walks in Central London to deepen appreciation of the many forms that visual culture takes, from the popular to the classical (James and Brookfield, 2014).

These activities had a range of purposes and effects, some more planned than others. The first, most obvious, outcome was a renewed awareness of the diverse potential of the spaces as resources for teaching and learning. As conference organizer this was a result I was hoping to see, and it was also revealed through the feedback from event attendees. Participants noted their heightened powers of observation, an ability to spot details that would normally be overlooked or ignored as irrelevant. This appealed directly to the instinct and abilities of art and design tutors to draw inspiration from any kind of shade, colour, shape or detail in the man-made or natural worlds to inform their creative process. For colleagues in non-design roles it prompted them to think again about making imaginative use of materials and 'props'.

The second outcome concerns the links and bonds – however small or slight – that can be forged during these kinds of experiences. These may be between people participating, between people and ideas, or a triangulation between thoughts, people and places that pique curiosity and deepen understanding. For example, colleagues admired the ability of the street art tour guide to update himself daily on the little variations and additions that had sprung up overnight. This made the walk as much a process of discovery for the guide as for his group. Admiration was expressed to the site officer who assiduously put up bird boxes in vertigo-inducing locations and patiently created tiny bee holes in brickwork to create protective shelters.

This sharpened awareness of space and how others use it combined in a third outcome, an increased sense of pride in university spaces (the simple and unsung ones, as well as the grandiose) and their history. Buildings take on their own lives and characters through the use that is made of them over time, and the events and people with which they are associated. This is effectively illustrated in the next example.

The Lime Grove Detective Tour

Serendipity often plays a part in the creation of new or alternative learning activities. The Detective Tour was a case in point, and sprang to life as part of the caravan conference. It was prompted by the reminiscences of a former technician visiting the building who started to recall what life had been like there 30 years earlier. A current technician alerted me to his stories of times past (and the photographs he had found), which captured our imagination as conference organizers and inspired us to turn his recollections into an event. There was something about the secret, lost life of the building that we felt was important to share with others so they could appreciate it too. We created a tour with clues, points of amusement, significance, revelation and nostalgia. It was designed to jolt participants out of their present-day, surface appreciation of their environment and to consider who had learnt in it before and how. The original building had been erected in 1907, to give technical trade instruction in cabinet making, home decoration and *repoussé* metalwork. It then became home to art and design students and its use evolved over time. The former BBC television studios were opposite and students were often cajoled with the offer of free breakfast to increase audience numbers. Tutors recollected seeing 'big name' film stars walking up the road and strange sights such as Darth Vader getting out of a taxi.

The charm of these encounters lay, in part, in the fact that you could not timetable them and they only happened due to the location. Their uniqueness was mirrored in the building's architectural features. Alongside sculptural woodwork, high ceilings, sweeping staircases and wide tiled corridors there were unexpected mysteries. A medieval window tucked within a 1970s partition, which could be seen from the garden but never found inside, and a door that opened into thin air.

These features conjured a theatricality of space, which is often only confined to parts of the campus designated as the grand, official spaces. How individuals move about and recognize and appreciate these spaces is part of how they perform their roles as staff and students. This theatricality can denote an emotional attachment to a space. Exploring the building in a guided tour brought the performance of past roles to life, but its structured form also gave participants a sense of permission to get closer to the building. This sense of relationship and authorization can inform use or non-use of spaces. Some people were reluctant to use spaces outside their usual routine in case they infringed a rule or protective boundary, others were more adventurous and lay claim to space – even if it was just a corridor.

Ways of inhabiting space relates to Barnett's evocation of interior space or the 'psychic' and 'ontological' drivers that encourage a student to 'venture forth' or 'explore the spaces open to her' (Barnett, 2011: 169). For students at Lime Grove in the 1970s, spaces and surfaces were integrated into their activities; the building was a learning canvas for students of surveying, with red and white paint rectangles on the external walls at regular spaces. Materials within the building were also recycled with entrepreneurial flair. The guide told of how you always knew when it was assessment time for the building students because the morning afterwards 20 miniature staircases would be dumped in a skip. By evening, the arts students would have reclaimed all of them, to be used as artefacts, materials and plant stands for offices. Textiles students were well known for going on raids for anything they could weave ... including electric cables. This natural sharing of resources and spaces is indicative of the communal life created within and beyond shared buildings and gardens. Trades courses owned a hut by the pond, which became a home for the Student Union, a café and the place for unofficial all-nighters when people had mural commissions. (The students had gone to the job centre and hired a chef, but the hut had to close down when it appeared to be in competition with the main canteen.) Students of public art made a mosaic concrete dragon by the pond area with local school children, which was later relocated to their school playground.

There were other memories of lives gone by, also conjured by the visitor who inspired the tour: a character sketch of the sales assistant in the college shop who had a phobia about knives and wouldn't sell scalpels; the caretaker's flat and balcony on the third floor, with small children and prams being carted along the corridor and washing hung out to dry; the life drawing room where Quentin Crisp was once a model; the airy staff room with its daily routines of fixed tea breaks and the chance to buy buns and tea from trolleys; the staff office which had a piano and billiard table, neither of which were ever used. (Over the years numerous different people reported they could hear a piano playing, but whenever anyone went to look no one was there.) These stories of previous inhabitants added layers of meaning to the physical character and atmosphere of the building. Each anecdote was recounted at a particular point on the tour and the combination of memory and place was powerful in helping participants imagine the scenes, senses and people.

The tour lasted about an hour, and as an exercise in active learning it was entertaining and thought provoking. Each participant felt inspired to look at their surroundings in different ways, and to find out more about the Lime Grove site and their own workspaces. Participants felt they had enjoyed a short but special adventure and been privy to learning the secrets of a building they thought they knew. As a means of encouraging a sense of ownership and community it was effective, although that outcome was an unexpected corollary of the event. It also stimulated participants to think about how else they might draw on the building as a resource with cultural, historical, sociological and design relevance. It inspired colleagues to consider how to incorporate such a tour into induction, imitating the tour for student benefit, helping them settle into their new arenas, rather than feel adrift in an alien place.

Reframing curriculum space
Barnett (2011: 170) argues that:

> The educational philosophy – as we might term it – behind informal learning spaces is one that diminishes the place of knowledge and instead throws its weight behind *being* and *becoming*.

This would seem to be true for much social learning design (comfy lounges and relaxing areas with plug points galore). However, its characteristics, while conducive to communal and collaborative working, are all directed at enabling students get to grips with knowledge or their relationship with it while being with others. This relationship between the subject, the space, collaborative working and the developing identity of the student as a practitioner or professional has been explored during our postgraduate certificate (learning and teaching) which is part of our staff professional development programme at the University of Winchester.

As part of an initial module, Engaging Students in Learning, students design a teaching activity in a non-traditional space on campus. This is driven by the desire of the teaching team to stretch conceptions of what constitutes legitimate space (real and virtual) for learning and teaching. Grouped randomly in threes or fours, they are given an hour to find the most unusual location in which to situate their activity. They must decide what will be taught, how and why, and the relevance of that location. They must also bring back a memento symbolizing the experience. On their return to the classroom they present their activity in whatever way they think fit. The students on this module are staff teaching diverse disciplines (this year these included criminology, psychology, politics, history, sports

Moveable feasts

science and journalism), so finding something mutually of interest is not necessarily obvious or natural.

During piloting, the exercise looked as though it had been a disaster because the first group returned clasping disposable cups, signs, we feared, of an early tea break. This was wrong, however. They had in fact chosen the student café as a location for teaching the sustainable production of coffee. The second group had set the scene for a dramatic performance in the rose garden (complete with handy pergola). The third group had found a curved stone bench and created a multi-layered reflection around it (Figure 4.1). This included consideration of geological formation, the bench as a visual symbol for a riverbed, glacier or some such, and then also as a metaphor for progress and learning – with students situating themselves at different points on the bends.

Figure 4.1: Curvy bench on campus, University of Winchester

Image: A. James

Notions of what constituted usual or unusual space also varied according to the discipline, and also what spaces mean within a discipline. Staff in the forensic studies department are used to burying animal carcasses (ethically obtained) in a designated area so that students can dig them up later to test for decomposition rates. To them, this is an everyday activity, although the 'cemetery' is off limits to other students and no doubt to them would seem highly irregular. It certainly brings new meaning to authentic learning and assessment.

The activities allowed for a rich interchange of ideas about what can be taught, where and why, and had a number of intriguing outcomes. Several of the group went on to build their main postgraduate certificate projects around the interpretation and navigation of space, and took elements of these projects back into their own classroom teaching. One project explored access to space on a criminology course to support student engagement with live cases. Others were about interior space in two distinct forms: one, gendered space, as translated into the arena of academics in global politics, the second about power relations in learning and teaching. These straddled both interior and exterior space and the notions of permission and authorization touched on earlier. Surprisingly, exploring inner and outer spaces also generated a rich discussion around what is covered by or restricted through the generic referents to teaching and learning activities (lecture, seminar, etc.). This sprang up when a class member's innocent question, 'what exactly *is* a lecture?' unleashed a wealth of diverse replies. The question seemed so powerful that I subsequently asked it on two HE discussions lists, including our NTF community, and received equally rich, complex and competing responses. Having these conversations about something so seemingly simple and basic was particularly useful in terms of unpacking the assumptions we may have about shared understanding of terminology in learning and teaching. The question and ensuing debate led to a year-long institutional conversation across the university, which explored how the lecture is interpreted across disciplines and what that means for the use (or not) of the traditional tiered lecture space. The findings from this are now being converted into a special issue of our in-house journal, including contributions from students.

Playing with, and in, space

Considerations of space featured both accidentally and intentionally in the Play and Creativity Festival hosted at the University of Winchester in April 2017. Devised to enrich the life of the university community, this five-day event encouraged staff and students to do something playful or creative all over campus. It aimed to re-energize morale and a sense of community at a busy, pressurized time in the semester and to reveal how important – and misunderstood – play is as an ingredient of HE. Its philosophy was steeped in theories of play, including Stuart Brown and Christopher Vaughan's (2010) work on play deprivation and delinquency, Bekoff and Byers's (1998) study of animal behaviour and inter-species play, Kane's (2004) radical manifesto for a play ethic in social redesign and Huizinga's (1949) view of play as visceral and pre-cultural. Over 60 sessions were scheduled, including ceramic painting, LEGO® building, games and puzzles, performance, sport, digital play, making activities with peas, sticks, collage, bunting and others.

Place was important for many events. In some, 'ordinary' things took place in unusual places, with creative writing, balloon chasing (Figure 4.2), a lecture and LEGO® workshop all happening in a darkened club space. In others, unusual things took place in 'normal' spaces, with maggot 'racing' (forensics again) and learning eighteenth-century hand gestures in a classroom.

Some sessions took space in a different realm, for example through mindful and contemplative activities which were about removing oneself from one kind of physical activity, but remaining alert and aware of sensations and processing experience in other ways. The practices of yoga and mindfulness invite participants to examine and extend the space within the body and mind. This also happened through the workshop on sensory drawing (including blindfolded and to music) and during outdoor labyrinth walking.

Figure 4.2: Balloon activity, Play and Creativity Festival, University of Winchester
Image: R. Cheetham

The quieting of the mind that these approaches engender also features in the recent adoption of contemplative pedagogies in HE (Barbezat and Bush, 2013). 'Uncluttering the learning space', as Barnett (2011: 170) refers to it, can be about physical clearance, but is also an interior act, as found through the restorative effects of play or meditative practices.

All of these activities were about easing, or jostling, people out of familiar or constrained conceptions of appropriate learning and teaching methods in an HE context. Over 350 staff and students took part in the festival and the organizing team went on to win a Senate Learning and Teaching Award for innovative and outstanding practice:

> A perfect example of research-informed pedagogy. Built upon the research into play as a form of learning, the festival provided a forum for imaginative, challenging and fun pedagogic practice which, in turn, inspired colleagues to review their own pedagogic practice and open themselves to the possibility of incorporating elements of play. (Deputy Vice Chancellor)

Barnett (2011: 168) talks of learning space as a radical concept that allows students 'space in which to become truly themselves, free from constraint'. The festival showed that staff also need that kind of space, whether on campus or off, as part of their sustenance and development as educators and practitioners (staff development is also discussed in Chapter 15). Feedback contained repeated comments about the fun, but also the value of stepping out of normal spaces (the office, classroom) to be surprised or soothed by novel activities. Some of these were performative, encouraging the audience to observe space in a particular way, such as Phil Stanier and Penny Newell's (2016) performance piece *The Naming of Clouds*:

> I feel very privileged to have seen this – This was a fascinating mix of art, theatre, exhibition, play and poetry reading as well as being a scientific treatise on the physics and chemistry of clouds.

In others, participants were more actively involved, as in the learning of hand gestures from eighteenth-century drama, or a vocal workshop:

> This was an excellent opportunity to engage physiologically, emotionally and socially to use our voices. We used our bodies and our voices to make sound in a way that was conscious, purposeful and self-aware.

Conclusion

In all these examples, space is reappraised and used in novel ways. They helped staff and students reframe space on campus in a variety of contexts, including considerations of alternative places for learning, and notions of legitimacy and authorization in the use of space, and of the kinds of activity conducted within it. Benefits noted included stress education, connectedness, a deepening of understanding, and fostering of surprise, curiosity and conversation. Through these innovations and experiments, preconceptions about appropriacy of location and method were challenged and new possibilities generated for teaching, professional activity and collaboration. At the heart of these has been the impact of space on the interior life of the learner, both in terms of subject study and self-awareness.

References

Barbezat, D.P. and Bush, M. (2013) *Contemplative Practices in Higher Education: Powerful methods to transform teaching and learning*. San Francisco: Jossey-Bass.

Barnett, R. (2011) 'Configuring learning spaces: Noticing the invisible'. In Boddington, A. and Boys, J. (eds) *Re-Shaping Learning: A critical reader: The future of learning spaces in post-compulsory education*. Rotterdam: Sense Publishers, 167–78.

Bekoff, M. and Byers, J.A. (eds) (1998) *Animal Play: Evolutionary, comparative, and ecological perspectives*. Cambridge: Cambridge University Press.

Boddington, A. and Boys, J. (eds) (2011) *Re-Shaping Learning: A critical reader: The future of learning spaces in post-compulsory education*. Rotterdam: Sense Publishers.

Boys, J. (2011) *Towards Creative Learning Spaces: Re-thinking the architecture of post-compulsory education*. London: Routledge.

Brown, S. and Vaughan, C. (2010) *Play: How it shapes the brain, opens the imagination, and invigorates the soul*. New York: Avery.

Huizinga, J. (1949) *Homo Ludens: A study of the play-element in culture*. London: Routledge and Kegan Paul.

James, A. and Brookfield, S.D. (2014) *Engaging Imagination: Helping students become creative and reflective thinkers*. San Francisco: Jossey-Bass.

Kane, P. (2004) *The Play Ethic: A manifesto for a different way of living*. London: Macmillan.

Keppell, M., Souter, K. and Riddle, M. (2011) *Physical and Virtual Learning Spaces in Higher Education: Concepts for the modern learning environment*. Hershey, PA: IGI Global.

Play and Creativity (2017) University of Winchester Play and Creativity Festival blog. Online. https://playandcreativityfestival.wordpress.com/ (accessed 8 October 2017).

Savin-Baden, M. (2008) *Learning Spaces: Creating opportunities for knowledge creation in academic life*. Maidenhead: Open University Press.

Stanier, P. and Newell, P. (2016) 'The naming of clouds: A performance'. Online. https://tinyurl.com/y6jgszhp (accessed 24 February 2019).

Chapter 5

Creative learning spaces: Facilitating student-led learning

Carrie Winstanley and Kirsten Hardie

We continue our journey to and through unusual and non-traditional learning places by exploring the learning opportunities afforded by museums and galleries. Locating learning away from the campus, in venues such as museums, art galleries, heritage centres and the outdoors can disrupt expected ways of working (Kenkmann, 2011). Without the resources typically available, both tutors and learners need to rethink how they should be working (Hannan *et al.*, 2013), how to make the most of where they find themselves, how to utilize artefacts or collections, the impact of being together in a public setting and the novelty of studying away from the campus (Boddington *et al.*, 2013). The educative nature of these places and spaces, how they are reimagined and repurposed and disrupt conventional learning spaces are key to their success. Ideas of disruptive innovation in terms of online learning are also discussed in Chapter 18. Moreover, how the use of space shifts and changes the power relationship in teaching and learning between the students and their tutors proves to be an essential ingredient in supporting and developing student autonomy in learning.

This chapter explores two case studies that use place and space for learning in creative ways and which enable and support student-led learning. Although there are qualitative differences and different student audiences, they share a common thread that links creative spaces, creativity and student-centred learning. These spaces and places for learning are powerful and empowering environments that enhance and unleash a liberating potential for student learning. Situated as they are outside the conventional physical space of the academy – in museums and art galleries – there is an aesthetic quality in the air that filters through, which materializes through the exhibits and artefacts that the students examine or have produced, for example in the second case, the wedding dress and the reimagining of the café as a romantic setting. We argue that these kinds of creative spaces for learning are potent, creating a kind of alchemy, which in turn liberates and makes possible learning that would otherwise not materialize in traditional academic settings.

The cases demonstrate the creation of an environment in which voice, a sense of self, the journey from silence to voice (see Belenky *et al.*, 1986) and the journey of developing student autonomy in learning (Boud, 1988) is reflected in the different ways that the learners and tutors engage and interact with the physical spaces portrayed. In the first case, the students appear somewhat tentative in their readiness to learn (Knowles, 1984). We see them together, waiting for each other alongside their tutor in the foyer of a museum, working out, perhaps, their place as learners in this new and unfamiliar space, and as they wait for everyone to arrive before they venture forth, we can see and recognize a felt sense of belonging together, an invisible but important social awareness of their collective learning relationship and the relative safety that it provides. We are also invited to see a democratizing process at play in which their tutor facilitates this learning opportunity for them to step into this space and explore it for themselves as equals, and which one student describes as 'an experience of getting lost in the museum together'. By contrast, the students in the second example have achieved a high level of personal and collective autonomy in their learning. They demonstrate this through their acquisition and organization of the museum space, claiming it as their own and making, through their artefacts, a unique contribution to learning that comes alive in this space.

Shifting spaces: The tutor's role in sharing learning spaces with students
Carrie Winstanley

This case study scrutinizes the role of the tutor in sharing new learning spaces with students, based on work with education studies undergraduates at a post-1992 institution over 15 years. Education studies attract students with diverse interests, ranging from a desire to work with early years and primary children to interests in mentoring disaffected teenagers or becoming educational psychologists or researchers. Many of the students are non-traditional entrants, often the first in their family to attend university and a large proportion come from minority ethnic backgrounds. This impacts on their experience and confidence at university, with their student identity, psychology and family dynamics all affected by their first-generation background (Davis, 2010). Students from these demographics are less likely than 'traditional' university students to make habitual use of museums and galleries with their families and are less likely to consider visiting heritage sites as a leisure pursuit (Harland and Kinder, 1999). Indeed, a recent commission into the future of cultural value expressed concern that arts, culture and heritage 'are predominantly accessed by an unnecessarily narrow social, economic, ethnic and educated demographic that is not fully representative of the UK's population' (Warwick Commission, 2015: 32). Some of our students are uncomfortable in museums because they feel that they do not belong since the exhibits do not represent their own cultural heritage, or they are perhaps unsure how to manage the experience, worrying about getting lost and being overwhelmed (Winstanley, 2013; Harland and Kinder, 1999).

When I first organized trips for students, I mistakenly assumed that they would prefer an independent, *laissez-faire* approach. I found that they were generally unenthusiastic about any type of visit and very worried about their perceived ignorance being embarrassingly and publicly revealed (Winstanley, 2013). However, after talking with students I soon discovered that they were actually keen to tour the galleries with me and appreciated any structure that I provided on the visit. So I changed my approach to a structured tutor-led trip in which I was embedded in the museum or gallery. Over the years I had tried different tactics: proposing short activities for students to complete independently, providing audio-guides or pairing students in teams for mildly competitive activities. On evaluation it was clear that all groups preferred a simple accompanied trip, where the tutor leads the groups around, in a fairly casual fashion, pointing out key exhibits and crucially linking things back to the module learning outcomes and assessment criteria. In the classroom, the tutor often stands apart from the learners, but this 'them and us' notion is dissipated on these trips, and it starts in the museum lobby.

The lobby space

The atmosphere of the lobby is simultaneously symbolic and functional, a liminal, permeable and transitional space.

> The lobby is a special space [...]. It is 'museum' because it is part of the building that houses the exhibition and 'not museum,' because it is not part of the exhibition. It is a transition zone, which links the exhibition with the surrounding world, and as such it plays an important but overlooked function. (cf. Carlsson and Ågren, 1982; Knudsen *et al.*, 2012: 1)

As the tutor meets the students in the museum entrance, the group begins to build a new identity as museum visitors about to embark on a shared journey. The tutor is therefore associated with the students. Together they are all *not* tourists, *not* museum staff and *not* other members of the public.

> I was pretty nervous about the gallery as it's not really my sort of thing, so it was a relief to find the others were already there and also that they were like, texting on their phones, or just chatting and that – I mean when we were waiting for you, just like normal. (Student evaluation)

The lobby demarcates the shift from the external urban hustle and bustle into a space dedicated to showcasing the best of human endeavour and marvels of the natural world: 'It is a transition zone' (Knudsen *et al.*, 2012: 1). Described as a passage or rite of separation, passing through the lobby has both 'physical and mental dimensions' (Sfinteş, 2012: 3) and the space can be characterized as a kind of heterotopia, which Foucault (1966) describes as 'somehow other' that is often disturbing, contradictory and transforming. Heterotopia describes particular cultural or institutional spaces that are worlds within worlds, disrupting what is outside; Foucault saw museums as a perfect example.

Compared to students arriving separately into a traditional lecture space, at the museum we all arrived around the same time, entering into a public space. Here, the tutor is identifiable as part of the group, not as museum staff, nor as another visitor or tourist. Typically, if feeling overawed by the opulence or grandeur of the space, students visibly relax as they see the rest of their group arrive, relieved to be among familiar faces, including their tutor, often verbalizing their relief saying things like, 'Oh, this place is huge, I'm glad I'm here with you lot!' or, 'I'd never come here on my own'. They are no longer alone in trying to decode what to do and how to behave, but instead they are part of a known group in which others may also be feeling overwhelmed. Decoding how to behave can be problematic for some students as they 'try to discern how to uphold the script created by the museum' (Knudsen *et al.*, 2012: 15). As they greet one another, they seem more inclusive than in the campus classroom, since their seating cliques are disrupted. They begin to engage with different classmates, recognizing them as being part of a larger group of peers, together sharing the transition into the new threshold-space.

Such settings require shifts to different behaviour (Falk and Dierking, 2000) similar to changes that occur when working in outdoor learning environments (Rickinson *et al.*, 2004). Gallery spaces require students and tutors to work in different ways from their habitual classroom-based approaches. There is a shift in power away from the tutor, as everyone is required to observe the demands of security guards and museum personnel, sometimes being unable to make independent decisions about where to assemble, or to where to lead their group.

> The teacher is no longer the gatekeeper of boundaries. The boundaries are not as narrow as in the classroom, and as the building is public, the teacher cannot make a claim over spaces in it. This is disempowering for the teacher. (Kenkmann, 2011: 285–6)

My experience was that this disempowerment worked to enhance the group ethos, as students became more open and relaxed, sharing concerns and expressing themselves more fully than in previous settings. This allowed us to help one another more effectively and, as I got to know them better, I was able to see what sort of support they needed. This resulted in the establishment of several peer-led study groups where, later, students booked regular slots in library study spaces, coming together to work on assessments.

There is also a need for physical closeness, since to hear what is being said in a noisy public setting, the group needs to gather closely both to one another and to the tutor, in a way that is not required in the classroom. This closeness has been shown to be positive in that a 'reduced physical and psychological distance between student and instructor, are positively related to student affective and cognitive learning' (Comadena *et al.*, 2007: 241–2). Students credited the closeness created by shared group experiences as the reason they felt comfortable to build the peer networks and some felt this contributed to gaining better grades.

> What happened is that we got to know other people much more because we weren't just in uni together, but we got lost in the museum together! It was a real experience. (Student evaluation)

Students talked about being 'in it together' and this fostered a comfortable atmosphere that persisted back on campus. There is a different relationship in the museum space which can be described as an 'immediacy' defined as 'the degree of perceived physical and/or physiological closeness between people' (Christophel, 1990: 325) which can 'modify motivation' and thus learning (ibid.: 323). Further research data suggests that 'teacher behaviours, especially teacher immediacy and teacher clarity, play complimentary roles in enhancing student learning' (Comadena *et al.*, 2007: 241). Indeed my own ability to support students improved as I understood them better. This had a positive impact as there was an increased willingness to attend tutorials and take on board feed-forward comments from ipsative assessments (see also Winstanley, 2014).

> It's not like other modules because I feel much more committed. I don't only care about the grades – although I do care about them – but I want to see people in the group to catch up with what they thought about the visits and even the reading. (Student evaluation)

These positive behaviours tend to increase in the museum setting, due in some part to the nature of the space and the removal of the traditional physical barriers – desks and screens – between teacher and learner (Comadena *et al.*, 2007). My own relationship with the museum was changed also, as I found myself more willing to explore out of my comfort zone, more willing to expose the gaps in my own knowledge and to learn with the students.

> The teacher is the one following behind to support individual participants and, thus, often explores the new space together with learners. There is no marked territory for the teacher on one hand and the students on the other hand. (Kenkmann, 2011: 286)

Moving around the gallery, making use of liminal, in-between spaces definitely provides opportunities for valuable informal conversations with learners, allowing tutors to strike up conversations with less forthcoming participants, and facilitating discussion between those who have not had a chance to meet one another. Walking along and chatting can be less intimidating than in-class conversations, since body language is less intense, with no need for constant eye contact.

  The structure of a teaching session is also altered. There is no pressure to leave to teach another timetabled group, as there may be on campus. The entire group need to make their way home. Just as we shared the transition of entering the museum space, there is an ending to the visit that the tutor can helpfully manage. Before closing the session, students find it helpful to have a clear closing activity, usually a reflection on the experiences. Focus group feedback suggests that this helps give the visit coherence and encourages students to analyse their experiences, which helps with the analysis required for their assessment.

Back on campus, we have found ways to reflect on and extend the positive effects of the trips. Student groups have created online galleries of images that further cement the group and are shared (with group consent) on social media.

Impact on students and staff

For education students, the impact of the visits has particular significance, as it will be these students who manage children's future experiences in museums, inspiring the museum audiences of tomorrow. Module evaluations note two key areas of learning: one is a new-found confidence in making use of museum spaces, the other a desire to share their interests in these spaces with friends, families and the children they care for in schools and other settings.

Evaluation shows that modules with most visits demonstrate a good set of grades, with very few fails. Such modules also buck the trend for attendance, with around 85–100 per cent attendance for all sessions. For me, however, the most significant impact of the visits is more subtle. At graduation ceremonies, the experiences from these visits are the ones that dominate conversations and remain memorable. Of all the modules I teach, this one provides the most long-term impact and each year I receive unsolicited emails from alumni who want to let me know about an exhibition that they think I will like, or to send me a picture of themselves with friends or family at a gallery we visited:

> That module is totally responsible for my love of museums and I take it upon myself to visit especially out of the way and obscure museums wherever I visit, dragging unsuspecting friends and family with me!

Colleagues who have worked with me have seen the value of accompanying students on visits and some have incorporated this into their work, rather than sending groups off to fend for themselves.

Gallery spaces require groups and tutors to work in different ways, disrupting their classroom-based habits. Sharing visits and trips and embedding the tutor in the new learning space, together with the students, strengthens group identity and provides valuable opportunities to foster positive and engaging learning experiences.

Be My ... Valentine exhibition: Museum spaces for creative collaborative learning
Kirsten Hardie who co-managed the project with Gabbi Hass, Arts University Bournemouth

Learning within a museum where students from different disciplines redesign and transform the space and determine design and curate exhibits can be distinct and innovative: a change in what is learnt, and how it is learnt, is made possible by a change of place and the changed use of its space.

The *Be My ... Valentine* exhibition project (2016–17) involved students and staff from five different art and design undergraduate courses working in partnership with the Priest's House Museum and Garden in Wimborne, Dorset, UK. The museum invited students to create an exhibition; to select a theme through investigation of its collections and to design and curate an exhibition within the museum's distinct spaces – the Georgian parlour, the seventeenth-century hall and the Victorian stationer's shop. The resulting exhibition *Be My ... Valentine* (4–28 February 2017) focused on the museum's important nineteenth-century Valentine's card collection. The use of a period museum building required students to consider a variety of dimensions when curating their exhibition: the constraints and protocols of working with and within a traditional museum and how spaces are used by staff and visitors.

The exhibition demonstrated the power of cross-disciplinary collaboration. Inspired by Valentine's cards, final-year interior architecture and design students created the exhibition's design as part of their final assessment work; second-year graphic design students designed its visual identity and promotion as part of their extra-curricular activities; work from creative writing students and local writers was interlaced across the exhibition; and costume and performance design students and staff created nineteenth-century-inspired bonnets and a wedding dress. Final-year creative events management students organized a live event on 14 February 2017 called 'Tea Hearts', which was a Valentine's Day-inspired romantic afternoon tea party that brought the local community together at the museum.

Tutorials, meetings and design work were undertaken in the museum's themed spaces. These places, initially unfamiliar to the students and far removed from their usual university learning territories of the studio or lecture theatre, became the students' blank canvases: the places in which they worked and the spaces their work was presented publicly.

Creative learning spaces

Figure 5.1: Exhibition information panel and exhibition curation by Nicole Dujardin, Sophie Walker and Elene Edisherashvili.

Image: K. Hardie

Students worked within spaces beloved by museum staff. To change the established aesthetic of the rooms required sensitivity to the emotional relationship that people have with space, as the interior architecture course leader comments:

> In appreciating the living context of their work, all the students involved in the project understood that their decisions would have an impact, that this was about more than cards; a learning experience to be cherished as deeply as the valentines themselves. (R. Gagg, email, 14 February 2017)

Students demonstrated that they understood the unique opportunities they had in working in these special places:

> We managed to create a sound narrative that explains the story of Victorian Valentine's Day cards that didn't disrupt the main narrative of the museum. This gave the museum a contemporary twist to their existing exhibits that didn't overpower the space, being sensitive to what the museum wants to present to the public. (N. Dujardin, email, 14 February 2017)

Impact

The spaces impacted upon students' learning in a variety of ways. Prior to the project the students had never visited the museum and were visibly surprised by the historical rooms and their rich contents. Their initial hushed voices and slow movement suggested a learnt behaviour when in a museum. As they grew familiar with the spaces and appreciated their significance and value, students worked in the spaces with confidence and respect. The freedom given to the students, by the museum director, to imaginatively reinterpret and reconfigure the established spaces and displays was surprising to both students and staff. The expected museum protocols of 'do not touch' and locked display cases were lifted, enabling students to transform into curators. Their learning was empirical and they evolved as curators through their hands-on experiences working within the spaces and with objects of which they initially had no knowledge. Through immersion in the museum's spaces and collections, experiencing the smell, light, colour, feel and sound of the rooms and their objects, the students design decisions matured and their knowledge and respect for the spaces developed:

> The biggest impact I was able to change was the environment of the rooms. The focus was not to take any of the rich history away from the rooms, but to add the elements of my design to create a story through the rooms. (Student evaluation)

Rooms were reshaped and transformed complete with text that students had researched and written. The students examined the ways that museum visitors meandered through the spaces and utilized their observations to inform their design plans. Established exhibits were repositioned or removed – original Valentines were displayed and easels presented creative information panels transforming the look and feel of the rooms. The students' ownership of the space developed their sense of being and belonging in a place that they had no knowledge of previously. Working closely together, each group took charge of key elements of the project and assumed responsibility for joint curatorship. Students inhabited the spaces, planning their design, creating artefacts and curating their exhibition, decisive in their selection and interpretation of artefacts. They worked in a space that was open to the public: their very making and doing was public. This remoulding of spaces directly influenced the way in which the public engaged with the exhibits and navigated the physical spaces. As curators, the students' decisions determined the visitors' experience.

Creative learning spaces

The students' appreciation of the museum spaces was evident in their curatorship. Their work interpreted and presented the spaces and artefacts in creative ways without impacting negatively on the museum's character or commitments, as the museum's director and deputy director comment:

> New ideas and techniques have been introduced to the museum space, which are sympathetic to the exhibition's period surroundings as well as enhancing the visitor's experience of these rooms. They have reconceptualised the Collection and this has inspired the curatorial staff to examine how this approach can be integrated into the permanent galleries and future development. (E. Ayling and J. Webb, email, 15 February 2017)

The students' design and the exhibition's success inspired museum staff to reconsider the use and presentation of their spaces. This coincided with the museum completing a Heritage Lottery Fund application that proposed a major redevelopment. As a result, students were commissioned by the museum to contribute designs and research to support what resulted in a successful funding bid. In this way the students' authentic learning experiences were extended and further reward for their creative endeavour was secured.

This project empowered students to undertake bold, active, experiential learning and repurpose spaces and exhibits to create courageous and original designs:

> Working with the Priest's House Museum has enabled me to gain more knowledge and understanding of how designs work in reality within museums and controlled spaces. Applying all the elements that I have learnt during my degree I was able to make well-considered decisions on how the exhibition would be produced and displayed to meet the desired outcome. It was my first experience of working with a live project and was a lot of fun. I learnt so much and was left with a desire to pursue a career in exhibition design. (S. Walker, email, 14 February 2017)

Challenges

While successful, both staff and students faced a number of challenges throughout the project. The majority of students and staff had never worked together before and were unfamiliar with the museum and its collections. This proved to be both a strength and weakness. Different experiences, knowledge and skill sets brought richness to the team, however, this required careful co-ordination. Working with unfamiliar team players within a tight project timeframe, where all had significant other commitments, required fast bonding activities – friendly meetings and cups of tea in the comfortable environment of the museum's café helped anchor trust and progress planning.

Unpreventable absences from staff challenged the balance of the team dynamics. Students assumed responsibilities with surprising gusto, confident in their ability to ensure that their plans would be successful. Staff learnt to let go, to stand back – a bold move, but one that was liberating for both students and staff – as the project's evolution developed student autonomy in learning (Boud, 1988).

Modifications to students' initial ideas proved to be necessary as time and a small budget shaped what could be realistically achieved. Rather than limitations that compromised student ideas, these challenges unleashed energetic creative problem-solving as students surged forward with alternative designs – and better solutions.

Lessons learnt

Some lessons were learnt by staff that could be transferrable to other contexts and disciplines. First, we learnt that collaborative cross-discipline learning can empower students to create diverse and innovative creative outcomes that can be shared and benefit others. We learnt that creating opportunities for collaborative learning to work with other organizations – 'true collaboration', which Herrington and Herrington (2006: 6) identify as 'solving a problem or creating a product which could not have been completed independently' – can energize learners and enable them to use their skills and expertise in new ways, as well as to learn with and from others.

Second, we learnt the importance of student-led learning and how student–staff partnerships can enhance learning and 'the importance of re-distribution of power and openness to new ways of working and learning together' (Healey et al., 2014: 10). We learnt that to enable and harness students' ideas, rich in diversity and ambitious in scope and scale, requires mutual confidence, trust and open discussion.

Finally, we discovered that museums are invaluable flexible places that enable a variety of learning and teaching activities and experiences that may not be immediately obvious. When learners are encouraged to take ownership of their space and repurpose and refashion it to create something different, the results and the learning can be original and rewarding for all. As Monahan (2002: 2) observes 'highly modifiable spaces invite imaginative experimentation to coordinate space and subject matter with the specific learning needs of different student populations'.

One of the great strengths, and pleasures, of the *Be My ... Valentine* project was that the exhibition was a 'realistic problem' (Herrington and Herrington, 2006: 4), an authentic learning experience that is highly relevant to students as creative practitioners. The integrated mix of students' specialist design skills and expertise created a hugely successful and cohesive exhibition that remodelled and redefined the spatial resources and impact of the museum. Students working collaboratively to redefine public spaces can provide valuable learning experiences that other disciplines may wish to explore too.

References

Belenky, M.F., Clinchy, B.M., Goldberger, N.R. and Tarule, J.M. (1986) *Women's Ways of Knowing: The development of self, voice, and mind*. New York: Basic Books.

Boddington, A., Boys, J. and Speight, C. (eds) (2013) *Museums and Higher Education Working Together: Challenges and opportunities*. Farnham: Ashgate Publishing.

Boud, D. (ed.) (1988) *Developing Student Autonomy in Learning*. 2nd ed. London: Kogan Page.

Carlsson, G. and Ågren, P.-U. (1982) *Utställningsspråk: Om utställningar för upplevelse och kunskap*. Stockholm: Prisma.

Christophel, D.M. (1990) 'The relationships among teacher immediacy behaviors, student motivation, and learning'. *Communication Education*, 39 (4), 323–40.

Comadena, M.E., Hunt, S.K. and Simonds, C.J. (2007) 'The effects of teacher clarity, nonverbal immediacy, and caring on student motivation, affective and cognitive learning'. *Communication Research Reports*, 24 (3), 241–8.

Davis, J. (2010) *The First-Generation Student Experience: Implications for campus practice, and strategies for improving persistence and success*. Sterling, VA: Stylus Publishing.

Falk, J.H. and Dierking, L.D. (2000) *Learning from Museums: Visitor experiences and the making of meaning*. Lanham, MD: AltaMira Press.

Foucault, M. (1966) *Les Mots et les choses: Une archéologie des sciences humaines*. Paris: Gallimard.

Hannan, L., Duhs, R. and Chatterjee, H. (2013) 'Object-based learning: A powerful pedagogy for higher education'. In Boddington, A., Boys, J. and Speight, C. (eds) *Museums and Higher Education Working Together: Challenges and opportunities*. Farnham: Ashgate Publishing, 159–68.

Harland, J. and Kinder, K. (eds) (1999) *Crossing the Line: Extending young people's access to cultural venues*. London: Calouste Gulbenkian Foundation.

Healey, M., Flint, A. and Harrington, K. (2014) *Engagement through Partnership: Students as partners in learning and teaching in higher education*. York: Higher Education Academy.

Herrington, A. and Herrington, J. (eds) (2006) *Authentic Learning Environments in Higher Education*. Hershey, PA: Information Science Publishing.

Kenkmann, A. (2011) 'Power and authenticity: Moving from the classroom to the museum'. *Adult Education Quarterly*, 61 (3), 279–95.

Knowles, M. (1984) *The Modern Practice of Adult Education: From pedagogy to andragogy*. Chicago: Follet.

Knudsen, L.V., Olafson, R., Kristiansen, E., Drotner, K., Simonsen, C.E. and Laursen, D. (2012) 'The museum lobby as a transformative space'. In Kristiansen, E. (ed.) *Proceedings of the DREAM Conference – The Transformative Museum: 23-25 May 2012, Roskilde University, Denmark*. Odense: Danish Research Centre on Education and Advanced Media Materials, 445–67.

Monahan, T. (2002) 'Flexible space and built pedagogy: Emerging IT embodiments'. *Inventio*, 4 (1), 1–19. Online. http://publicsurveillance.com/papers/built_pedagogy.pdf (accessed 14 January 2016).

Rickinson, M., Dillon, J., Teamey, K., Morris, M., Choi, M.Y., Sanders, D. and Benefield, P. (2004) *A Review of Research on Outdoor Learning*. Shrewsbury: Field Studies Council.

Sfinteș, A.I. (2012) 'Rethinking liminality: Built form as threshold-space'. In Jöger, B.-G. and Comșa, D. (eds) *Proceedings: ICAR 2012: International Conference on Architectural Research – (RE)writing history*. Bucharest: "Ion Mincu" Publishing House. Online. https://icar2012.uauim.ro/ (accessed 24 February 2019).

Warwick Commission (2015) *Enriching Britain: Culture, creativity and growth: The 2015 report by the Warwick Commission on the Future of Cultural Value*. Coventry: University of Warwick. Online. https://tinyurl.com/y58kjkm3 (accessed 24 February 2019).

Winstanley, C. (2013) '"Museums and galleries? No thanks, not for me": A critical review of attitudes to museum and gallery visits among university students on an education degree programme'. In Boddington, A., Boys, J. and Speight, C. (eds) *Museums and Higher Education Working Together: Challenges and opportunities*. Farnham: Ashgate Publishing, 123–34.

Winstanley, C. (2014) 'Spaced out: The impact of museum spaces on teaching and learning'. *Education Sciences and Society*, 5 (2), 65–82.

Chapter 6
Making learning spaces: Working with architects and estates

Ingrid Murphy, Gareth Thomson, Kevin Singh and Tim Bilham

Academic staff are invariably responsible for the choice, and development, of learning spaces such as field locations (see Chapter 2), work-based learning (Chapter 12) and extra-mural and community spaces (Chapter 3) yet not for their *on-campus* teaching spaces. Similarly, many teaching staff, and particularly academic developers, are frequently directly involved in the design and development of virtual teaching spaces, yet overlooked in advising upon physical teaching spaces, a situation that is surprising considering the growing adoption of blended learning approaches.

A major reason often cited for this exclusion of involvement is the lack of evidence that location is influential in the learning process (Temple, 2009). However, Brooks (2011), in a controlled study, found that achievement of learning outcomes was significantly improved in student cohorts that experienced learning in an active learning space, including technology-enhanced learning, over a traditional classroom. In an Australian research study, Sheringham and Stewart (2011: 110) report that design of university teaching space in the past has been driven by 'high-level agendas and institutional values' and that the specific requirements of stakeholders and of practitioners using these spaces were frequently discounted because they were unknown to decision-makers. As a result the traditional didactic and teacher-centric model of university teaching has been entombed by the constructed spaces of the campus, by rigid lecture theatres and formal classrooms (Jamieson, 2003). The transmission mode of teaching is so prevalent that teaching and assessment systems are based upon it worldwide, and 'teaching rooms and media designed specifically for one-way delivery' (Biggs, 1999: 21). Such architectures, in themselves, significantly determine the teaching style; as learning and teaching approaches become more flexible these same structures, especially the dominance of particular classroom types, arguably constrain the development of innovative, student-centred and flexible pedagogies.

Jamieson (2003) argues that the design and development of new learning spaces and the refurbishment of existing ones fundamentally impact upon the student experience and should be a priority for practitioners. He further contends that traditional university teaching-space architectures are manifestation of the pre-eminent form of power relationship between lecturer and student, and that more progressive relationships require less rigid spaces (Jamieson, 2003). Consequently the opportunity to be involved, as an academic teacher, in the process of the design and specification of physical teaching and learning spaces is an invaluable and all too rare privilege. In this chapter three NTFs recount their experiences of being closely involved in new builds, or renovations, and how they were able to bring their requirements and expectations for their learning spaces to the design, development and build process.

Our first case looks at maker spaces. Maker spaces in education are formal and informal spaces for creative production of artefacts or products. Frequently seen in the creative arts, in studio spaces, they are also common in science and engineering disciplines, where students blend physical and digital technologies to develop skills, explore ideas and create products often in communities of practice (Sheridan *et al.*, 2014). Our second case is from the engineering discipline and explores the need for practical and flexible space to comply with externally imposed professional requirements, and illustrates the importance of getting correct the small details and practical functions such as power and aesthetics. While there are examples of student engagement in many university activities and processes (Trowler, 2010) there are far fewer instances of purposeful student participation in campus redevelopment. In considering the development of communities of practice in learning, Kornberger and Clegg (2003) call these 'generative buildings' – in other words, they are buildings designed in collaboration with the users of the spaces. Hillier and Hanson (1984: 2) propose that the 'ordering of space in buildings is really about the ordering of relations between people'. The final case considers such a participatory approach to developing informal learning spaces, in this instance, for a library and a social space for students.

The making of a maker space
Ingrid Murphy
The physical environment that students experience in design subjects can have a profound effect upon their creativity and their performance.

However, the design of the spaces themselves often receives scant attention, and insights from users, teachers and students are sometimes not sought (Thoring *et al.*, 2017).

The development of a new building for the Cardiff School of Art and Design (CSAD) in 2013 presented us, as users, with a rare opportunity to influence from the outset the design of the building and subsequent learning spaces for students. CSAD was formerly housed in a city centre six-storey building, designed by Cardiff City architect John Dryburgh in 1966. Although a purpose-built art school, after 47 years both the building and the spaces within bore witness to the silo'ed practices of a bygone era. Academic programmes were located in defined physical spaces and students rarely transgressed boundaries as they were inextricably linked to human and physical resources. This compartmentalization of practice not only resulted in a duplication of resources but the architecture itself became a barrier to collaborative or interdisciplinary activity. As the school had grown new blocks were added; these disconnected structural entities contributing to the sense of fracture. For example research staff and doctoral students were housed separately from teaching activities, creating a perceptual divide between the diverse practices of the school. Fine Art students occupied the top floor with lofty north-lit studios while many ceramics' students were in terrapin huts in the car park. The location and quality of space operated within a value system, but it was not only the physical space that has this currency, area and hierarchical space metaphors within educational practice also infer value such as determining who has access to particular forms of knowledge (Paechter, 2004).

In 2013 the school undertook a comprehensive review of its undergraduate provision, changing the portfolio of courses and including interdisciplinary delivery. It became evident a change in nomenclature as well as architectural design would be required to meet the needs of this newly designed curriculum.

Co-designing the building

The design was informed through a detailed consultative process. The project lead and his team visited the original building to view working practices, scoping out the requirements of each stakeholder group, visiting teaching sessions and meeting with students and staff. Key aspects included:

- flexible spaces to accommodate changing student numbers and curricula
- ease of movement between spaces

- communal space for interdisciplinary learning and socializing
- natural light throughout the building
- highly functional non-decorative design
- industrial workshops that are inviting to the novice, yet meet expert needs
- proper equipment of the building to promote a strong studio
- ergonomic design – for example the doors must swing so that work going to the kilns can be easily transported.

The resulting building won the RIBA regional award for Wales for 2015:

> Here is an exercise in efficient, transparent inter-departmental connectivity, planned around a central atrium using its concrete frame and exposed services as an object lesson in value for money. (Stirling Prize Awards, 2015)

Although the architectural space was important in changing our practices, care in naming the areas played a significant role too. Within the school, we renamed physical resources/workshops by the relevant material or process rather than proprietorial disciplines: product design became soft modelling, sculpture became wood and metal and textiles changed to stitch. This proved an inexpensive but hugely influential change, as ownership of resources shifted from being course specific to being school-wide. It reframed how students both perceived and used these spaces and the students' sense of accessibility and opportunity increased.

> For me, the interior architecture of the CSAD building seems to breed opportunities for critical dialogue. The vast central atrium above the heart space gives a feeling of accessibility to every studio and workshop. While the open plan balconies and studios allow for more spontaneous dialogue across spaces and disciplines. (2017, CSAD student focus group)

The ground floor holds our industrial-level workshop while the other three floors contain light airy studios, which surround a central atrium – the Heart Space (Figure 6.1). This design allows for cross-building vistas, a single glance offering a plethora of learning scenarios and the four-metre ceiling height, large windows and the lack of internal walls give a wonderful sense of space.

Making learning spaces

Figure 6.1: CSAD Heart Space and atrium

Image: I. Murphy

The maker space

While the building itself met its design brief, our newly acquired spacious studios provided little infrastructure, either to ignite our imagination or determine the nature of the teaching and learning. The BA Artist, Designer: Maker course team designed a multi-modal learning space, which encompassed:

- delivery of lectures, seminars, workshops and tutorials
- a 3D-making space for casting processes, small metalwork, resin ceramics, enamelling and glasswork
- 120 individual dedicated workspaces
- collective teaching/making space
- a digital studio for CAD, scanning, 3D printing and physical computing
- the ability to convert to a white cube exhibition space annually to house degree shows.

Fundamentally we wanted this space to promote creativity and be a physical manifestation of a community of making practice, ensuring that students would maximize their time in the studio.

Following research into creative learning spaces based upon an initial typology of functions, Thoring *et al.* (2012) developed a space development toolkit (Thoring *et al.*, 2016, 2017). Their 'Design for Campus' toolkit identifies five different types of space that promote creative working and learning activities:

- spaces for *deep work*, providing personal space for focused concentration and reflection
- spaces for *collaboration*, for group work, workshops and student-teacher consultation
- spaces for *presentation*, places to share ideas, present and exhibit
- spaces for *intermission*, transitional and liminal spaces (cafés, corridors, etc.) for transit and informal learning
- spaces for *making*, for experimentation, play and production.

Figure 6.2: Individual student workspace

Image: I. Murphy

As a result we give every student their own dedicated workspace for *deep work*. Students fill their spaces with their objects, design sheets and research images (Figure 6.2) so each space is frequently the most readily accessible indicator of engagement. As these spaces become visual microcosms of students' learning, they are a critical space for teaching delivery. Having continuous access to a space containing bespoke stimuli, trials and outcomes also enables students to reflect on their progress and promotes a sense of security that is beneficial to creative engagement. Students have access to these spaces until midnight and at weekends, which is critical to promoting a strong studio culture and to fostering a sense of community.

> I feel part of a community of staff and students. (2018, unanimous student opinion, NSS)

Individual spaces are grouped by year and surround more communal and process-orientated spaces, enabling peer-to-peer learning and providing a space for collaboration. These communal spaces are used for field teaching, where interdisciplinary groups work on collaborative projects. These interdisciplinary field projects are central to ensuring that students move freely through the building, and can access all the school's resources. Through this approach students engage with different disciplinary approaches and communities of practice actively working collaboratively.

> [We have] brilliant studio space, offering a collaborative making environment, resulting in an amazing creative atmosphere. (2016, Artist, Designer: Maker, NSS, open comment)

Figure 6.3: Breakout space

Image: I. Murphy

Transparency is key to successful communication in any space. Staff/student meetings, assessment presentations and vivas are held within a glass-walled space adjoining the studio. Students can clearly see when academics are engaged in non-studio activities, programme committees or student interviews, making the full machinations of programme delivery visible. This also provides a formal space for presentations.

Directly outside the studio space there is a breakout space for students (Figure 6.3), with sofas and reading materials and a shared kitchenette. This space for intermission provides a quiet and isolated space moving social interaction away from the working areas, and helping students cope with long working hours. Placed strategically next to the programme office, it keeps the academic team close to where struggling students may seek solace from a noisy studio environment.

In designing a space for making, it is important that the environment itself promotes a culture of making. In our case the architectural functionality of the exposed concrete walls and cabling trays emphasizes an aesthetic so closely allied to material and process that it is practically instructional. Over our four years of occupancy our 'space for making' has undergone many iterations. What began as a space for maker and ceramics students now also houses BA courses in interior design and architectural design technology. Collectively, our making processes span from the very clean and digital to the very dusty, not ideal practices to share a working environment. To address this we created the 'Arc of Making', moving from the hi-tech to the low-tech, and from the very clean to the very dirty. The arc spans two halves of separate studios while the linking corridor provides a natural dust and sound barrier.

Impact

In April 2018, as part of a British Council funded Living Research project in China, I visited 38 maker spaces in the cities of Chengdu and Xi'an, with the aim of identifying a network of making practice. Bringing makers from different cultures to work together is not unlike students from different disciplines sharing the same physical resources; frequently the language or terminology of tool use or process is different. However, making is a universal language and tools can unite makers across cultures and disciplines.

To facilitate tool use learning we developed an augmented reality (AR) co-creation project with maker students. Each student created instructional video content on how they specifically used their tool of choice and the online content was accessed by scanning each tool image (an AR marker) with a smart device. These images cover our studio walls (Figure 6.4) allowing for a very dynamic way to access a large amount of instructional or contextual information. Not reliant on language, it can quickly familiarize a maker with the capabilities of their environment, or a novice with the potential of a new tool. Currently this resource is being developed for local schools in a campaign to promote making.

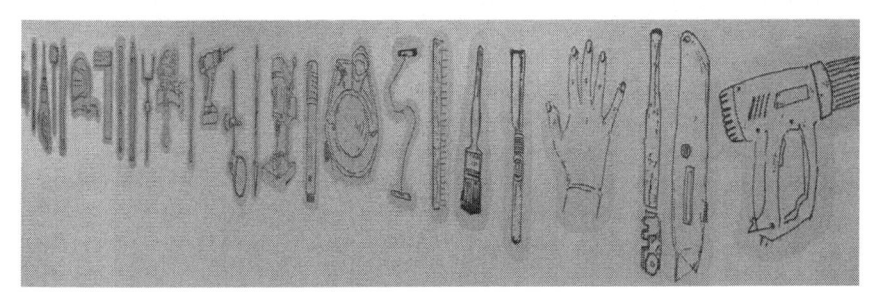

Figure 6.4: AR interactive tool wall

Image: I. Murphy

In 2017, another project between our FabCre8 research group and third-year maker students co-created a radio frequency-identifiable material library (Figure 6.5), which links physical materials to digital content. Again, this enables students to access online content from their studio space; students take test tubes of materials to a digital reader and view student-generated video content of how the material can be used in related making processes. Repeated visits to this material library helps understanding more lengthy processes like bronze casting as a student learns the various stages, in turn helping to scaffold learning and promoting creative applications of process and material. Importantly, the content is accessible at any time and at the point of need in the studio. As the content was produced by fellow students in our workshops, it has high levels of fidelity with a new student's own learning experience, promoting a more immersive interaction with content than untrusted sources.

> The interaction between the physical object and the digital content makes you want to explore more, viewing both the material and the process in a new light. It helps to develop my learning allowing me to see new avenues for developing my work. (2017, CSAD focus group)

Ingrid Murphy, Gareth Thomson, Kevin Singh and Tim Bilham

Figure 6.5: RFID interactive material library
Image: I. Murphy, J. Pigott and A. Taylor, 2017

Our latest initiative is to create an immersive making environment seamlessly linking physical space and artefacts with digital content, in which a virtual reality (VR) studio can be accessed via a headset and haptic tools can be used to sculpt virtual clay that can be directly exported to a 3D printer.

Lessons learnt

These projects employ the principles of 'placemaking' (Harrop and Turpin, 2013), which strategically places resources for greater social interaction and revitalizes underutilized space. Placemaking principles can help meet the diverse needs of students, helping to establish a learning community promoting collaboration and interdisciplinary practice.

We have found that co-designing with students the spaces that they use is critical to their sense of place (see also Chapter 1 in this volume) and, as needs change, involving them in empirical problem-solving is inclusive and empowering, ensuring that their voice is heard.

Our £14 million, 8,575 m^2 CSAD building opened in 2014 and our biggest problem has been in asking the students to leave!

Collaborative development of a learning space for active project-based engineering

Gareth Thomson

The mechanical engineering and design group at Aston University is an active player in the Conceive, Design, Implement and Operate (CDIO, n.d.) initiative, a global educational framework aimed at producing the next generation of engineers. The aim of this initiative is to help universities develop programmes that better equip engineering graduates with the breadth and integration of technical and non-technical skills required by employers. Participating universities agree to follow a set of 12 standards that broadly foster a culture of active, often project-based learning, with integrated curricula and a commitment to the continuous improvement of provision. They must support this activity with appropriate learning spaces.

The curriculum challenge

For the CDIO methods to impact learning outcomes, students need creative spaces to experience authentic practice (Zabudsky et al., 2015). In adopting CDIO, we moved from a traditional intense and assessment-heavy teaching approach to a culture where students are given space, encouragement and skills to become independent learners and successful and impactful professional engineers. We initiated substantial curriculum changes, including introducing major, structured, group projects undertaken by full cohorts in both years one and two, necessitating suitable workspaces in order to comply with the CDIO framework.

The space challenge

Aston University is largely housed in a single, eight-storey building dating from the mid-1950s with the main engineering laboratories housed in the basement. This imposed a number of technical challenges and constraints, including immovable support pillars that challenged sight lines, building services running through the space and no natural light or ventilation. In its previous form the space had been functionally adequate, but given its location it was seen as 'the dungeon' by many students. It was therefore vital to make the space more appealing. It needed air, water and power and because the floor level was sunken, it would need to be built up around 3 m to make it easily usable. In addition to physical constraints the team also had budgetary and timing issues with the strip-out, build and commissioning to be completed within the three-month summer vacation period to avoid disruption to classes. CDIO engineering workspaces must provide for conceptual development and reflection, digitally supported design, systems integration and testing and operation. We knew such competencies were best nurtured in spaces that are student-centred, interactive and that support collaborative learning (Zabudsky et al., 2015).

The plan

Experiences in the existing space largely informed the practical requirements for the new space. A cohort of 150 would need to be accommodated, seated in groups of five or six around 24 workbenches, which needed to allow for a range of activities, including meetings, group work, prototype fabrication and assembly.

The benches should not be fixed to allow for repurposing the space for trade-show type activities, for example. There was a requirement for power supply to the benches via pull down mains sockets, room-specific AV and WiFi, a technician cabin to house support staff, tools and consumables, and additional storage for student work-in-progress. Additionally, adjoining space was required to allow for overspill project space and a flexible engineering teaching laboratory.

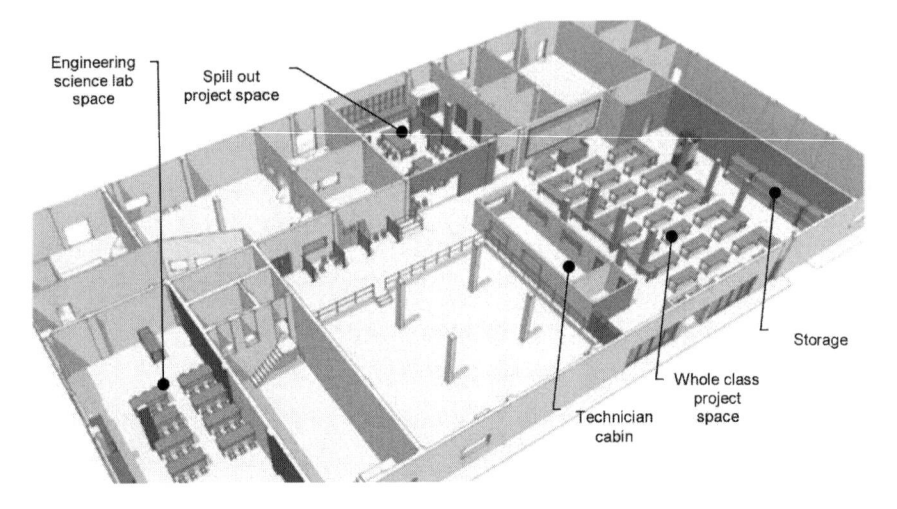

Figure 6.6: Final pre-production plan of proposed working space development
Image: ADP Architecture Ltd

The team

This was a major project, the execution of which involved a wide-ranging planning and execution team, including academics, students, support staff, estates staff and a plethora of external contractors and consultants. From a learning space perspective, a core team consisting of two academics and the manager of the technician team, who support the student activities, set the requirements and co-designed the space. The academic team followed best practice, modified by reflection upon their own experiences and drawing upon ideas and opinions from the wider programme teaching team and students. Student opinion was gathered from reflection forms for those classes who experienced the space, via feedback on flexible project spaces especially among final year students and via direct dialogue with students. The students in particular felt the existing space was very dingy with particular practical issues related to sight lines and access to technicians.

The overall requirements were co-ordinated by the estates project team, who worked with the central facilities team to ensure the building work and the final outcome would not have an adverse impact elsewhere. The estates' team incorporated third-party contractors including architects and structural engineers. The build had to be completed between mid-June and the start of the new academic year at the end of September. Planning began around February, centred on fortnightly meetings of a core project planning team consisting of representatives of the academic and estates' teams with each of the key contractors.

It was important that the academic team and the contractors had direct contact to ensure a clear understanding of the teaching requirements achieved under the stewardship of estates. While the overall project team was quite large, this structure ensured that decisions could be made quickly – changes necessitated by structural engineering concerns, for example, which might have an impact on teaching, power, fire safety or ventilation issues could very quickly be resolved with all parties present. While the estates' team generally acted as an intermediary, it was not uncommon for contractors to contact academics directly for clarification (emails copying in the entire team were stored in a central cloud to ensure visibility to all).

Evaluation

In the main project area the space is now bright and airy while retaining a desired professional and industrial feel. A large window and graphics area create impact and engender ownership and pride among students and staff.

> It now feels far more like an actual university engineering space, whereas before we couldn't help but feel that we were simply in the basement.

> The change in lights and (introduction of) colour to the room automatically changed it from a dull, underground lab to a more inviting workspace.

The space is very flexible, which is important for a space-constrained university, as it allows for a range of different uses from conventional lectures, project work, physical design and build and presentations and shows. Crucially, it is also well-suited to open learning, with students free to come and go to work on their project supported by peers, on-site technicians and academics.

The technicians booth helps separate the workspace and conversations are easily heard, rather than trying to talk over the background noise of the class.

The additional facilities for hand tool work have proved beneficial, and with the over-spill classroom facilities has enabled final year project work, and other activities to take place simultaneously with main room teaching, so we have a beneficial efficiency improvement.

Lessons learnt

Clear communication between the academic team, the internal estates' office and the contractors was essential in understanding the need and fully exploring the opportunities on offer. Critical factors include:

- insist on being a core part of the team with contact with lead contractors
- be prepared to commit significant time and you may need to get down to more detail than you might anticipate
- make sure estates and contractors are clear about your goals but then allow them to work on the detail and negotiations
- compromise to keep the project on budget – make sure you are involved in these decisions
- be clear on the extent of your obligations regarding a development – for instance, do benches, stools and other new items come out of the development budget or the operating budget?
- insist on post-development snag meetings and that estates include you in these – give yourself the time to appraise any outstanding issues among the teaching and student support team as they will be much harder to resolve after sign-off.

The space has been operating in its new format for over a year now and the careful work of all parties in the run-up to the development have meant there have been very few issues on the ground. The development has proved a significant change for the better delivering a much stronger student experience and a more effective working environment for both academics and supporting technicians.

Student involvement in design of their learning spaces
Kevin Singh

The opportunity for architecture students to follow a live design and construction process over a two-year period is an invaluable learning tool that allows them to witness 3D construction complementing their study of generally 2D drawings. In developing our campus, Birmingham City University (BCU) took the unusual step of contractually requiring all building contractors to engage students in the construction process, including site visits, work placements, research opportunities and live design competitions. Construction site hoardings have even been used to display student design. Live projects (which are also considered in Chapter 13 in this volume) have a long tradition at the Birmingham School of Architecture. Indeed, the school is credited with being the first to embed live projects in the curriculum in the 1950s: a housing project working with the local authority.

Today this tradition lives on via Co.Lab (Collaboration: Practice), which provides innovative modules for both undergraduate and postgraduate students across the disciplines of architecture, landscape architecture, interior architecture and design, and product and furniture design. Co.Lab (n.d.) is an award-winning design and research initiative within the Birmingham School of Architecture, as part of which students and staff work collaboratively with a multitude of community and professional organization. It provides students with opportunities to collaborate with community groups, commercial entities and others on live projects.

As an extension we created Co.Lab Consult, a vehicle for staff to continue to practice and retain currency and support local and regional small and medium enterprises. The creation of Co.Lab Consult has also allowed the school to fill the perennial void that exists in the vast majority of universities, that of estates and facilities departments not engaging with their schools of architecture and design.

Because we know learning is made more effective as a result of interactions between students, the design of spaces needs to consider spaces where students work and socialize together (Kuh *et al.*, 2010). The library offers an obvious space where learning is undertaken in a social context, supported physically, technologically and remotely. Bennett (2003), in *Libraries Designed for Learning,* proposes that library design (and redesign) should not be dominated by information resources, but should incorporate strategies that support independent, active learning behaviours. Co-design with users is critical to successful outcomes:

> Learners' views are key to getting the balance of the design right, and their opinions should be sought at an early stage in its development. (JISC, 2006)

Alongside this, the university itself has been a leader in student engagement through its OpportUnity scheme led by the Centre for Enhancement of Learning and Teaching (CELT) and run in partnership with our Students' Union. The work has gained sector-wide recognition, including a 2010 *Times Higher* Award for Outstanding Support for Students. The simultaneity of Co.Lab Consult and OpportUnity has created a perfect opportunity, opening up new possibilities for collaboration between the estates and facilities teams, the School of Architecture and Design and our students. This partnership was applied to two critical learning spaces, a student learning centre and the redesign of areas of the main library.

The Den – student centre

The Den, located on the BCU North campus, was commissioned to support students who live in the 'out-of-town' halls of residence. Taking an overarching brief from the student accommodation team, we worked with a group of student assistants from several courses – motorsport technology, mental health nursing, psychology and media – in a process that developed details of the brief and ultimately the design of the centre.

The focus group consultations were in two parts, firstly with the facilities team and then with myself, as the designer. The different priorities of the two sessions meant that students were able to discuss and identify functional requirements, but also personal and psychological needs such as a 'hangover'/chill out room, or, for a student who did not return home for the Christmas vacation, somewhere which felt like home.

Figure 6.7: The Den at BCU North Campus

Image: Emphasis Photography

Making learning spaces

A noticeable aspect of these stakeholder meetings was how seriously students undertook this role, focusing on study spaces but appreciating that spaces that encourage social interaction and collaboration are just as important (JISC, 2006). This resulted in a design proposal that was articulated in three distinct areas relating to work, rest and play (Figure 6.7).

Redesign of Curzon Library

This project came directly at the request of the university's vice chancellor following negative student feedback about the lack of available seats in the new library and the imbalance between social learning spaces and individual and small group-study areas, which generated a noisy 'social club' feel rather than a place of study:

> Not enough resources or quiet spaces to work in. Very restricted areas with limited working spaces as people who just socialise in areas where people are trying to work, and taking up resources ... It is not a very relaxing space to work. (2017, NSS, open comment)

The original design was problematic in that large communal seating areas would be colonized by an individual student or perhaps a small group that prompted a response of not feeling welcome to use other adjacent seating places. I was therefore tasked with undertaking a design review and space and furniture audit of the library to address the problems being experienced. The student union played a key part in the design consultation, participating in walking observations, briefing sessions, reviewing interim designs and critically communicating the proposals, final outcome and benefits to their members in conjunction with the library team (BCU, 2016). As the project was led by the Students' Union, the estates team primarily concerned themselves with practical and logistical issues such as power and data installation, the removal of superfluous items and the procurement of the furniture.

> Involving learners in aspects of the design is important. This signals that they can have a measure of control over the learning environment and over their own learning. (JISC, 2006)

During the consultation it became clear that students wanted a space with a defined territory, regardless of whether it was in a communal setting and so the use of low desk dividers helped define each space.

> The Students' Union had lots of complaints from students with regard to the library layout ... lack of seating areas, quiet study

> spaces and laptop areas; this was an issue we highlighted to the university. They actively sought our guidance and ideas in order to improve this space, with students' needs at the forefront of the design. This was a great win for us, and the students, as they felt listened to and it proved that they had a say in their education and their university. (Vice President for Student Engagement, BCU Students' Union)

The redesign provided an additional 107 study places, but just as importantly it found a more appropriate balance between social and group spaces, providing a variety of learning spaces from communal tables to smaller group study spaces in pods.

> Our [library] NSS satisfaction score rose from 83 per cent in 2016 to 86 per cent in 2017. Although space remains a challenge, there were fewer negative comments in the NSS this year. Undoubtedly the improvements made to the Curzon Library in 2016 were impactful. They created more space for individual study, and the reconfiguration of group study spaces by replacing sofas with the very popular power-enable pods resulted in the full utilisation of these areas. (Deputy Director of Information Services, Library and Learning Resources)

Reflections

The success of these two projects has led to academic involvement in further significant build projects. My unusual faculty estates role has allowed me to influence a wide range of university functional areas, including timetabling, room use strategies, the reorganization of the Arts, Media and Design building, as well as multidisciplinary co-working spaces. My involvement adds an academic learning and teaching perspective as well as experience of being a practising architect. My colleagues, and the students, find comfort in working with me, knowing that I can interpret for them the terminology of design and construction, and represent their views within the institution.

References

BCU (Birmingham City University) (2016) 'Space, glorious space!'. BCU Library and Learning Resources blog, 2 September. Online. https://tinyurl.com/y6okwqc9 (accessed 24 February 2019).

Bennett, S. (2003) *Libraries Designed for Learning*. Washington, DC: Council on Library and Information Resources.

Biggs, J. (1999) *Teaching for Quality Learning at University*. Buckingham: Society for Research into Higher Education and Open University Press.

Brooks, D.C. (2011) 'Space matters: The impact of formal learning environments on student learning'. *British Journal of Educational Technology*, 42 (5), 719–26.

CDIO (Conceive Design Implement Operate) Initiative (n.d.) 'About CDIO'. Online. www.cdio.org/about (accessed 5 November 2018).

Co.Lab (n.d.) 'About Co.Lab'. Online. https://birmingham-colab.org/about/ (accessed 5 November 2018).

Harrop, D. and Turpin, B. (2013) 'A study exploring learners' informal learning space behaviors, attitudes, and preferences'. *New Review of Academic Librarianship*, 19 (1), 58–77.

Hillier, B. and Hanson, J. (1984) *The Social Logic of Space*. Cambridge: Cambridge University Press.

Jamieson, P. (2003) 'Designing more effective on-campus teaching and learning spaces: A role for academic developers'. *International Journal for Academic Development*, 8 (1–2), 119–33.

JISC (Joint Information Systems Committee) (2006) *Designing Spaces for Effective Learning: A guide to 21st-century learning space design*. Bristol: Joint Information Systems Committee. Online. https://tinyurl.com/yysabygu (accessed 24 February 2019).

Kornberger, M. and Clegg, S. (2003) 'The architecture of complexity'. *Culture and Organization*, 9 (2), 75–91.

Kuh, G.D., Kinzie, J., Schuh, J.H., Whitt, E.J. and Associates (2010) *Student Success in College: Creating conditions that matter*. Rev. ed. San Francisco: Jossey-Bass.

Paechter, C. (2004) 'Metaphors of space in educational theory and practice'. *Pedagogy, Culture and Society*, 12 (3), 449–66.

Sheridan, K., Halverson, E.R., Litts, B., Brahms, L., Jacobs-Priebe, L. and Owens, T. (2014) 'Learning in the making: A comparative case study of three makerspaces'. *Harvard Educational Review*, 84 (4), 505–31.

Sheringham, S. and Stewart, S. (2011) 'Fragile constructions: Processes for reshaping learning spaces'. In Boddington, A. and Boys, J. (eds) *Re-Shaping Learning: A critical reader: The future of learning spaces in post-compulsory education*. Rotterdam: Sense Publishers, 105–18.

Temple, P. (2009) 'From space to place: University performance and its built environment'. *Higher Education Policy*, 22 (2), 209–23.

Thoring, K., Luippold, C. and Mueller, R.M. (2012) 'Creative space in design education: A typology of spatial functions'. In Buck, L., Frateur, G., Ion, W., McMahon, C., Baelus, C., De Grande, G. and Verwulgen, S. (eds) *Design Education for Future Wellbeing: Proceedings of the 14th International Conference on Engineering and Product Design Education, Artesis University College, Antwerp, Belgium, 6–7 September 2012*. Glasgow: Design Society, 475–80.

Thoring, K., Mueller, R.M., Desmet, P. and Badke-Schaub, P. (2016) 'Design the campus: Introducing a toolkit for developing creative learning spaces'. Paper presented at the Cumulus Association International Conference, Nottingham, 27 April–1 May 2016.

Thoring, K., Mueller, R., Badke-Schaub, P. and Desmet, P. (2017) 'A creative learning space development toolkit: Empirical evaluation of a novel design method'. In Maier, A., Škec, S., Kim, H., Kokkolaras, M., Oehmen, J., Fadel, G., Salustri, F. and Van der Loos, M. (eds) *Proceedings of the 21st International Conference on Engineering Design (ICED17), Vancouver, Canada, 21–25 August 2017: Volume 9: Design education*. Glasgow: Design Society, 245–54.

Trowler, V. (2010) *Student Engagement Literature Review*. York: Higher Education Academy.

Zabudsky, J., Rayegani, F. and Katz, Y. (2015) 'The power of creative space in engineering education'. In *Proceedings of the 11th International CDIO Conference, Chengdu University of Information Technology, Chengdu, Sichuan, P.R. China, June 8–11, 2015*.

Part Two

Spaces for the self

2

Chapter 7
Borderland spaces: Moving towards self-authorship
Jennifer Hill, Helen Walkington and Pauline Kneale

The borderland spaces concept offers a powerful means for representing and reframing educational discourses (Hill *et al.*, 2016). The borderland is used as a metaphor for the condition of living between spaces and cultural norms, displacing the learner and learning (Thomas, 2010) and opening up the interstices within traditional arenas and/or practices of pedagogy (Elenes, 1997). In higher education (HE), borderland spaces can be defined as unfamiliar physical or metaphorical territories whose novelty and ambiguity offer a challenge, which seems daunting to students and faculty. In this way, the borderland concept encourages a relational examination of pedagogic spaces, identities and practices, interweaving the three socio-spatial perspectives of Barnett (2011): physical and material, educational and interior.

Through exploration and exemplification of borderland spaces we demonstrate that learning is both situated and embodied (Boddington and Boys, 2011). Physical locations are used in different ways by a variety of staff and students, and this can establish productive relationships between space and learning. This chapter presents a case study of undergraduate students disseminating their research in a novel professional setting, exposing and demonstrating their experiences of learning in a borderland space.

Theoretical context: Self-authorship and borderland spaces
Self-authorship
Self-authorship, in essence, is the ability to know oneself, to know what one knows, to reflect upon it and to base judgements on it (Baxter Magolda, 2004). It can be conceived across three levels: epistemological, concerning the nature and certainty of knowledge; intra-personal, concerning an individual's sense of who they are and what they believe; and inter-personal, concerning the construction of relationships.

We begin with an initial premise that higher education educators should strive to move undergraduate students towards self-authorship. Rather than adopting formulaic approaches to learning, self-authorship provides a personally referenced way of knowing that draws on experience, knowledge and values related to learner identity, and how that relates to others. It facilitates the development of skills including critical analysis, evaluation and reflection and the development of mature working relationships that embrace and value diversity and the consideration of multiple perspectives. It increases learner self-efficacy and self-regulation (Hawe and Dixon, 2014; Ritchie, 2016), and thereby enhances student learning, performance and development. Students move towards self-authorship when they are able to balance their understanding of the contextual and partial nature of their knowledge with personally-grounded goals, beliefs and values, defined by relating to others.

Undergraduate students are more likely to develop self-authorship when faculty (academics) offer sufficiently novel spaces and encounters that compel their students to consider new conceptions of self and personally referenced ways of knowing (Baxter Magolda, 2004). As such, we argue for the creation of learning spaces where students are challenged to become 'border crossers', displacing them from the familiar pedagogic contexts of their undergraduate experience, to situate them in new, and hence, more challenging spaces. Such spaces can be created at the heart of the curriculum or in the less formal, co-curricular spaces in between. This transition into the borderland may involve entry into a novel learning space, such as a virtual world, or through adopting an unfamiliar pedagogy in a familiar space, such as student-led seminars, field activities, laboratory and studio work (there are many examples throughout this volume; see, for instance, Part 1 and Chapters 11 and 19).

Defining the borderland

Borderland spaces of learning are liminal, foregrounding a sense of becoming and ambiguity (Turner, 1974). When entering a liminal space, participants become 'neither here nor there, betwixt and between all fixed points of classification' (ibid.: 232). Expected norms are disrupted so transitions will not be easy. Initial discomfort and uncertainty is to be expected in both faculty and students as they move into these 'messy' spaces (Felten, 2011). Students can feel confused by emerging re-formulations in their ways of knowing, doing, practising and being, causing them to avoid or postpone entry into these spaces (Savin-Baden, 2008). However, crossing a threshold into the borderland permits new and previously inaccessible ways of thinking and practising (Meyer and Land, 2006) and it can promote the evolution of identity from a singular point of reference to something more expansive (Beech, 2011). This makes borderland spaces potentially transformative (Mezirow and Associates, 2000). There may be a reformulation of the learner's frame of meaning; prevailing views are discarded and alternative forms of personal understanding are accepted (Land *et al.*, 2014).

Generally, these spaces destabilize traditional academic power hierarchies (Freire, 1970; Giroux, 1992; Kincheloe, 2004). Students work with peers and faculty, and draw more freely on their own experiences, which prompts the construction of new identities (Giroux, 1992). The division between teaching and learning becomes blurred as students adopt the role of tutor and tutors become facilitators, learning from and with their students. Borderland spaces are fluid and non-prescribed, remaining open to being shaped by the processes of learning experienced by their participants. They act against the essentialism of educational identities, encouraging hybrid forms of teacher–student and student–teacher, each gaining a greater understanding of themselves and each other.

Importantly, the permissive spaces of the borderland allow genuine dialogue to take place, offering opportunities for co-inquiry and reflection among students and between students and faculty (Lodge, 2005). In such spaces, students can be empowered to participate in their learning so that they might actively shape their own learning experiences and possibly those of succeeding cohorts. Borderland spaces can therefore be viewed as 'contact zones' for creative possibility (Askins and Pain, 2011), with perhaps the most important result for students being a movement towards self-authorship.

Table 7.1 highlights ways in which physical and virtual spaces might be used by faculty and students as borderland spaces for learning. Learning spaces are not automatically borderland spaces – they have to be used as such, ontologically, epistemologically and practically. Encouraging students to take on new roles and identities can transform traditional spaces into borderland learning locations.

Table 7.1: Higher education spaces and their potential borderland roles

Physical – Euclidean spaces	Conventional use	Example use as borderland space
Lecture theatres, seminar rooms, classrooms	Transmissive faculty-led presentations, seminars and workshops	Flipped classroom – student-led breakout discussion/critique; use of collaborative technology (e.g. clickers, smart devices) Student-led, faculty-facilitated collaborative debate and critique Group role play and other experiential learning
Laboratories and studios	Directed experiments and exercises, performance, dance; faculty demonstrate equipment/techniques	Student-directed/informed experiments, productions, dance, theatre, exercises and small group explorations
Libraries, resource rooms	Faculty-directed study	Collaborative, dialogic, self-directed meaning-making Student research-led reading and learning
Field, campus spaces	Faculty-led tours Small group inquiries and exercises following stipulated techniques	Students generate new knowledge through research (using relevant technologies) Student field presentations and interpretations
Transit spaces: cars, trains and buses	Directed reading and thinking Informal conversations	Individual and small-group sharing and reflection Group learning via smart devices
Communal campus spaces: auditoria, corridors, refectories, student accommodation	Directed reading, watching audio and video podcasts Informal conversations	'Think stops' for peer sharing and group learning face-to-face and via smart devices
Exhibition and conference spaces	Transmissive presentation of faculty-directed student materials	Faculty–student–employer multi-way dialogue enabling critical interaction with student research Networking

Physical – Euclidean spaces	Conventional use	Example use as borderland space
Classroom and corridor walls	Passive displays of materials	Interactive critique of materials
Collaboratories: pods for breakout sessions	Faculty-initiated group inquiries	Student-led problem-solving and critical reflection via dialogue
Faculty offices	Formal tutorials Faculty-led feedback	Formative discussions between faculty and students, directed by the latter
Peer-mentoring spaces (PAL)	Revision of faculty-delivered material by PAL leader	Student-led participative inquiry and shared meaning- and identity-making
Off-campus informal spaces: coffee bars, cafés, student accommodation, libraries, museums, galleries, parks, theatres, malls	Directed personal reading and watching audio and video podcasts Performances Informal conversations	'Think stops' for peer-sharing Small group exploration and discovery
Virtual Learning Environments: synchronous (chat rooms, virtual worlds) or asynchronous (discussion boards, blogs, wikis, emails)	Faculty communicating with individual students and student groups Resource repositories	Peer production of knowledge, resources and meaning Peer questioning and answering in class/field/studio/immersive environment Peer assessment
Online undergraduate research journals	Student reading and authorship	Student video reflections on personal research Reflective blogs
Social media (e.g. Twitter, Facebook, Instagram)	Faculty communicating with students and student groups	Two-way iterative developmental dialogue between faculty–students and students–students
Personal (head) space	Thinking within comfort zone	Thinking 'outside the box'

(Adapted from Hill *et al.*, 2016)

Engaging students in a borderland conference space: A case study

Context

Undergraduate research conferences are growing in number at institutional, national and international levels (Walkington *et al.*, 2017). The National Conference on Undergraduate Research (NCUR) started in the USA in 1986 and the UK British Conference of Undergraduate Research (BCUR) was initiated in 2010. We use BCUR as a national multidisciplinary undergraduate research conference to explore the opportunities, benefits and challenges of engaging students in borderland spaces in higher education. This space and the pedagogic practices it allows, intersect with both learner and teacher identities at intra- and inter-personal levels, highlighting the fundamental role of space as a representational medium (Sagan, 2011). In our case study students are travelling to another, unfamiliar campus to present their research to a wholly unknown audience. The borderland space is physical, in terms of campus setting, and virtual in challenging personal thinking. The situation is outside the comfort zone of the 'expected' HE experience, providing disruption and challenge, and promoting deeper, more engaged learning.

Case study methodology

Between 2012 and 2014, the authors undertook 90 interviews with students who presented a poster or paper at three BCUR conferences, thereby capturing views from 14 per cent of the participants. Respondents were drawn from all undergraduate disciplines (STEM, social sciences, medicine and allied health disciplines, law, arts and humanities). These interviews, averaging 30 minutes in length, focused on the students' experiences of preparing for the conference, presenting their paper or poster and being a conference participant. Interviews were audio-recorded, transcribed and entered into the data analysis software NVivo to assist coding based on interpretive readings of the responses. The use of double blind coding was employed to reduce bias. This constructivist grounded theory enabled salient themes to surface from data during the analytical process. The majority of respondents were final-year students presenting their dissertation, summer research project or independent research (Kneale *et al.*, 2016; Walkington *et al.*, 2017).

Conference findings

The analysis demonstrated that the physical space of the conference was fundamental in shaping the learning experience of the participants. Students perceived the conference space as clearly distinct from their own campus space, offering different educational experiences. The conference space was often described as transitional, helping students to develop their academic journey:

> Coming here I see as a stepping stone ... this is practice for the next step and I'm constantly trying to build and develop myself.

For many students, the public context represented a shift to a more authentic 'real-world' environment compared to the classroom, allowing some to glimpse their future:

> It's a taste of what my professional life could be like.

> In regards to furthering my own career and my own ambitions, I suddenly realised they're much more attainable than I thought they were.

As students moved into the borderland conference space, with its intrinsic novelty and challenge, they expressed feelings of apprehension. They frequently spoke of being pushed beyond their 'comfort zone', articulating feelings of vulnerability, mediated by a consensus that persisting in this space gradually dissolved their concerns due to the safe and nurturing environment:

> In the beginning I was really nervous, I didn't want to talk, but people come up to you and ask you questions, they make comments and then you relax and want more of it.

The students described how they had thought critically about their research, repurposing it to suit the multidisciplinary context. Notably, they selected and prioritized material that conveyed their core messages in a manner that would be comprehensible to a diverse audience. The students detailed how they made conscious decisions about including or omitting content in the process of summarizing their research projects:

> A ten-minute presentation forced you to look much more closely at what's necessary for the argument ... you learn to define what's important about your work.

The authenticity of the conference space promoted intellectual autonomy in the participating students. The majority carefully regulated their preparations to ensure they were ready to present their work to an external audience. Before the conference they rehearsed in front of peers and tutors, sought feedback and subsequently improved their presentations:

> I sent my poster to my friends and my family who know little about what I do. I said 'Do you understand this? Is there anything in there that the average person would not get?' They gave me advice and I interpreted it.

This self-review process continued throughout the conference as the students benchmarked themselves against their peers. Situating themselves against others, the students considered how to proceed with the best aspects of what they had witnessed and strengthen their own performances:

> I listened to what the other papers were about, got tips, worked out how they were presenting it and then went home and re-evaluated my presentation.

The relationships between faculty and students were perceived very differently to those in their home institutions. During the interviews, students often gestured with their hands that faculty were positioned higher than students, but they noted that the conference made this relationship more equal. Hierarchies were accordingly broken down in this borderland, which was empowering:

> At university there always seems to be that student–teacher barrier ... at something like this you feel more on a par with people and you can just discuss things.

Encounters between students and reciprocal dialogue were important in the conference space. The poster presentations, in particular, provided discursive spaces that encouraged students to negotiate their thoughts with one another, engaging them in 'deeper' critical thinking:

> Difficult questions move you forward ... If you're thinking for yourself you just continue to strike forward in a line, but if someone stops you and asks you, 'What's going on here?' Then you ask yourself and you improve.

> The way I learn best or when I think I understand something is when people come and ask me lots of questions about it and then I have to re-explain it.

These conversations were points of contact where individuals offered multiple perspectives from equal power positions. The students shared agency, speaking for themselves about their own and each other's research. These conversations sometimes unsettled the presenters as their existing viewpoints were challenged, but they came to realize that there was not just one story of, or understanding derived from, their research (Wahlström, 2010). These conversational negotiations helped the students to cross a threshold of understanding and to deepen their comprehension about the construction, nature and utility of their knowledge (Land et al., 2014):

> I'm quite aware that my perspective may not match other people's perspectives, and so the more perspectives I can get, the more robust, grounded and relevant the argument becomes.

Students described how they began to understand that knowledge is partial, continually created and re-created in response to new research, ideas and perspectives from a range of disciplines. The students also reported their ability to see synoptically and to make connections across disciplines, and they perceived themselves as having agency in this process through disseminating their research:

> Speaking to people in other disciplines, seeing the kind of parallels, what you're doing is actually just a subset of a higher scientific framework. That brings a more holistic approach to research.

Presenting research in the egalitarian BCUR spaces reconfigured the grounds on which knowledge was legitimated, away from expert tutors who were benchmarking students against assessment criteria to award a grade. Here, there was engagement with audiences of peers who were genuinely interested in learning from their fellow students:

> When you're taking your research to a conference it's more tied in with yourself ... people are going to judge me ... as a person, as a researcher, as someone who's trying to be a scientist.

The students described a strong sense of ownership of their research because what they created from it, whether a poster or verbal paper, mattered to them beyond tutor-assigned assessment criteria. They benchmarked themselves against an exposition of self and self-directed research appropriate to a diverse audience. They constructed personal values, balancing the alternative perspectives of others as co-ordinating referents, demonstrating the developmental maturity of self-authorship (Baxter Magolda, 2004). The conference thereby became a space for experimentation and creative expression:

> The BCUR experience has been a greater learning experience than anything I've had on the course because it's something that comes from you ... you get a feeling of satisfaction when you create something from scratch.

The conference offered a liminal space, beyond the cultural norms of the classroom, in which students experienced a process of becoming (Cook-Sather and Alter, 2011; Todd, 2014; Kneale *et al.*, 2016). They repositioned themselves in an unfamiliar role as research disseminators and they began to emerge as authors of their own lives:

> I feel like a mini professional, it's really strange, not feeling like a student.

> You can become who you want to be, rather than what you think a piece of paper says you should be.

Some respondents anticipated an oscillation between their old and new identities. They talked of developing a new identity at the conference, but they expected to lose it once they stepped back into the classroom:

> You do get into the mindset of being a researcher rather than a student, but I'm not sure this will last when I go back to my classes. Will I revert to simply being a student again?

Some students clearly perceived their emerging identities to be slippery and dependent upon returning to the pedagogic conditions offered by borderland spaces in the future.

Borderland spaces and self-authorship: Reflections

This study revealed benefits from engaging students in teaching and learning partnerships in borderland space by challenging understanding, identities and perspectives. The novelty of entering the unfamiliar and challenging borderland resulted in antithetical feelings for students at the start. They recognized anxiety mixed with excitement as they moved beyond their comfort zones. However, as they became accustomed to the space and embraced its liminality (Cook-Sather and Alter, 2011), they gained confidence in their new roles and began to embrace new responsibilities. The conference offered a space for opportunity where participants, from a multitude of disciplines and through interactions with one another, were able to cast off the fixed identity of 'student' to become nascent research professionals. This was a future-facing, authentic 'space of practice', where students implemented the taught and the learned and reframed themselves.

They demonstrated enthusiasm for, and increased confidence in, accepting agency in learning. In the borderland conference space learning was shared and generative. Through a process of reciprocal elucidation (Foucault, 1984) students mutually interrogated and co-created understanding across disciplines. They developed a form of conference 'citizenship', a sense of belonging professionally and legitimately in that space (Walkington et al., 2017).

Entering the borderland, and persisting in it, can be transformative, as students acquire new frames of meaning and facets to their identity (Land et al., 2014). They mature into multi-dimensional individuals as they experience learning from a novel vantage point. The students at the conference demonstrated adaptability to their surroundings, to this new space, becoming self-aware and engaging meaningfully with their learning. They reported becoming receptive to alternative viewpoints, and exercised critical thinking and reflective judgement. These are facets of self-authorship (Baxter Magolda, 2004). Some students crossed conceptual thresholds (Meyer and Land, 2006), opening up previously inaccessible ways of thinking, knowing and doing. They progressed beyond 'bare pedagogy' (Giroux, 2010) to engage with aspects of critical pedagogy. Visiting borderland spaces at a number of points during their learning journey can allow students to engage further with, and progress beyond, their disciplinary identities, to express complex and intersecting personalities, and to trust their judgement in order to make informed decisions.

The study also identified challenges with regard to teaching and learning in the borderland. The conference students felt anxious and vulnerable as they entered the space, taking on new roles and adopting an ethos of socially constructed pedagogy. Partnership between student peers, and between students and faculty, can mean letting go of familiar ways of learning, requiring trust in a process that is inherently unpredictable (Healey et al., 2014). As such, borderland spaces are inherently risky. Students and tutors adjusted to accommodate the altered identities and reciprocal dialogic pedagogies they found. This adjustment is fundamental to enabling such spaces and practices to thrive effectively. Tutors leave behind the security of the lectern and transmission-based pedagogies, becoming more personally involved in their students' learning. This includes candid conversations about what students expect from them and it demands significant investments of time, which will probably not appear in workload models. Students, with their identities in flux as they move between borderland spaces and more traditional education spaces, can feel confused about their roles and behaviour (how they should act) with different tutors across a variety of learning contexts. Support for these transitions requires receptive academic and professional staff (Johansson and Felten, 2014).

Borderland spaces are also emotional spaces for students and faculty. As a consequence, appropriate, and contextually specific, guidance and training should be available so that both parties can develop their knowledge and skills to ensure successful navigation into, and out of, these challenging environments. Faculty are responsible for encouraging and supporting inclusivity in such spaces, particularly for those lacking confidence and cultural capital (Felten *et al.*, 2013). Adoption of this responsibility needs to be genuine. Minimal support for student engagement could lead to students feeling disillusioned and alienated (Mann, 2001), and could reinforce existing power hierarchies (Robinson, 2012). Disruption and borderland activity should promote individual agency in real terms, moving students away from a homogenized academic experience (Sabri, 2011).

The messy spaces of the borderlands generate issues that are difficult to resolve for all concerned and this has implications for any conclusions about their effectiveness. There needs to be consideration of actively promoting the 'disruption' generated by the movement of students and faculty into and out of borderland spaces through strategies and policies. In an era of accountability, we argue for productive disruption in our embodied spaces of learning, offering fluidity and connection between the formal curriculum and the more flexible co-curriculum. Care needs to be taken in evaluation style and timing. If student views are sought during the initial unsettling experiences that occur within borderland spaces, when cognitive dissonance precedes sense making, there is likely to be negative feedback.

If the greatest impact on learning occurs in these boundary-crossing, integrative and socially embedded experiences, then we need to create these experiences through effective learning design. There should be adequate supporting infrastructure, promotion of co-creative approaches in academic development fora, and personal development opportunities and recognition for students and faculty to engage successfully in borderland spaces. There are many opportunities to encourage effective and inclusive learning experiences in the potentially transformative spaces of the borderland, but they need careful and creative thinking, planning and action.

References

Askins, K. and Pain, R. (2011) 'Contact zones: Participation, materiality, and the messiness of interaction'. *Environment and Planning D: Society and Space*, 29 (5), 803–21.

Barnett, R. (2011) 'Configuring learning spaces: Noticing the invisible'. In Boddington, A. and Boys, J. (eds) *Re-Shaping Learning: A critical reader: The future of learning spaces in post-compulsory education*. Rotterdam: Sense Publishers, 167–78.

Baxter Magolda, M.B. (2004) 'Preface'. In Baxter Magolda, M.B. and King, P.M. (eds) *Learning Partnerships: Theory and models of practice to educate for self-authorship*. Sterling, VA: Stylus Publishing, xvii–xxvi.

Beech, N. (2011) 'Liminality and the practices of identity reconstruction'. *Human Relations*, 64 (2), 285–302.

Boddington, A. and Boys, J. (2011) 'Reshaping learning – an introduction'. In Boddington, A. and Boys, J. (eds) *Re-Shaping Learning: A critical reader: The future of learning spaces in post-compulsory education*. Rotterdam: Sense Publishers, xi–xxii.

Cook-Sather, A. and Alter, Z. (2011) 'What is and what can be: How a liminal position can change learning and teaching in higher education'. *Anthropology and Education Quarterly*, 42 (1), 37–53.

Elenes, C.A. (1997) 'Reclaiming the borderlands: Chicana/o identity, difference, and critical pedagogy'. *Educational Theory*, 47 (3), 359–75.

Felten, P. (2011) 'From the advisory board: Monet moments and the necessity of productive disruption'. *Teaching and Learning Together in Higher Education*, 1 (2), Article 1, 1–2. Online. https://repository.brynmawr.edu/tlthe/vol1/iss2/ (accessed 20 February 2019).

Felten, P., Bagg, J., Bumbry, M., Hill, J., Hornsby, K., Pratt, M. and Weller, S. (2013) 'A call for expanding inclusive student engagement in SoTL'. *Teaching and Learning Inquiry*, 1 (2), 63–74.

Foucault, M. (1984) 'Polemics, politics and problematizations: Based on an interview conducted by Paul Rabinow'. In Foucault, M. *Essential Works of Foucault: Volume 1: Ethics*. Trans. Davis, L. New York: New Press.

Freire, P. (1970) *Pedagogy of the Oppressed*. Trans. Ramos, M.B. New York: Continuum.

Giroux, H.A. (1992) *Border Crossings: Cultural workers and the politics of education*. New York: Routledge.

Giroux, H.A. (2010) 'Bare pedagogy and the scourge of neoliberalism: Rethinking higher education as a democratic public sphere'. *Educational Forum*, 74 (3), 184–96.

Hawe, E.M. and Dixon, H.R. (2014) 'Building students' evaluative and productive expertise in the writing classroom'. *Assessing Writing*, 19, 66–79.

Healey, M., Flint, A. and Harrington, K. (2014) *Engagement through Partnership: Students as partners in learning and teaching in higher education*. York: Higher Education Academy.

Hill, J., Thomas, G., Diaz, A. and Simm, D. (2016) 'Borderland spaces for learning partnership: Opportunities, benefits and challenges'. *Journal of Geography in Higher Education*, 40 (3), 375–93.

Johansson, C. and Felten, P. (2014) *Transforming Students: Fulfilling the promise of higher education*. Baltimore, MD: Johns Hopkins University Press.

Kincheloe, J.L. (2004) *Critical Pedagogy Primer*. New York: Peter Lang.

Kneale, P., Edwards-Jones, A., Walkington, H. and Hill, J. (2016) 'Evaluating undergraduate research conferences as vehicles for novice researcher development'. *International Journal for Researcher Development*, 7 (2), 159–77.

Land, R., Rattray, J. and Vivian, P. (2014) 'Learning in the liminal space: A semiotic approach to threshold concepts'. *Higher Education*, 67 (2), 199–217.

Lodge, C. (2005) 'From hearing voices to engaging in dialogue: Problematising student participation in school improvement'. *Journal of Educational Change*, 6 (2), 125–46.

Mann, S.J. (2001) 'Alternative perspectives on the student experience: Alienation and engagement'. *Studies in Higher Education*, 26 (1), 7–19.

Meyer, J.H.F. and Land, R. (eds) (2006) *Overcoming Barriers to Student Understanding: Threshold concepts and troublesome knowledge*. London: Routledge.

Mezirow, J. and Associates (2000) *Learning as Transformation: Critical perspectives on a theory in progress*. San Francisco: Jossey-Bass.

Ritchie, L. (2016) *Fostering Self-Efficacy in Higher Education Students*. London: Palgrave Macmillan.

Robinson, C. (2012) 'Student engagement: What does this mean in practice in the context of higher education institutions?'. *Journal of Applied Research in Higher Education*, 4 (2), 94–108.

Sabri, D. (2011) 'What's wrong with "the student experience"?'. *Discourse: Studies in the Cultural Politics of Education*, 32 (5), 657–67.

Sagan, O. (2011) 'Between the lines: The transitional space of learning'. In Boddington, A. and Boys, J. (eds) *Re-Shaping Learning: A critical reader: The future of learning spaces in post-compulsory education*. Rotterdam: Sense Publishers, 69–79.

Savin-Baden, M. (2008) *Learning Spaces: Creating opportunities for knowledge creation in academic life*. Maidenhead: Open University Press.

Thomas, H. (2010) 'Learning spaces, learning environments and the dis"placement" of learning'. *British Journal of Educational Technology*, 41 (3), 502–11.

Todd, S. (2014) 'Between body and spirit: The liminality of pedagogical relationships'. *Journal of Philosophy of Education*, 48 (2), 231–45.

Turner, V. (1974) *Dramas, Fields, and Metaphors: Symbolic action in human society*. Ithaca, NY: Cornell University Press.

Wahlström, N. (2010) 'Learning to communicate or communicating to learn? A conceptual discussion on communication, meaning, and knowledge'. *Journal of Curriculum Studies*, 42 (4), 431–49.

Walkington, H., Hill, J. and Kneale, P.E. (2017) 'Reciprocal elucidation: A student-led pedagogy in multidisciplinary undergraduate research conferences'. *Higher Education Research and Development*, 36 (2), 416–29.

Chapter 8

Space for the self: Creating my academic identity

Mary Hartog

Creating a space for the self has been integral to my development as an academic. Through a discipline of reflective practice and practice-based research I have gained a deeper understanding of my pedagogy of teaching and learning and my educative values, which in turn have informed my own scholarship of teaching and learning. This chapter explores my process of creating space for myself in the context of my professional development journey as a higher education (HE) teacher.

Barnett's (2011) model of learning spaces suggest a dynamic interaction between the material/physical spaces in which learning takes place, the curriculum and pedagogic space, and the interior space of the student. He describes these spaces as cloudy and fuzzy, increasingly cluttered, if not full, and leaving little space for students to breathe or reflect. For this chapter, my conception of space is concerned with my interior life, in the development of a reflexive sense of self, and pedagogically through my learning relationships with students. I illustrate this by telling my story about becoming a teacher in HE, presenting examples from my practice to illustrate my emerging discipline of enquiry, punctuated by cycles of action and reflection. In this instance, I am the learner and thus a student.

Inspired by Celia Hunt and Fiona Sampson (1998) (see also Chapter 9 in this volume) I began to discover my writing voice by experimenting with creative life writing in constructing my PhD (Hartog, 2004) using stories (Richardson, 1994) to explore the study of my practice. Richardson tells us that writing is a way of knowing, and a method of discovery and analysis. She suggests that through writing we may discover things we didn't know before, most importantly, our relationship to the stories we tell.

Usher (1998) tells us that there are two stories of the self that can be told. The first, a modernist one, assumes the autonomy of a developing ego and is typically a hero's tale in which we overcome the challenges of life. The other, a post-modern story, recognizes that we do not control life itself and that the past is recoverable only in traces. Usher suggests, therefore, that we think of the self as an interplay between the two. Sagan

(2011) similarly adopts a post-modern perspective of the self. Taking up Winnicott's (1965) ideas of a transitional space for learning, Sagan suggests that although Winnicott held to the belief of a 'true self' as opposed to a 'false self', he accepted that self was 'a work in progress'.

There is a similarity between Winnicott's transitional space and the borderland space described in Part 2 (particularly in Chapter 7), in that they both create space betwixt and between old and emerging identities. Like Hill's students, I am on a learning journey; in my case, to become a HE tutor and a professional. In the process I am working out what I know or think I know, reflecting on it and evaluating and making judgements about my work and practice. In other words, getting to grips with the knowledge and educative values that are to become central to my practice as a HE tutor.

Introduction (my story)

I began working in HE over 25 years ago. I was working in human resources in the public sector, teaching part-time at Middlesex Polytechnic as well as completing a part-time postgraduate programme in personnel management. While this course was strong in theory and gave me the language to articulate my experience of personnel management in the workplace, some of my teachers had little or no understanding of the application of theory to practice. This direct practical experience was where I was seen to have something to offer. By the end of the course I was asked to apply for the full-time position of senior lecturer and attended for interview. During the interview, and perhaps because I was not a conventional academic, I was asked: 'How are you going to become an academic?' I set about thinking about my own personal development and after my first year of teaching learning and development to postgraduate practitioner students, I began a (part-time) MA in management learning. The course I selected was designed using a unique experiential learning programme incorporating 'action learning' (Revans, 1971). This approach encouraged students to focus on real issues that they faced in their work and that directly informed the teaching and learning strategy, in contrast to a predesigned or prescriptive curriculum. This approach enabled me to use my teaching practice and the challenges I faced as a new teacher in HE as the basis for my development.

A few years later, I began my PhD at a centre for action research in professional practice, where I opted to undertake a self-study of my practice as a HE teacher. Creating a space for myself (Hartog, 2004) had helped me to appreciate what is important in my work and how to create safe and enabling learning relationships that nurture student development and enrich the learning of my students. With each stage of my development I was reconstructing my sense of self and creating my identity as a teacher and academic, and in 2006 I was awarded a National Teaching Fellowship. Had I not embarked on this journey of development in my PhD through self-study and the creation of space for the self, I doubt very much that I would have achieved the recognition of teaching excellence that comes with the National Teaching Fellowship award.

In self-study (a form of practitioner action research; Whitehead and McNiff, 2006), the self is both the 'subject and object' of the enquiry. This is quite different to a traditional positivist approach to research where the researcher is expected to be objective and detached from the enquiry. Self-study can seem counterintuitive to many academics. However, with the rise in doctoral research programmes in professional practice, self-study in the form of practitioner research has become more established.

Action research is concerned with improvement and change to practice. It is particularly suited to the process of planning and implementation of a project, testing out ideas for practice, stepping back and reflecting on what works, or doesn't. It is distinguished by iterative cycles of action and reflection that emerge in the process of enquiry. Action research is particularly appropriate for the scholarship of teaching and learning because teachers tend to know what they are trying to achieve, they invariably plan their curriculum and step back at key points, for example at the end of term, to review and evaluate the impact of their learning intervention. Lessons learnt can be taken forward and changes made to teaching practice, which can then be explored in the next iteration/cycle of inquiry.

Winter (1997) asks the question 'Where does "theory" come from in action research?' and poses a concern about the relationship between theory and practice, problematizing the vested interest of universities in separating theory from practice and the concerns of practitioners. Winter argues that theory in action research 'is a form of improvisatory self-realisation', where theoretical resources are not predicted in advance but are drawn in by the process of inquiry. In other words, theory emerges in the process of an action research study, rather than in the form of a traditional literature review.

Stand and deliver

My first lecture was scheduled for three hours. I had a projector, a marker pen and a roll of transparent film. I was anxious to convey all the points of my prepared lecture. Despite my brain telling me to invite some student participation, the words kept tumbling out!

They were part-time evening students on a postgraduate programme in personnel management attending class after work. Preoccupied with lecture content, I had failed to consider that a break would be an essential component of their teaching and learning experience. Furthermore, I was not focused on their needs as learners but on myself as the teacher, focused on teaching them theory and filling their heads with knowledge about the subject, rather than drawing out the experience they had gained through their work practices. I had wrongly assumed that I had to be the expert to be judged competent in doing my job.

A short while later I was asked to lead a residential weekend for the same group of students. The theme was 'equalities-based' interviewing, aimed at helping learners incorporate an equal opportunities approach to their work and apply equalities' legislation in recruitment and interview practice. I determined that their learning could best be enhanced if they were to learn from the experience of undertaking such an exercise (after all, this was how I had learnt – on the job).

I assigned each student to a group and set out the tasks to be carried out (covering each stage of the interview process). I began the day with a briefing, informing them that they would be engaged in a process of 'learning by doing'. I explained that we would reconvene, all together, at the end of day, in order to reflect on their group process and learning. I thought the day had gone well. Student feedback suggested they had enjoyed it. But my euphoria was short-lived, when I was summoned to the course leader's office to explain myself. One of the students had complained that there was not enough teaching. The course leader concluded that I had been remiss in my duties. I knew this because she told me so. She ended the meeting with an unequivocal instruction: In future, my job was to 'stand and deliver'!

My learning

I share these early examples of my teaching practice because they represent my quest to begin to understand my practice. When I started working in HE, teaching and learning qualifications were not the norm. Hence, my learning about what worked and what didn't emerged from my experience and reflection on my practice. At that stage, I knew little about how best to structure and scaffold student learning or how much I should direct it. Just as I had assumed the role of the expert in my first lecture, my expectations that the students would find experiential learning liberating was both a mistake and a generalization.

Theory and practice

Critical incidents in my early practice of teaching and learning provided excellent opportunities for me to learn from my experience and, more importantly, to learn from reflecting on that experience. Schön's (1983) seminal work on the reflective practitioner had opened my eyes in helping me to think through the steps that I had taken in my work and to see what choices and assumptions I had made. Schön demonstrated the value of reflective practice by illustrating how a trainee architect deconstructs the process of their drawing (on the board) through a reflective conversation with a coach (which he termed 'talk back'), through which the trainee unpacks the steps they have taken. Since discovering this approach I have often employed 'talk back' by having a conversation with myself. This reflection on practice is a form of reflective storytelling where we explain and justify to ourselves why we have taken the course of action we have, and in so doing, reflect on whether we might have been better taking a different path.

Developing a discipline for self-study and inquiry

While critical incidents and Schön's writing had set me on the road to becoming a reflective practitioner, my journey was to be further informed by the development of a discipline of self-study during my PhD training. As a full-time employee, I was undertaking my PhD on a part-time basis. At the same time I was working on the design and implementation of a new MA in management and organization development for practitioner part-time students. The development and delivery of this programme became the focus of my work-based research project, with my practice as a HE teacher at its centre.

Rogers (1983) had helped me to see how important relevance and meaningfulness are in engaging students in learning. With colleagues, I had designed a learning framework that was flexible and responsive to student needs rather than producing and prescribing a syllabus in advance. The programme was marketed as a 'partnership in learning', working with the students to meet their needs and involving them directly in the assessment of their work, through self-peer and tutor assessment. It acknowledged that in practice we were not the only experts in the room. A key feature of this programme was action learning (Revans, 1971), in which students worked on live work-based projects that are important to their organization and their personal development. They worked in small groups called action learning sets, facilitated by the tutor team, coming together to reflect on their practice.

Living theory

Later I was inspired by Whitehead (1989) who promoted the self-study of teachers, encouraging them to ask questions of the kind: 'How do I improve my practice?' He proposes that a living educational theory emerges and evolves in the context of teaching practice and that teachers are best placed to study their own practice because they knew best what their intentions are in relation to their work in their classrooms. He challenges the tradition of social science researchers of studying teaching practice 'objectively' in classroom settings and propounds that not all knowledge is confined to a disciplinary form. Teachers, he argued, are motivated by their actual reality and experience and are perfectly capable of researching, and evaluating, their own practice, as they respond to the needs of their students.

Whitehead (ibid.) argues that teachers develop their own sense of living theory, informed by their educative values. Moreover, he does not believe that values and qualities can be communicated solely through the propositional form, rather, he believes that teachers embody their values in their practice and communicate them in the course of their practice, as their practice unfolds and emerges. I recognized that I was trying to live my educative values in my practice, in so far as I was engaged in an authentic partnership in learning with my students, by valuing their prior experience and encouraging them to share that experience in the programme through their leadership of and contribution to the learning workshops.

However, there is another aspect to Whitehead's conception of living theory, the idea that we notice ourselves as living contradictions, when we experience a negation of our educative values in our practice. This negation can be of our own doing and sometimes that of the system or organization we are working in. But in this chapter, I will confine my account to my own contradictions.

Educative values and reflective practice

The values that I aspired to live out in my practice and articulated in my PhD research (Hartog, 2004) included:

1. *Listening and learning to hear* by 'holding' my students in an educative space, in which they are heard as persons by the teacher and their peers as they grapple with their learning and come to know what they already know more clearly

2. *Being mindful*, attentive to my thoughts and engaged in a process of reflection in practice that is attuned to the students' needs as learners, in the moment
3. *Developing an ethic of care* in my teaching and learning relationships
4. *Valuing the emotional* as well as the cognitive processes of learning
5. *Developing a practice of 'connected teaching'* by getting alongside my students to understand them as people, their point/s of view and to enable them to find their own voice.

Living these values in my practice has proved to be an ongoing challenge. I learnt that there was often a gap between what I said and what I did, and thus, I experienced myself as a living contradiction. For example, in the first workshop I offered no structure in getting the programme underway, believing that the students would rise to the challenge and take an active lead in the introduction of this learning event (based on their work experience as training and development practitioners), but I had overestimated their readiness to reverse the power dynamics of teacher and student. By not breaking the ice and allowing the anxiety to mount, I was failing to live my values in my practice and I was challenged to reflect more deeply on what connected teaching might mean.

Noddings (1984, cited in Belenky *et al.*, 1986: 214) expressed connected teaching as a 'time for the voice of the mother to be heard in education.' This quotation frames the final chapter of Belenky *et al.*'s (1986) book, which is concerned with 'connected teaching', a concept illuminated by the metaphor of teacher as midwife and informed by Friere's (1972) critique of the so-called 'banking model' of education, which is critical of the process of depositing information into the heads of students, as one might deposit money in a bank. Belkenky *et al.* argue that midwife teachers aim to help students' to think and speak in their own active voice.

As I reflected and learnt from my experience, I paid more attention to what Knowles and Associates (1984) describes as the students' 'readiness to learn'. I listened more carefully to their stories about their prior experience of education and relationship with teachers, and in response I learnt to meet them where they were, and create a dialogue that shared our reflections on our experiences of learning and expectations of how we might learn differently on this programme. I had begun to create a space for myself to build an emerging living theory of my practice. By articulating the educative values that I thought I was trying to live and practice by, I was also identifying yardsticks by which the integrity of my research and claims to know could be measured. Building on Schön's (1983) proposition that

Space for the self

professional knowledge is formed through a reflective conversation in a situation that is both unique and changing, Eames (1993) suggests that reflective practitioners think and act through an interplay of questions and answers. Dialogue, according to Eames, is fundamental to the development of a living form of knowledge.

The project

The programme known as the MA in personal and organizational development had been designed for practitioners with responsibilities for learning and development in organizations. Cohorts consisted of 20 students. The educational philosophy of the programme was to honour the experience and expertise of the students and to encourage them to share their knowledge and create opportunities for learning based on their individual and shared needs. The programme was validated with indicative module titles that spoke to the themes of personal and organizational development, but without a specified syllabus or content. The assignments were framed as 'relevant work- or practice-based assignments' to be produced as reflective essays or mini projects. The aim of the programme was to encourage self-directed learning with the students co-creating their collective syllabus, choosing their own individual topics for their assignments, and engaging in self, peer and tutor assessment. Despite a few false starts, by the second cohort the student voice was becoming increasingly powerful.

The first two cycles of action and reflection followed the implementation of the programme and the experience of cohorts one and two. The purpose was to evaluate, to what extent we had been successful in employing our espoused philosophy of freedom to learn and self-directed learning. This second story provides a further glimpse into my experience with that programme, illustrated by another critical incident that calls into questions my educative values in action and showing me up, once again, as a living contradiction.

'Who is Spartacus?'

One particular cohort had decided to explore the role of reflection in workplace learning during one of their modules, producing a group reflective assignment as an outcome.

The module was led by two of my colleagues and as the programme leader I was invited to attend the final session.

I observed a creative session in which students performed a play and recited poems about their learning. Later, I was handed a package that contained a collection of handwritten reflections and artefacts of their learning. I was told that this constituted their group assignment submission. However, when I saw that the reflections were anonymous, I expressed concern that the external examiner would be unwilling to approve it in its current form. I was unprepared for the uproar that followed!

Both students and tutors reminded me of the core philosophy of our programme and claimed that any requirement to unravel the submission would undermine the learning of the entire group.

Someone called out: 'Whoever is Spartacus,[1] step forward.' One by one they rose, determined to stand or fall together!

My learning

We were claiming to be helping our students to think for themselves and find their voice but we had failed to establish clear boundaries between what we intended by 'freedom to learn' (Rogers, 1983) and what the expectations and rules of assessment were. While these students felt able to challenge the authority of the academy, I had reinforced the power dynamic of academic authority.

Through my inquiry I was learning about myself as a teacher and how difficult it was at times to live by my educative values. In creating a space for myself through action and reflections on my practice, I was only beginning to understand the true complexities of power, authority and equality in the learning relationship.

Conclusion

Witherell and Noddings (1991: 3) suggest 'that to educate is to take seriously the quest for life's meaning and the meaning of individual lives'. Creating a space for myself has enabled a transformation in my development as a HE teacher, shaping and reconstructing my identity as a teacher over time. It has led to a lifelong commitment to learn to teach well, even when I still experience myself as a living contradiction in my efforts to do so. Teaching excellence is a felt experience, contained in and between the spaces for teaching and learning that are created in the teacher–student relationship. Creating space for the self enables the teacher to strive to re-create those moments of excellence in the student experience.

In my first story, I had acted in the belief that students would learn best through experiential learning, rather than checking with them what they needed. In my second story, I failed to appreciate inequalities in the learning relation or contain their expectations accordingly.

What I have learnt is that I am still 'a work in progress'. I am clearer about why my educative values are important, understanding now what

Noddings (1984) meant by bringing the voice of the mother into the academy in relation to 'connected teaching'. It is about caring, holding and containing a transitional space for learning that is safe, where learners' can explore, experiment, find their voice and discover who they are, or might become, in the process.

Acknowledgements

I would like to acknowledge the inspiration I found in Hunt and Sampson (1998) on using creative writing in my personal development. Celia Hunt is one of the other authors in this book.

Notes

[1] Spartacus was the leader of slaves who revolted against Roman in 73–71 BC. When he was asked by the authorities to make himself known to them, all the other slaves stepped forward, making it impossible to single him out.

References

Barnett, R. (2011) 'Configuring learning spaces: Noticing the invisible'. In Boddington, A. and Boys, J. (eds) *Re-Shaping Learning: A critical reader: The future of learning spaces in post-compulsory education*. Rotterdam: Sense Publishers, 167–78.

Belenky, M.F., Clinchy, B.M., Goldberger, N.R. and Tarule, J.M. (1986) *Women's Ways of Knowing: The development of self, voice, and mind*. New York: Basic Books.

Eames, K. (1993) 'A dialectical form of action research-based educational knowledge: A teacher researcher's view, conversation one'. In Ghaye, T. and Wakefield, P. (eds) *C.A.R.N. Critical Conversations: A trilogy: Book one: The role of self in action research*. Bournemouth: Hyde Publications.

Hartog, M. (2004) 'A Self Study of a Higher Education Tutor: How can I improve my practice?'. Unpublished PhD thesis, University of Bath.

Hunt, C. and Sampson, F. (eds) (1998) *The Self on the Page: Theory and practice of creative writing in personal development*. London: Jessica Kingsley Publishers.

Knowles, M.S. and Associates (1984) *Andragogy in Action*. San Francisco: Jossey-Bass.

Noddings, N. (1984) *Caring: A feminine approach to ethics and moral education*. Berkeley: University of California Press.

Revans, R.W. (1971) *Developing Effective Managers: A new approach to business education*. London: Longman.

Richardson, L. (1994) 'Writing: A method of inquiry'. In Denzin, N.K. and Lincoln, Y.S. (eds) *Handbook of Qualitative Research*. Thousand Oaks, CA: SAGE Publications, 516–29.

Rogers, C. (1983) *Freedom to Learn for the 80's*. Columbus, OH: Merrill.

Sagan, O. (2011) 'Between the lines: The transitional space of learning'. In Boddington, A. and Boys, J. (eds) *Re-Shaping Learning: A critical reader: The future of learning spaces in post-compulsory education*. Rotterdam: Sense Publishers, 69–79.

Schön, D.A. (1983) *The Reflective Practitioner: How professionals think in action*. New York: Basic Books.

Usher, R. (1998) 'The story of self: Education, experience and autobiography'. In Erben, M. (ed.) *Biography and Education: A reader* (Social Research and Educational Studies Series 19). London: Falmer Press, 18–31.

Whitehead, J. (1989) 'Creating a living educational theory from questions of the kind, "How do I improve my practice?"'. *Cambridge Journal of Education*, 19 (1), 41–52.

Whitehead, J. and McNiff, J. (2006) *Action Research Living Theory*. London: SAGE Publications.

Winnicott, D.W. (1965) 'Ego distortion in terms of true and false self'. In Winnicott, D.W. *The Maturational Processes and the Facilitating Environment: Studies in the theory of emotional development*. New York: International Universities Press, 140–52.

Winter, R. (1997) 'Action research, universities, and theory'. Revised and abridged version of a paper originally presented at the annual CARN Conference.

Witherell, C. and Noddings, N. (eds) (1991) *Stories Lives Tell: Narrative and dialogue in education*. New York: Teachers College Press.

Chapter 9

Creating space for the self: Thinking differently

Celia Hunt

> When you get to PhD level, you're expected to know how to write. You can't ask. (PhD researcher)

In this chapter I discuss the concept of space in two different ways: first, internal space, in the sense of a space for the learner's self, and second, external space, or the kind of learning environment in which space for the self can be generated. I illustrate this through a 15-credit module for doctoral researchers called 'Self, Voice and Creativity in Research Writing', which I and others have been teaching since 2008. The module offers participants an opportunity to reflect on their academic writing and on themselves, as academic writers, particularly to help them identify helpful and unhelpful thinking processes in relation to their academic writing. Participants engage in creative life writing exercises focused on academic writing and research, creative life writing being understood as writing that consciously uses poetic and fictional techniques to capture self-experience (Hunt, 2010). Most participants choose the module from a range of options within an MSc in social research methods in preparation for doctoral study; others already doing doctoral research can also participate.

The chapter also reports upon our evaluation of the experience. A qualitative research project into the learning experience of eight students from the 2014 and 2015 modules indicated that participants experience beneficial change in their understanding of their academic writing processes and in their sense of self and agency as academic writers, as illustrated by the exemplar case study of one participant. The research data was generated through questionnaires and semi-structured interviews, and re-reading end-of-module, reflective essays. It was analysed using an interpretive phenomenological methodology within a weak constructivist paradigm. I am grateful to participants for permission to discuss their experience. Where used, names have been changed.

Creating a safe space for learning

My research with the doctoral students has revealed how fraught with anxieties academic research and writing can be (see the case study of Elizabeth that follows). This is in addition to anxieties already present, such as juggling the PhD with a demanding job or looking after a young family, or coming to study in a foreign country. It was striking how few of the students I interviewed had had any formal training in academic writing during their higher education. Until recently, there was clearly an assumption that you just learn how to write by producing essays for tutors, but feedback at undergraduate level usually focuses on subject matter rather than style or voice, and certainly not on understanding one's own writing and thinking processes. One student told me in an interview that she settled on a style for essays that got her good enough marks, even though she didn't feel comfortable with it. This inevitably becomes more challenging when students write at doctorate length in greater isolation. While doctoral study, particularly in social research, involves a series of training courses in research methods, there is often no formally designated space where students can reflect on the process of doing and writing the doctorate, and on the fears and anxieties they themselves bring to it. So, the module provides a safe space where students can be more open about their concerns about both their writing and completing a doctorate at what is invariably a very demanding and stressful time.

One of the most important aspects of this work is to create a learning space in which participants feel comfortable enough to relax into reflective mode. In a paper discussing the workshops on which the module is based, Phyllis Creme and I (Creme and Hunt, 2002) talk about creating a hybrid learning environment – part academic seminar and part play-space that can open students up to different kinds of learning experiences. This sort of environment is different from those that students expect to encounter in a research-training context, and for some it can be daunting or discomforting. Students are more used to learning about specific subjects than reflecting on themselves in the process of learning. Writing autobiographically and sharing this with others is also not the norm, and sometimes puts learners in touch with sensitive personal material. Allowing time at the outset for participants to get to know each other can help them to settle into this hybrid learning space. It is also important for participants to formulate a group contract, agreeing upon things they want to be borne in mind while they work together in this more personal way, for example the importance of mutual listening, giving constructive critical feedback, respecting each other's writing and confidentiality regarding personal material. Working in small groups to share writing as it is produced can also be helpful, as it generates another level of reflection, allowing participants to receive feedback from people outside their field, who bring a different perspective. The groups themselves also serve as the safe space where participants can share their experience of PhD work and express their fears and anxieties.

Practice

The module consists of four weekly sessions of three hours, each focusing on a different theme, as follows.

Session 1 – Freeing up the writing process

We brainstorm conceptualizations of academic writing, finding keywords and phrases, for example, gruelling, stimulating and so on, then finding metaphors; for instance, academic writing is a corset – it gives you a nice shape, but is quite constraining. Then participants choose a word or phrase from the brainstorm and use it as a starting point for several stages of open-ended 'freewriting' (Elbow, 1998: 50–8), culminating in the crafting of a short piece of prose or poetry to share with the group. We explore the concept of 'creativity in writing' (Hunt and Sampson, 2006: 58–72), and then participants write an imaginary dialogue with a key concept from their research, as if it is a 'person' (Elbow, 1998: 92–3) (see an example in the case study below).

Session 2 – The role of the body in writing

We explore Eugene Gendlin's (1992) concept of 'felt sense', which is the idea that we can always extend our thinking by paying attention to the 'source of thought' (Petitmengin, 2007) at the bodily-felt edge of language. Participants engage in a writing exercise (adapted from Perl, 2004), which takes them through stages of relaxing into the body and turning their attention to what their thinking feels like (Johnson, 2007) (the case study illustrates this).

Session 3 – Exploring writing voice and writing identity

We explore what it means to have or develop a writing voice or writing identity, bringing theory to bear (Elbow, 2000; Hunt and Sampson, 2006). Participants then work in small groups analysing extracts from published academic texts, identifying where and how the author is most present or authoritative, or engaging most effectively with academic field(s) or discourses, or with the reader (Hyland, 2000; Kamler and Thomson, 2006).

We share findings, then the participants analyse their own writing and that of their group members in a similar way.

Session 4 – Imagining the reader

We explore the role of readers on the page and in the mind when one is writing (Elbow, 2000; Ong, 1977; Hunt and Sampson, 2006: 73–93), then participants write an imaginary dialogue about their academic writing with what they conceive of as their critical reader(s) for the thesis, for example a supervisor or potential examiner. Finally, they create an exchange of letters between themselves and an imagined ideal reader such as a friend or family member, or someone from history or their culture who has been important to them.

In each of these sessions, participants share, in small groups, the writing they have produced. They also keep a journal to record reflections on their learning, notes on their reading and other useful material. At the end of the module they write a critically reflective essay on what they have learnt about their writing and learning processes, drawing on the learning journal and analysing their creative practice (with examples) in the light of the theory studied.

These various activities can be thought of as 'soft structures' – an idea that comes from the field of management but one that is also useful in education. Soft structures are framing devices that guide activity and thinking in a human way, as opposed to bureaucratic or managerial structures that tend to be more impersonal and controlling (Tomer, 1999). In an educational context they can work towards lessening the intrinsic competitiveness of the academic environment, creating a more benign learning space, where students can feel 'safe-enough' (Winnicott, 1971) to loosen control over their usual ways of thinking and to explore issues beyond familiar territory. The tutor's soft structuring of the environment is also key here, in that she/he needs to be able to 'hold' (ibid.) the learning space flexibly in its different guises: leading writing practice, guiding participants in how to work in the small reading groups, generating whole-group discussion of how creative practice can be understood theoretically and allowing time for reflection in learning journals and discussion of the end-of-module essay.

'Holding' is psychoanalyst D.W. Winnicott's term for the way a mother creates an environment for her baby that feels supportive and contained and enables the child to develop a sense of independence even when the mother is absent (ibid.). It involves an internal stepping back on the mother's part, while remaining alert and able to step in when needed. Adapted to the teaching situation, this involves teachers to step back from the tendency to be at the forefront of the learning process, listening and feeling their way into what students need for their learning from moment to moment, letting them have the space while subtly managing it, and moving them onto different kinds of learning activities (Wyatt-Brown, 1993). This back-and-forth movement between 'multiple ways of knowing' (Yorks and Kasl, 2006: 44) – from practice to theory to reflection – opens space for thinking and, if the learning environment is effectively 'held', students will begin to trust the learning process, to be alert to the contingency of learning rather than focused primarily on the end product and the expectations of academic readers or examiners.

The focus on academic readers is highly visible in my research data, with a majority of respondents talking about their concern to 'get things right', as if there is one definitive way to present their findings. This concern is not always fully conscious at the outset of the module and, if conscious, often not unpacked, and is not just anxiety about the bibliographical conventions or how much of oneself to make visible in the writing. When I probe beneath the surface of this concern, I often find uncomfortable feelings about looking inadequate or stupid. As one respondent put it, when talking in interview about her anxieties around doing the doctorate:

> I suppose at [PhD] level there's that expectation that you know. It's ok when you're an undergraduate because you can always ask, but as a postgraduate doing a PhD, you can't.

A psychodynamic (see Leiper and Maltby, 2004) way of understanding this is that anxiety-laden preconceptions freeze thinking so that it cannot move freely (Bion, 1962), and a fixed focus, such as on getting things right for supervisors or examiners, is needed to keep anxiety under control. This can generate learning or writing blocks, what I have referred to elsewhere as 'excessive cognitive control' (Hunt, 2013: 16–19). What is centrally important in the work of the module is to help students to learn how to loosen control in the process of learning and writing, while simultaneously – like the 'good-enough' mother or teacher (Winnicott, 1971) – holding open the space of their own learning so that the imagination can get to work. Psychoanalyst Marion Milner (1934: 102) describes this as cultivating the stance of 'benign observer of one's thinking'. Not surprisingly, seeing that there is an explicit focus on 'letting go' in the writing exercises and the readings, this is a large theme in my research data, and there is a marked shift, in students' reported experience, from an over-abundance of high-level intentionality to a more workable balance between high- and low-level intentionality (see Hunt, 2013: 132–45), as demonstrated for example in the case study below. This is not to suggest that high-level intentionality is not important. Indeed, it is vitally necessary for focused thinking, but if it cannot be relaxed it can lead to trying to force writing into being. The all-important creative distancing (Hunt, 2001) involved in low-level intentionality enables thought to become grounded flexibly in what learning and writing feel like, rather than governed by fixed, anxiety-laden preconceptions of, for example, what writing should be, thus allowing thought to move reflexively back and forth between high and low-level intentionality (see also McGilchrist, 2009, on the relationship between the hemispheres of the brain and Siegel, 2007, on reflexivity).

Reflection on a case example: Elizabeth

As an illustration I present the case of one student, Elizabeth, a professional researcher and writer undertaking commissions for different organizations, who had returned to university as a mature doctoral student and joined the module in her second year. As a professional, she had developed a method of writing up her assignments in the same way as she wrote reports to fulfil her clients' brief within the specified time-frame. This involved locking herself away from her family for ten hours at a stretch, and focusing on 'whatever I think the audience needs, or wants, or expects', editing each word and sentence before she moved on to the next, until the piece is complete and 'perfect' in one go. This 'seemingly rational and somewhat mechanistic' reader-orientated method is successful in that it gets the job done on time, although it puts 'a huge strain' on herself and her family.

When she has to start writing her PhD she expects to be able to proceed in her usual 'detached' way, but finds that this method doesn't work. Not only is this a matter of length of the thesis, the longer time-frame and the huge amount of data she has generated, the topic – young mothers' experience of leaving their children in daycare nurseries – is also quite personal to her; it needs more of her own self-presence than she is used to. To add to this, she feels intimidated by the requirements of academic writing – the need for 'citations, literature, positioning' – and what she sees as the expectations of her academic readers. Being unable to take time out to reflect on what is happening, her anxieties mount up and she becomes blocked. She is 'not an academic', she says, and is simply unable to write. As an experienced professional writer she finds this humiliating, and her confidence plummets.

For Elizabeth, the module is an important vehicle for change. It encourages her to take a step back in the way described previously, to create some mental space, and address the difficulties she is having with moving

Creating space for the self

'from data to [writing up my] findings'. Practising freewriting, following Peter Elbow's (2000) advice on setting audience aside in the early stages of writing, gives her a more flexible strategy for getting words onto the page 'unencumbered by thoughts of citations and literature and positioning', as well as by her perfectionist need to 'get it right first time'. Creating a written dialogue with one of her key concepts – 'identity' – as if it were a person (see the description of Session 2 above) enables her to work collaboratively with her imaginary interlocutor 'to arrive at an almost shared definition' of this term. Here is an excerpt from this exercise:

> Elizabeth: Hello Identity, how are you? No, what I really mean to ask is what are you? I was being polite.
>
> Identity: I am who you feel you are.
>
> Elizabeth: Who *I* am? Who am I? So you mean the way I describe myself when I meet someone new?
>
> Identity: Not exactly. The way you describe yourself will depend on who you are meeting and the impression you want to give them.
>
> Elizabeth: Right, so not that so much.

Having practised the 'felt sense' exercise in class in Session 3, finding out what words come spontaneously when she focuses on the feeling of eating cake – 'watery mouth filling/Pulling on the inside/Clenching, twisting, waiting, anticipating/Aroma drifting/Closer/Swallowing sweet scent' [extract] – Elizabeth then applies this method to an 'unexceptional' but emotionally difficult event that both she and her research participants experience every day: dropping off their children at nursery. Here is an extract from her poem:

> Wet cheek pressed firmly against mine
> Small strong fingers gripping wherever they can: my neck, my arm, my fingers
> Twisting, squirming, and climbing back inside me
> Legs flailing
> Shoes flying
> Face raining
> No words, only sounds
> No words needed, cries say everything
> I untwist and prise him off of me into another's arms
> His arms rigid and reaching

> Red face streaming
> Big breath
> Slowly
> In
> I bite my cheek
> I blow out, quietly. Stopping my tears before they fall.

Writing this up as a poem enables her to 'reference the body and bodily signals much more than I might have done', so that it conveys the experience in a much more emotionally felt way to the reader. 'I will put it into my thesis,' she says.

In the 'writing voice' exercise in Session 3 (see above), the group of students with whom she shares her writing each week give her a different kind of feedback from that of her supervisors, which makes her more aware of her self-presence in her writing:

> They said they could hear me as if I was speaking, which was quite revealing ... because ... I'm not sure you could hear me in the things that I'd produced for my thesis.

These various writing and group exercises open a space for thinking differently, as does creating a visual mind map (Buzan and Buzan, 2010), a drawing technique Elizabeth knew before taking the module, but as she says:

> Somehow I put all this knowledge and all these different techniques, I'd kind of held them back from the PhD, because I had such an idea that there was one way to do it and I wasn't sort of letting all that in or even applying it to how I was approaching the PhD.

The module's creative environment gives her 'permission' to use this technique, she says. Her first mind map includes all the ideas arising from her first set of interviews with 30 research participants; it is 'beautiful', extremely detailed and completely overwhelming:

> It's as full as my brain was with all the nuggets and links and umm, I think that was it, I was just absolutely full [laughter] and didn't know how to get all this stuff out.

Having now got all this material out onto one large sheet of paper in diagrammatic form, she is able to benefit 'from the [mental] space that it left behind':

> I elected to pick a single element of my first version and expand it [which] helped me see five different stories in my research around which I created five categories. I finally had something to write about!

She then moves on to 'loopwrite' (an extended form of freewriting; see Elbow, 1998: 59–77) a complete first draft of her analysis chapter, without the academic paraphernalia of references and footnotes:

> Forcing a draft and willing myself to pretend I knew all the things I didn't, to act as though I had made up my mind when really I was uncertain, and even to leave out large chunks of my extensive research, really helped me find a beginning to get hold of.

She finds this 'a highly agentic process', and now feels 'as if potentially I could be an academic writer after all'. What has happened here, I think, is that the mental space generated by the combination of literary and visual techniques, and the collaborative learning space of the module, enable Elizabeth to step back creatively from the writing process as discussed above, loosening the cognitive control necessary to keep at bay the fear of not knowing how to do this piece of writing – hence feeling stupid as a professional researcher and writer – and developing a bodily-felt place to stand from which she can make her case. In other words, she is discovering Milner's reflexive stance that enables her to move back and forth more readily between high- and low-level intentionality, and this enables her to be a more self-directed learner (Knowles, 1975).

Conclusion

I have demonstrated the importance of providing a formal, structured and guided space for self-reflection as doctoral researchers embark on what might be a very daunting and difficult new experience. But such spaces can be as useful at undergraduate level as at postgraduate, and for new academic faculty and staff as well. And it is critical that these *are* formal spaces, an 'officially recognized time and place for reflection', as one of the research participants put it. Another said that without the framing role of the module and the requirement that she spend time reflecting on her thinking and learning, she would not have done so. As we have seen above, the more personal play-space of the module gives Elizabeth 'permission' to think outside her usual boxes and to focus for a while upon herself in the writing and researching process, rather than just on the PhD as an end-product to be judged by academic readers. This shift of focus from end product to self-process, which, my research reveals, happens for most research participants, is facilitated primarily by using creative life writing and/or visual arts techniques (on the latter, see James and Brookfield, 2014), as they encourage us to engage more deeply with the emotional and bodily-felt dimensions of learning, and therefore to experience feelingly what is happening to ourselves when we write or learn.

Of course, this approach to teaching and learning is not easy. It sometimes involves opening people up to challenging uncomfortable feelings and requires that tutors can render the learning space sufficiently 'held', so that students feel 'safe-enough' to engage in this work and to begin to trust their own learning processes. This, in turn, requires that tutors be more open than is usual in academic teaching and trust the (sometimes) challenging process of personal learning. Academic institutions also need to formally recognize the value of this kind of learning, and the reflective essays that flow from them as valid demonstrations of that learning. There are different kinds of learning, but learning better how we, as individuals, learn and think, must surely be a crucially important part of any academic study.

References

Bion, W.R. (1962) *Learning from Experience*. London: Heinemann.

Buzan, T. and Buzan, B. (2010) *The Mind Map Book: Unlock your creativity, boost your memory, change your life*. Harlow: Pearson/BBC Active.

Creme, P. and Hunt, C. (2002) 'Creative participation in the essay writing process'. *Arts and Humanities in Higher Education*, 1 (2), 145–66.

Elbow, P. (1998) *Writing with Power: Techniques for mastering the writing process*. 2nd ed. New York: Oxford University Press.

Elbow, P. (2000) *Everyone Can Write: Essays toward a hopeful theory of writing and teaching writing*. New York: Oxford University Press.

Gendlin, E.T. (1992) 'The wider role of bodily sense in thought and language'. In Sheets-Johnstone, M. (ed.) *Giving the Body its Due*. Albany: State University of New York Press, 192–207.

Hunt, C. (2001) 'Assessing personal writing'. *Auto/Biography*, 9, 89–94.

Hunt, C. (2010) 'Therapeutic effects of writing fictional autobiography'. *Life Writing*, 7 (3), 231–44.

Hunt, C. (2013) *Transformative Learning through Creative Life Writing: Exploring the self in the learning process*. London: Routledge.

Hunt, C. and Sampson, F. (2006) *Writing: Self and reflexivity*. Basingstoke: Palgrave Macmillan.

Hyland, K. (2000) *Disciplinary Discourses: Social interactions in academic writing*. Harlow: Longman.

James, A. and Brookfield, S.D. (2014) *Engaging Imagination: Helping students become creative and reflective thinkers*. San Francisco: Jossey-Bass.

Johnson, M. (2007) *The Meaning of the Body: Aesthetics of human understanding*. Chicago: University of Chicago Press.

Kamler, B. and Thomson, P. (2006) *Helping Doctoral Students Write: Pedagogies for supervision*. London: Routledge.

Knowles, M.S. (1975) *Self-Directed Learning: A guide for learners and teachers*. Englewood Cliffs, NJ: Cambridge Adult Education.

Leiper, R. and Maltby, M. (2004) *The Psychodynamic Approach to Therapeutic Change*. London: SAGE Publications.

McGilchrist, I. (2009) *The Master and His Emissary: The divided brain and the making of the Western world*. New Haven: Yale University Press.

Milner, M. (ps. Field, J.) (1934) *A Life of One's Own*. Harmondsworth: Chatto & Windus.

Ong, W.J. (1977) 'The writer's audience is always a fiction'. In Ong, W.J. *Interfaces of the Word: Studies in the evolution of consciousness and culture*. Ithaca, NY: Cornell University Press, 53–81.

Perl, S. (2004) *Felt Sense: Writing with the body*. Portsmouth, NH: Boynton/Cook.

Petitmengin, C. (2007) 'Towards the source of thoughts: The gestural and transmodal dimension of lived experience'. *Journal of Consciousness Studies*, 14 (3), 54–82.

Siegel, D.J. (2007) *The Mindful Brain: Reflection and attunement in the cultivation of well-being*. New York: W.W. Norton and Company.

Tomer, J.F. (1999) *The Human Firm: A socio-economic analysis of its behavior and potential in a new economic age*. London: Routledge.

Winnicott, D.W. (1971) *Playing and Reality*. London: Tavistock Publications.

Wyatt-Brown, A.M. (1993) 'From the clinic to the classroom: D.W. Winnicott, James Britton, and the revolution in writing theory'. In Rudnytsky, P.L. (ed.) *Transitional Objects and Potential Spaces: Literary uses of D.W. Winnicott*. New York: Columbia University Press, 292–305.

Yorks, L. and Kasl, E. (2006) 'I know more than I can say: A taxonomy for using expressive ways of knowing to foster transformative learning'. *Journal of Transformative Education*, 4 (1), 43–64.

Chapter 10
Space for belonging: Induction and beyond
Ruth Matheson and Mark Sutcliffe

The need to 'belong' is fundamental to our human experience (Wood and Waite, 2011). Maslow (1954), in his hierarchy of needs, recognized belonging as essential and foundational in building self-esteem, respecting self and others, developing confidence and underpinning our ability to become creative, spontaneous, problem-solving humans with an acceptance of others (self-actualization).

In higher education (HE) student identity, engagement and motivation are strongly determined by the degree to which students feel they belong (Ostrove *et al.*, 2011; see also Chapter 1 in this volume). This 'sense of belonging' is a critical driver for academic success (Meeuwisse *et al.*, 2010), requiring academic and social systems that provide students with a learning environment that is activating, co-operative and promotes integration. It is the combination of these factors that deepens the sense of belonging and promotes academic success, increased retention and higher completion rates (Sheader and Richardson, 2006). So, whether a student believes they belong on a programme of study or not is crucial in shaping their subsequent success on that programme.

This chapter explores the importance of creating space for developing belonging. Specifically it considers the critical transition point when students from many differing countries and cultures first embark upon British study in a new institution. Drawing on a longitudinal study of a cohort of 52 international postgraduate students over one year, it explores the impact of an induction programme designed to promote belonging and the lessons learnt. The study reveals the transformational impact that creating space to develop belonging had on the student experience. It explores the perception of students and the ways in which the creation of a learning space that valued the diversity of the student group, demanded self-reflection and encouraged creative thinking, challenged students to explore their collective and individual sense of belonging.

Transition

Much of the current literature relating to transition has focused upon educational transition at school or undergraduate level. Tobbell *et al.* (2008: 8) have identified a 'significant omission in transition between undergraduate and postgraduate study'. Leonard *et al.* (2006) noted that existing literature on transition tends to ignore the student voice, focusing on the views of the academic rather than gaining insight into the perceptions of the students. This study sought to address these imbalances by triangulating data from multiple sources of student feedback.

Heussi (2012) has also recognized this scarcity of literature relating to the transition needs of students who are entering taught postgraduate study, identifying that insufficient support is given to facilitate postgraduate students in their transition. Cluett and Skene (2006) suggest that 80 per cent of postgraduate students feel overwhelmed with coursework expectations, while 63 per cent of students find the transition to postgraduate study difficult (West, 2012). This lack of understanding of postgraduate transition is compounded by a prevailing, but erroneous view that students entering taught postgraduate study are 'experts' (see also Chapter 9 in this volume), having been successful undergraduates. They are expected to understand the requirements of the educational system, have developed their own personal and academic identity and are ready to 'go it alone' (Tobbell and O'Donnell, 2013: 129). There is a false expectation that little adjustment is needed as students are just embarking on the next step of a natural progression (West, 2012).

Recent research challenges this view of postgraduates as 'experts' and proposes that not enough support is given to students making this transition (Tobbell *et al.*, 2010; West, 2012; Heussi, 2012). In their study of postgraduate students from five UK universities, Tobbell and O'Donnell (2013) highlight a number of aspects that postgraduate students value and that aid their transition, including: opportunities to learn with other students, an informal atmosphere with emphasis on group interaction, and support to develop academic skills and understand new educational practices enabling academic identity. Their recommendations also emphasize that postgraduate students need a clear induction programme (Tobell and O'Donnell, 2015).

Krause and Coates (2008) suggest that universities need to adopt a more holistic view to aid the smooth transition of students, requiring the development of curricular and extra-curricular activities that deliver both academic and social activities. Adopting this approach enables students to recognize and address the expectations of university, see themselves as central to the academic and social community and begin to shape their self-identity as postgraduate students. Central to this development of 'self' is the need for students to experience early success through formative or summative assessment and feedback, building towards familiarity with academic practice. This increases their self-efficacy (O'Donnell and Tobbell, 2007) and is crucial in promoting a positive 'academic self-concept' (Lent et al., 1997: 313).

Our sense of self is derived from our relationship to others, and the imposition of social norms, values and customs. So feeling that you belong is 'fundamental to who and what we are' (Miller, 2003: 217) and in establishing self-identity. This belief in the importance of creating a sense of belonging, and the impact it has on the students' ability to establish an individual, collective and academic identity underpinned the practice within our induction programme and evaluated in this chapter. All of the activities that comprised the induction programme sought to recognize the characteristics of adult learning (Knowles and Associates, 1984): being task-orientated (problem-centred), recognizing individuals' different backgrounds and experiences, promoting discovery, developing students as independent learners and making the purpose of learning explicit.

The induction programme

The MSc in international business management at Cardiff Metropolitan University was designed to be student-centred with creativity at its core. Aimed at international students from different cultures and with different educational experiences, our challenge was to provide a learning experience that encouraged creativity and risk taking, valued students' voices and facilitated their active participation.

Previous research by the curriculum designers (Matheson and Sutcliffe, 2017) had identified that, to achieve these aims, students needed to feel a sense of belonging to their programme and to their institution, which would help them identify with their fellow students, be clear about the expectations regarding participation and take ownership of their own learning. Our solution was to create an induction programme that provided the foundations for belonging and inclusion. The resultant programme promoted social interaction, set expectations regarding active participation, increased motivation through engagement and explored the individual and group identity of the students. This is achieved through a series of experiential learning induction activities.

Concurrently a one-year longitudinal qualitative study was established to explore the factors that promoted belonging and the impact on student learning and identity. Focus groups, final reflective accounts of their learning journeys and individual interviews were used to create a source of data, which was analysed thematically to provide recommendations for practice.

Creating belonging

The induction to our MSc programme begins with a variety of experiential learning activities to encourage student engagement, build trust, openness and collaboration and provide a platform to develop both a robust 'community of practice' (Wenger, 1998) and a collective sense of belonging (Matheson and Sutcliffe, 2018). Fundamental to this is the creation of a learning environment that values students' opinions, diversity and cultural differences, and the methodology involves providing physical learning resources, including a cardboard cube, a T-shirt and an outdoor environment. These experiential activities are designed to reduce anxiety and encourage students to share their experiences and scaffold their reflections, enabling them to share their social and personal habitus (Bourdieu, 1977). Many postgraduate students tend to keep their anxieties locked in – while really feeling like impostors, and thinking they are the only ones feeling this way (Parkman, 2016). Anxiety gets in the way of learning – Barnett (2011) talks about opening up the students' psychic space – so the space created aims to open up the students to learning both for themselves and for each other and the activities provide not only a social space for learning but also space for collaboration and reflection.

The belonging cube

The 'belonging cube' (Sutcliffe and Matheson, 2015) requires students, post-enrolment but prior to starting the course, to select pictures that represent where they come from, their expectations and their future goals. In an induction session students select six images representing their past, present and future and place them on the sides of a cardboard cube. The cubes are shared with other students, with an explanation on the choice of images and their representation. The activity aims to create openness and a deeper understanding of each individual, their hopes, fears and aspirations. This visual autoethnography allows different stories of self to emerge, some that represent a confident and known self-grounded and secure in their home settings, as well as the vulnerable telling of self in this new and unfamiliar setting (Ellis and Bochner, 2000). The idea of the belonging cube was inspired by Professor Clive Holtham, who introduced the idea of storytelling through pictorial cubes at an Association of National Teaching Fellows' annual symposium. (Clive Holtham is one of the authors of Chapter 19 in this volume.)

Sharing via the cubes enables the students to realize that they are not learning alone, and that their motivations and fears are broadly similar, irrespective of cultural difference (Ryan, 2005).

> Analysing and looking inside me, being honest and putting these thoughts on paper is one of the hardest things that I have ever done. Looking back, I realise that it gave me important insight into who I am, who I want to be and how I can become that person. (Evaluation from reflective account)

For many students the realization that their opinions, past experiences and personal ambitions would be valued by academic staff was revelatory, as it differed so much from their past undergraduate experiences, where the lecturer was seen as expert and the student as a novice with little to offer. However, for some, immersion into this approach created cognitive dissonance (Matheson and Sutcliffe, 2017) so much so that their new learning strategies conflicted with their older ingrained approaches. Such students required more learning scaffolding within the curriculum space (Barnett, 2011), and so creating social learning space within which the students felt valued was fundamental in putting in place a learning environment that promoted belonging and the development of the individual.

> At the beginning ... I feel alone. I was in a group in a foreign country, in another language and I was very scared. They make belongingness for all of us. So now I think I belong to this group, I am more confident in this group and I am happier. (Focus group participant)

The T-shirt exercise

In another session students were given a white T-shirt and a marker pen on which they were asked to depict their hobbies and interests in pictorial forms. Wearing the completed T-shirts, they were invited to form groups with similar interests, comprised of four to five students from different geographical areas and representing a gender mix. These same groups formed the basis for action learning sets that would run throughout the year. The aim was to break down cultural and language barriers through commonality in a seemingly diverse population. Action learning (Revans, 2017) was created to support the process of learning from experience and is often used to support learning alongside traditional classroom spaces. The set or small learning group can be facilitated by a tutor or peers and the reflective learning process helps learners to explore and work through issues they are finding challenging or are grappling with in their learning. The focus on real-life issues and the support set members provide each other with help to develop confidence, reflection on action and trust and a solid bond among learning set members. It is a space in which learners are helped to find their voice, which in turn creates space of inclusion and belonging. Communicating with others, through their shared experience and interests provided a catalyst for students to get to know each other, and was not solely reliant on language skills (Ryan, 2005). Students appreciated the opportunity this provided, allowing time to think and plan introductions before engaging verbally, which was especially important for those not communicating in their first language. The importance of this T-shirt exercise in relation to overcoming language barriers cannot be over emphasized.

> I think that it was challenging for me, I never experienced such ways to introduce myself. It was really difficult for me and for Chinese but looking back it was perfect! (Evaluation from focus group)

In a recent Postgraduate Taught Experience Survey 86 per cent of students considered that their ability to communicate information effectively to diverse audiences had developed during their study. Providing multiple opportunities to communicate to different audiences, through different media and in various spaces, was fundamental to this increasing confidence.

Outward bound activity days

At the end of the second week of induction, students undertake a two-day outward bound (OB) residential to further develop group cohesiveness. This is another form of experiential learning that serves to reinforce a sense of belonging and teamwork through personal and team learning. All students are encouraged to attend, but they are also reassured that participation or withdrawal from any activities is fine, thereby providing opportunities to still experience the social aspects and group cohesion.

> The Outward Bound, it was a challenge! We did things that we had never done before. It was a challenge being open to new things and to new people. The people who wanted to be integrated were integrated. Those who didn't participate, unfortunately and if it sounds harsh, are going to be left behind. (Evaluation from interview)

Team working and co-operation were essential in tackling a learning environment that was both physically and mentally challenging. For many of the students, this was their first experience of outdoor activity, challenging cultural norms and taking them far out of their comfort zone.

The groups quickly identified the importance of reliance upon each other and the need to identify the individual strengths of group members if they were going to be able to complete the tasks. However, it was the residential aspect of the OB activity that provided the opportunity to integrate socially, outside the formal educational environment, enabling bonds between individual students and the group to develop, helping to bridge cultural differences.

> The OB was a turning point for me. We were taught about stepping out of the comfort zone, being creative, leadership and team working. I discovered I am a very good team worker but also can demonstrate good ideas to other team members. (Evaluation from interview)

This demonstrates the importance of moving the focus from *task* to *relationship*. The initial focus is on a shared task or problem to be solved, but quickly shifts to the performance of the team, achieving the shared goals and learning from that experience. Students learn about the roles they can play in a team, whether for example they are natural leaders or effective followers. These OB 'games' help break down cultural and social barriers because individuals are recognized for what they contribute to achieving the task. The breaking down of barriers opens the way for overcoming differences and discovering similarities (Frame *et al.*, 2006), of a more interpersonal nature – belonging based not solely on what you are, within your team role (Belbin, 2012), but for who you are as a person.

Lack of participation is a key concern. Applying substantially Western educational norms, such as active learning, constructivism and peer learning, to students unfamiliar with these expectations can lead to disengagement and disillusionment and thus its application needs careful thought, preparation and student support (Heussi, 2012). Yet we should not assume that these are necessarily inappropriate methodologies. Ryan (2005) found that it was more to do with a gap in expectations between lecturers and international students and a stereotyping of students according to their language or culture (Valli *et al.*, 2009). Ryan (2005) also found that many staff had significant misconceptions about international students assuming a homogeneous group with similar learning styles and a tendency to rote and surface learning, reluctance to learning in groups and a preference to only interact with those from similar backgrounds. In fact, her analysis of international students found that they did want to learn new skills, to demonstrate their experiences and they enjoyed group work and independent approaches to learning. However, they reported feeling undervalued and misunderstood and wanted help to speak up and to fully engage in group activities.

As independent learners our students have choice, and for those students who choose not to participate initially, we have implemented a number of support and confidence-building interventions, including the production, by existing students, of vodcasts that demonstrate the value of the OB activity and its importance to their future study, as well as the scaffolding of learning in more conventional spaces within the academy, including the learning sets.

Beyond induction

Central to the success of the induction in creating belonging, and importantly maintaining this sense of belonging throughout the year, was the formation and use of action learning sets. These small groups provided the basis for the sharing of ideas and problems and a platform for the peer review of reflective pieces of writing, providing a pedagogic and collaborative space (Barnett, 2011) for problem-solving and discovery. However, such learning journeys are neither straight nor smooth: Revans (1982: 720) refers to learning set members as 'comrades in adversity', denoting a type of group identity or belonging occasioned by a common situation. What became apparent to students was the value placed on their past experiences and the individual ideas they brought to the group. This not only enhanced their overall engagement but also impacted on their willingness to take risks and experiment, thereby increasing their creative thinking.

> One of the most important things of all that I have learnt was reflecting as it contributed massively to my self-development. Not being judged but being valued for my personal perspective motivated me to integrate reflective thinking into my everyday life. (Evaluation from reflective account)

Having created space and activities for the development of belonging within the induction programme, there was a need to maintain and build on this throughout the rest of the year. The teaching methodologies used within the programme, the assessment methods and the emphasis on reflection and self-discovery were all contributing factors to the development of belonging and the subsequent changes that occurred within the students. Feedback from the induction focus groups led to the development of a further programme of social events aimed at promoting intercultural exchange and celebrating diversity. These included a world food day, a running club and a further OB activity day. Course representatives, who were drawn from different cultural groups, were given responsibility for driving forward the 'belonging' agenda throughout the remainder of the course, transferring the responsibility from the programme director to the student group.

> The Programme Director, I think that he did a really great job at the beginning of integrating everyone. He was pushing us all the time, like it was our job to integrate, and I must say thank you because it really worked. (Evaluation from interview)

For many, the major obstacle that needed to be overcome was their largely passive prior learning experiences (Matheson and Sutcliffe, 2018). Active engagement requires confidence, and picking up the new rules that translate such engagement into academic success. Thus, the early days of the programme led to students identifying a range of issues, which were compounded by uncertainties about language and a basic understanding of procedures. Many began to express doubt about their self-worth, and the value of their previous education in preparing them for this moment. Congruent with Bourdieu's (1977) institutional habitus, those students coming from outside a largely Western educational setting expressed even greater feelings of uncertainty, and a need to be 'shown the way' and 'told what to do'. The importance of early scaffolding of the programme to create this security has led to more of an emphasis on academic skill development. Creating belonging within the cohort served to reduce competitiveness and, in doing so, increased collaboration, lessening anxiety about judgement within the group. This lack of judgement, and building of trust, appeared significant in facilitating both independent and group learning, helping to set the foundations of the students' communities of practice and the principles upon which they are based.

The art of reflection is a complex and high-level skill and one that needed to be developed alongside other academic skills (Bolton, 2010). Writing about 'self' was alien to many of the students, seemingly self-indulgent and boastful at first. Learning to trust in both the tutors and their own judgement took time and openness. The nature and honesty of reflection alters depending upon the audience to which it will be presented. Belonging to a community in which there is a sense of security and trust provides the environment for a level of reflection that can be truly transformational.

> In the course of the module and with increasing practice I felt comfortable to express my arguments and views, building a relationship of trust with the tutors, encouraging me to reflect and be truly honest; knowing they would never judge me. (Evaluation from reflective essay)

In fact 86 per cent of students agreed that they were more confident about independent learning and that their confidence to be innovative or creative had developed during their study.

Changing student approaches to learning, from being self-orientated to being collaborative, was an outcome not foreseen at the outset. Much was achieved through the communities of practice that emerged from the action learning sets, and from the facilitation of debate that value the development of personal opinion and critical thinking.

Lessons learnt

The transition of students from different educational backgrounds and cultures into a community of active learning is a challenge in many programmes. Fundamental to achieving this is the need for students to feel that they belong to the academic and social community.

Our study highlighted the need to create space in the curriculum (Barnett, 2011) for a holistic induction programme, where activities not only address the students' academic needs, but also focus on social needs and security, and start to break down both language and cultural differences. Designing induction activities that promote an understanding of each other's individual cultures, values, expectations and motivations provide students with the basis for developing an understanding of self, the importance of belonging and the nature of diversity. An understanding of self provides the driver for the development of 'belonging' to a cohort, programme or institution.

The importance of space to develop skills of reflection primarily through formative activities is recognized by both students and academic staff as being of primary importance. For many this proves difficult and highlights the struggle to adjust culturally and to a new educational environment. Inadequacies of integration and difficulties created because of language barriers often hamper early engagement. Thus, it is important to 'scaffold' struggling students in the first few weeks to increase self-esteem and provide a variety of experiences so that they can make choices as to what is comfortable for and appropriate to them.

For students to feel both academically and socially secure, they need to feel they belong and induction should also help break down both language and cultural barriers. However, this should not stop at induction, but should be addressed throughout the curriculum and programme duration if learning is to be truly transformational.

Being mindful of different cultural norms is essential, but it is also important not to shy away from challenging students to step out of their comfort zones. This also needs careful consideration and empathetic support through the creation of appropriate spaces and environments and full explanation of purpose, as we enable students to become independent adult learners. Opportunities to communicate to varied audiences, valuing the difference that students come with and utilizing it appropriately and embedding formative feedback opportunities are critical activities that are transferable to every level of higher education.

References

Barnett, R. (2011) 'Configuring learning spaces: Noticing the invisible'. In Boddington, A. and Boys, J. (eds) *Re-Shaping Learning: A critical reader: The future of learning spaces in post-compulsory education*. Rotterdam: Sense Publishers, 167–78.

Belbin, R.M. (2012) *Team Roles at Work*. London: Routledge.

Bolton, G. (2010) *Reflective Practice: Writing and professional development*. 3rd ed. London: SAGE Publications.

Bourdieu, P. (1977) *Outline of a Theory of Practice*. Trans. Nice, R. Cambridge: Cambridge University Press.

Cluett, L. and Skene, J. (2006) 'Improving the postgraduate coursework student experience: Barriers and the role of the institution'. In *Proceedings of the Australian Universities Quality Forum 2006: Quality Outcomes and Diversity, Perth, Australia, 5–7 July 2006* (AUQA Occasional Publications 7). Melbourne: Australian Universities Quality Agency, 62–7. Online. https://tinyurl.com/y36o2p5w (accessed 17 October 2017).

Ellis, C. and Bochner, A.P. (2000) 'Autoethnography, personal narrative, reflexivity: Researcher as subject'. In Denzin, N.K. and Lincoln, Y.S. (eds) *Handbook of Qualitative Research*. 2nd ed. Thousand Oaks, CA: SAGE Publications, 733–68.

Frame, P., O'Connor, J., Hartog, M. and Kyprianou, A. (2006) 'Which diversity domains have most impact on student learning? An exploration of the inhibitors and facilitators of learning', *International Journal of Diversity in Organizations, Communities and Nations*, 5 (4), 111–18.

Heussi, A. (2012) 'Postgraduate student perceptions of the transition into postgraduate study'. *Student Engagement and Experience Journal*, 1 (3), 1–13. Online. https://tinyurl.com/yxrhtr4p (accessed 20 February 2019).

Knowles, M.S. and Associates (1984) *Andragogy in Action*. San Francisco: Jossey-Bass.

Krause, K.-L. and Coates, H. (2008) 'Students' engagement in first-year university'. *Assessment and Evaluation in Higher Education*, 33 (5), 493–505.

Lent, R.W., Brown, S.D. and Gore, P.A. (1997) 'Discriminant and predictive validity of academic self-concept, academic self-efficacy, and mathematics-specific self-efficacy'. *Journal of Counseling Psychology*, 44 (3), 307–15.

Leonard, D., Metcalfe, J., Becker, R. and Evans, J. (2006) *Review of Literature on the Impact of Working Context and Support on the Postgraduate Research Student Learning Experience*. York: Higher Education Academy.

Maslow, A.H. (1954) *Motivation and Personality*. New York: Harper and Brothers.

Matheson, R. and Sutcliffe, M. (2017) 'Creating belonging and transformation through the adoption of flexible pedagogies in masters level international business management students'. *Teaching in Higher Education*, 22 (1), 15–29.

Matheson, R. and Sutcliffe, M. (2018) 'Belonging and transition: An exploration of international business students' postgraduate experience'. *Innovations in Education and Teaching International*, 55 (5), 602–10.

Meeuwisse, M., Severiens, S.E. and Born, M.P. (2010) 'Learning environment, interaction, sense of belonging and study success in ethnically diverse student groups'. *Research in Higher Education*, 51 (6), 528–45.

Miller, L. (2003) 'Belonging to country – a philosophical anthropology'. *Journal of Australian Studies*, 27 (76), 215–23.

O'Donnell, V.L. and Tobbell, J. (2007) 'The transition of adult students to higher education: Legitimate peripheral participation in a community of practice?'. *Adult Education Quarterly*, 57 (4), 312–28.

Ostrove, J.M., Stewart, A.J. and Curtin, N.L. (2011) 'Social class and belonging: Implications for graduate students' career aspirations'. *Journal of Higher Education*, 82 (6), 748–74.

Parkman, A. (2016) 'The imposter phenomenon in higher education: Incidence and impact'. *Journal of Higher Education Theory and Practice*, 16 (1), 51–60.

Revans, R.W. (1982) *The Origins and Growth of Action Learning*. Bromley: Chartwell-Bratt.

Revans, R. (2017) *ABC of Action Learning*. London: Routledge.

Ryan, J. (2005) 'Improving teaching and learning practices for international students: Implications for curriculum, pedagogy and assessment'. In Carroll, J. and Ryan, J. (eds) *Teaching International Students: Improving learning for all*. London: Routledge, 92–100.

Sheader, E.A. and Richardson, H.C. (2006) 'Homestart – a support for students in non-university accommodation'. In Cook, A., Macintosh, K.A. and Rushton, B.S. (eds) *Supporting Students: Early induction*. Coleraine: University of Ulster, 51–72.

Sutcliffe, M. and Matheson, R. (2015) 'The Belonging Cube: An induction activity to recognise and celebrate diversity'. In Kneale, P.E. (ed.) *Masters Level Teaching, Learning and Assessment: Issues in design and delivery*. London: Palgrave Macmillan, 76–8.

Tobbell, J. and O'Donnell, V.L. (2013) 'Transition to postgraduate study: Postgraduate ecological systems and identity'. *Cambridge Journal of Education*, 43 (1), 123–38.

Tobbell, J. and O'Donnell, V.L. (2015) 'Transition to postgraduate study: Overlooked and underestimated'. In Kneale, P.E. (ed.) *Masters Level Teaching, Learning and Assessment: Issues in design and delivery*. London: Palgrave Macmillan, 57–61.

Tobbell, J., O'Donnell, V.L. and Zammit, M. (2008) *Exploring Practice and Participation in Transition to Post-Graduate Social Science Study*. York: Higher Education Academy.

Tobbell, J., O'Donnell, V.L. and Zammit, M. (2010) 'Exploring transition to postgraduate study: Shifting identities in interaction with communities, practice and participation'. *British Educational Research Journal*, 36 (2), 261–78.

Valli, Y., Brown, S. and Race, P. (2009) *Cultural Inclusivity: A guide for Leeds Met staff*. Leeds: Leeds Metropolitan University.

Wenger, E. (1998) *Communities of Practice: Learning, meaning, and identity*. Cambridge: Cambridge University Press.

West, A. (2012) 'Formative evaluation of the transition to postgraduate study for counselling and psychotherapy training: Students' perceptions of assignments and academic writing'. *Counselling and Psychotherapy Research: Linking Research with Practice*, 12 (2), 128–35.

Wood, N. and Waite, L. (2011) 'Editorial: Scales of belonging'. *Emotion, Space and Society*, 4 (4), 201–2.

Chapter 11

Spaces for performance: Becoming a professional

Laura Ritchie and Ben Hall

We continue our consideration of learning spaces that form transitional or liminal spaces within a student's educational journey. While the previous chapter was concerned with the transition of students into university, this chapter focuses upon the transition from university and into professional roles. Furthermore, while Chapter 10 stressed the importance of *belonging*, here we consider the importance of *becoming* a professional (see also Chapter 14 in this volume).

'Becoming' is considered a useful metaphor for professional learning as it stresses that learning and the development of practice is a continuous process (Hager and Hodkinson, 2011). This contrasts with other conceptions that simply see professional learning as having a final end point that involves the acquisition of a set of skills from an educational environment that are then deployed in a professional workplace. The idea of a continuing and unending search for mastery locates professional learning within the concept of lifelong learning (Scanlon, 2011).

Becoming is also concerned with the development of identity and self. Scanlon (ibid.: 14) argues that 'becoming' is an evolutionary and iterative process from which students develop a 'sense of professional self – a professional identity'. Their learning journey involves students moving from expert students to becoming novice professionals (Reid *et al.*, 2011).

This chapter explores the student journey through learning spaces by considering the process of becoming a professional and, using Barnett's (2011) taxonomy of learning spaces, how these 'permeable' spaces are aligned throughout the curriculum, where the boundaries between the educational space, the physical place of learning and the interior space of the students meld in developing individuals as performers and as a community of musicians. Although describing practices within music at the University of Chichester, the principles applied here are widely transferable to other disciplines and domains.

Becoming a professional

Like many professionals, musicians develop their craft over the course of several years of study, and the journey through higher education (HE) takes students through a number of spaces, from entry, through the audition space, into practice and the rehearsal space. Private study then becomes public when students are tested in a performance space, and some embark upon the entrepreneurial space as they prepare to enter professional roles. There is no threshold moment at graduation when students transform into professionals who are ready for the working world. This happens gradually over the course of years, as students journey to autonomy, ingenuity and self-reliance. Teaching staff serve as role models, grounded in professional practice, utilizing and embedding innovation and creativity in their teaching and curriculum.

The theory of skills development that leads to successful transitions into expert status is not unique to music. Acquisition of mastery and skill can be paralleled with sporting performance and also with the mental acuity developed through study in physics, or the knowledge and applied skill in medicine. For example, Boshuizen (2004) discusses specific examples within medical training, but the overall concepts can transfer to business, music or another area of study. Boshuizen (ibid.: 74) claims that 'building up domain knowledge, in combination with learning the required skills, is the key'. This accumulation of knowledge is not a linear process and gathering information is only the first step, which leads to understanding so that students can connect ideas and processes in order to use them effectively in practical settings. In HE there are inherent expectations of students that they will persist with learning in order to reach the goal of becoming a professional, and this requires resilience (Ritchie, 2016). Gu and Day (2007) highlight that teachers must also be resilient to model, mentor and change the students' perspective from one of impending risk to opportunity for growth.

In all subjects learning requires metacognitive processes, the thinking about thinking (Azevedo, 2009). Musicians also need to learn how to learn, from understanding pattern and detail and committing these to memory, to training the fine motor skills and embedding strength and stamina in different muscle groups. Learning to learn develops a self-reflexive capacity within the interior space of the student (Barnett, 2011), enabling the learning to become deeply felt and embodied in the process. In performance the proficiency and level of technical skill, expression and overall professionalism of the performance are assessed. The musical material learnt at university is a small component of what is encompassed across a professional career; the skills required to perform a specific repertoire can be learnt in class, but understanding their wider application is essential. A musician may learn repertoire, but it is the facility of their musical vocabulary that will hold them securely within the profession, just as the adaptability of an engineer allows her to find a solution instead of being perplexed by something new.

The programmes at the University of Chichester are designed around the students and the development of skills that transcend the focused goals of becoming an orchestral musician or solo performer. In many conservatoires students are trained intensely in soloistic and orchestral repertoire; at Chichester they gain these skills but also develop a wider and holistic array of adaptable skills that combine performance and musicianship with communication, entrepreneurial, creative and employable skills that are essential for community outreach, teaching and less formal or traditional performance settings. This enables them to gain confidence in becoming professionals both in traditional stage and non-traditional community or private performance settings.

Graduates need to be adaptable, possess insight and have strong self-efficacy that allows them to be creative with how they use their skills in order to establish themselves in their chosen profession. Just as few who study astronomy or history become astronomers or historians, few musicians who study performance go on to have careers as soloists (Comunian *et al.*, 2010). Nevertheless, like many professionals their journey begins with an audition.

The audition space

The transition into a professional space begins as a pre-undergraduate when applying to enter HE, and can feel like the first bridge into the adult world. Each year over 800 students travel to Chichester for their auditions in the university chapel. The physicality of bringing people onto the campus is an important step in marking the beginning of each student's relationship with the university. Candidates perform in the chapel, which is the heart of the music department. It is a large, open, square-shaped building with floor-to-ceiling windows on two sides. As a performance space it combines enormity with intimacy, connecting the potential within this auspicious physical setting with the interior learning capacity of the student. Students are presented with a concert-grand Steinway piano, an audience of critical listeners, and over 200 cu ft/ ft^3 of space to project their sound both out and up. Although a new and often daunting experience, the audition and individual interviews create a positive, nurturing environment that acts as an invitation for the student to enter the space of HE, take the stage and engage with performance. During his first week at the University of Chichester in 2013, one student reflected on the process and wrote:

> My most memorable musical experience was auditioning in the Chapel for the Instrumental Teaching course at this university. Throughout the 90-minute train ride I was completely focused on the audition, telling myself, 'You'll be fine. Try not to make a mistake.' It's memorable to me because passing the audition in that space has led me one step closer to my career.

Auditions and interviews are not merely an exercise to identify candidates with a desired skill set, but are valuable as initial student experiences in the university. In audition students begin to develop qualities that educators and future employers want to see, such as being confident, self-critical and self-reliant (Pegg et al., 2012).

Throughout their school years, students are taught to take tests and generally to conform to predetermined procedures (Illeris, 2007), so it is a significant challenge to move from years of training in compliance to a higher education environment requiring autonomy and independent thought, characteristics synonymous with maturity and professionalism. Consequently it is important that the interviewed candidates feel, and believe, that the audition is a first step in crossing over into a new space that is about *them* and their development.

For educators, recognizing students as individuals with unique potential, as opposed to viewing a cohort en masse, allows students to begin to realize that their education is about them. For us, as educators, this process begins at the very first meeting when auditioning candidates are challenged to see themselves as active participants and learners.

For the student, truly believing in their individual potential helps them make the transition to university. This transitional space of learning, as discussed by Sagan (2011) is a significant point in the psychosocial journey of the student (Barnett, 2011), enabling students to separate from their past, let go of anxieties and step forward with an emerging sense of a future self (also see Chapter 10 in this volume). This is a moment of 'positive mirroring' (Winnicott, 1965) in which students recognize their future self in the teacher in the same way that infants see an image of themselves in the face of their caregiver or mother (Sagan, 2011: 71).

The learning and rehearsal space

Understanding the component processes in learning and performance helps students to develop positive self-efficacy (Ritchie, 2016), and these self-beliefs will help carry students forward towards achievement, whatever their discipline. Students who have high self-efficacy beliefs see tasks as progressions of hierarchical goals instead of insurmountable blockades, use more critical thinking skills to navigate challenges, are less deterred by failure, become more resilient and tend to be more successful (Zimmerman, 2000). Music provision at Chichester presents performance as a series of stepwise goals, embedding stages of learning and exploration, feedback and reflection in 'safe' spaces before performance on a public stage. This process allows for both the acquisition and demonstration of skill, as well as the nurturing of belief. Students foster a positive outlook towards achievement throughout their course, making the prospect of success more believable, and thus more attainable. This is enabled by a flexible and unconventional use of space. An example is the Head of Department's office, which has a sign on the door: 'This is Ben Hall's office. It is also a practice room. If he is not here, please feel free to use it.' Such redefining of space allows students, who are frequently uncertain in new spaces, to become more confident as their skill and familiarity increases.

Moreover, learning space becomes transitional, moving from the rehearsal space to the public performance and providing opportunities for self-validation. This is first reinforced by teachers and peers and then mirrored by public audiences as students move beyond their student community towards a professional community of musicians. Various formal and informal performance opportunities are included in the curriculum space to encourage students and to provide experience and accomplishments in which to take pride. For example, those in the chamber orchestra wear ball gowns and dinner jackets; they perform in professional venues, sound professional, look professional, and they *feel* professional. One student explained:

> Playing in Chamber Orchestra is not just about playing an instrument, it's like an actor's play: your body language is very important as well as your energy, and how you are dressed. Like all the artists we leave behind our thoughts, life problems and trainers before coming on stage. Our dresses help us reincarnate from a simple person to a professional artist.

In music, the technicalities of the discipline are requisite, but musicians must be adept in communicating, applying and delivering across a range of settings and spaces. Performance is more than playing your part in a concert. It is a watershed for students to understand that their accrued skills also transfer to other spaces, from formal performance halls to the impromptu stage of a converted barn. Professional musicians bring performance to these spaces.

Moving into the performance space

The transition to a professional performer takes time. Music students spend considerably more time practising than performing, and developing effective methods of self-directed learning are essential (McPherson and Zimmerman, 2002). Perception, organizational and analytical skills, perseverance to secure and refine mechanical and musical production skills and the specific self-efficacy beliefs and general security required for the pressurized settings of auditions and performances are all crucial attributes. As students adopt new processes, they need time to see the purpose and application of various methods, and to select which to adopt and make part of their own daily routines (Zimmerman and Schunk, 2001).

Both individual tuition and performance seminars provide space where students deliberately observe processes demonstrated by teachers and peers. They *test* their musical ideas, reproducing them in a public space, receive feedback from staff and peers, and reinforce these experiences through further reflective practice as the learning cycle continues. The transition from student to professional is facilitated when the boundaries of walls and the traditional staff–student divide is transcended.

Students experience the iterative stages of learning first-hand and the learning process is modelled through the different interactions in the course in ways similar to the stages of modelling outlined by Bandura (1977) of attention, retention, reproduction and reinforcement. Whether in musical theatre, jazz or pedagogy studies, the lecturers actively model performance with the students, and this breaks down traditional boundaries and hierarchies between staff and students. For example, the Head of Jazz transforms a lecture space into a jazz club every week where he and other staff perform in front of and alongside students. The media often portray performance on a grand scale, and the distance from the inexperienced student to the stage can seem insurmountable. At Chichester the perceived barriers to these spaces are broken down from the outset; students are welcomed onto the stage and supported by staff throughout, experiencing both traditional and often extraordinary, non-traditional spaces.

It is essential that students have real-world experience in all stages of performance, finding venues, creating programmes, attracting and communicating with the audience and delivering a successful event. This practical experience combined with the technical musical training develops world-ready whole musicians who present music in new and often entrepreneurial ways.

The entrepreneurial space

Professional skills are developed during the undergraduate music courses as tours and performance events move into external spaces, giving students experience with professional practice. Their personal development also moves closer to self-actualization as they develop and participate in a wider community of practice (Wenger, 1998). Teaching in this way involves careful preparation, sensitive facilitation and trust, but can have far-reaching impact. One example involves third-year musical theatre students who audition and form one of three companies: a touring company that self-organize and promote a multi-city tour, a consignment company that co-write and produce a musical off campus and a festival company that take shows to festivals across the country. The concept of these tours and of including student companies in the curriculum was devised by our musical theatre co-ordinator to 'extend the exploration of musical, dance and acting styles by offering, not just ambitious repertoire, but creating as close to a professional context for its presentation as it was possible to get within our formal learning environment'. The staff are West End professionals with dozens of credits, including *Cats, Wicked* and the original cast of *Billy Elliot*. They are involved in mentoring and coaching rehearsals in preparation for each year's productions, thus expanding further the professional space and experiences.

Emerging as a professional

Promoting resilience in identity encourages a readiness to learn and helps students move toward professionalism. In 2011, and building upon the curriculum and entrepreneurial spaces they had experienced, two music students came together and formed the operatic production company City Wall Productions, specializing in Baroque opera and providing bespoke live music for events across the south coast of England. There are few traditional, 'ready-made' jobs that a music graduate would apply for, and this example of student entrepreneurship took considerable planning, risk and tenacity to be successful. The impact has been significant, including these alumni providing invaluable performance opportunities and experiences for our current students:

> Our own experiences in the classroom gave us enough to produce the product. We entered the University's Business School Award

> Scheme for entrepreneurs and beat all the business students to some funding and free office space. We endeavour to maintain and subsidise a student contingency in our troupe, to encourage them to feel validated while studying and experience a taste of professional life. We hope this passes onto students the need for self-regulated, well-balanced and resilient performance practice and a healthy understanding of the business side of art. (Co-director and founder, City Wall Productions)

Similarly, students on our international experience module create a bespoke curriculum that gives them experiences within the professional teaching, recording, and performing industry. In 2017 students travelled to California and met with a music lawyer and a member of the Board of Governors for the Grammys to discuss copyright and licensing, gave public concert performances and delivered workshops to school children aged 5–18.

> The opportunity to learn outside a typical educational environment is something every student should take instantly. I was able to change the way I taught from leading one workshop to the next and improve. Seeing the joy and excitement on the children's faces when playing a DooD (NUVO beginner Clarinet), was more than I could have hoped for, something you cannot be taught in a classroom. (International experience student)

Speaking about the impact and the confidence gained from these experiences, one student commented:

> Hands on experience gave us the opportunity to put skills we learnt into practice, opened our eyes to the real world of teaching, and prepared us to think with great creativity and imagination. Now, I am director of my own music academy.

These reflections speak of the 'safe' space, which Barnett (2011) describes as vital for being and becoming. Such unconventional teaching spaces, both engage the student in pedagogic challenges and ontological risk. However, not all students wish to be either entrepreneurs or to tour or travel abroad. Stepping outside requires confidence, personal exploration and risk, and some prefer the safety of the known. The students who choose not to travel undertake an alternative module where each student designs their own professional teaching website. Although not involving physical connection and outreach in the same way as the international experience, populating a website with posts, videos and articles about teaching and performing does encourage them to develop an outward-facing and networked professional profile while remaining comfortable among peers in familiar spaces.

These curricula open up a plethora of rich and distinctive spaces for learning, taking the student on a journey of becoming, where the validation of self is reflected and seen, in the company of others and through social learning spaces, from rehearsal to performance and beyond into professional roles.

Lessons learnt

It is not enough today to provide students with a foundation of skill. Technical competencies are prerequisites in the workplace, and there is a much wider portfolio of professional skills needed by today's graduates. The experiences at university prepare students to continue on their own and the most important contribution teachers in HE can give is to show students how to learn, while providing facilities and resources to develop them for their future roles.

We have learnt not to assume that students understand how to engage in such learning. Consequently it is necessary to clearly outline our expectations of student engagement, as opposed to outcomes or assessments, in order to encourage deeper learning and reflection. However, it takes time for students to become autonomous thinkers and to confidently develop their own professional networks, so educators need to be patient, persevere and believe in their students. Providing learning spaces for students to experience and assume responsibility as professionals will reinforce their skills and build their sense of self.

Our experience is that students value the empowerment that comes from the visible outcomes of their learning from authentic experiences. Hence we create curriculum spaces for a variety of projects, activities, performance opportunities and experiential learning that directly represent professional roles.

Change is often challenging, disrupting our security as learners and as teachers. As educators we cannot dictate, mandate or timetable change; however, we can facilitate, foster and scaffold resources and experiences to enable students to learn and become professionals.

References

Azevedo, R. (2009) 'Theoretical, conceptual, methodological, and instructional issues in research on metacognition and self-regulated learning: A discussion'. *Metacognition and Learning*, 4 (1), 87–95.

Bandura, A. (1977) *Social Learning Theory*. Englewood Cliffs, NJ: Prentice-Hall.

Barnett, R. (2011) 'Configuring learning spaces: Noticing the invisible'. In Boddington, A. and Boys, J. (eds) *Re-Shaping Learning: A critical reader: The future of learning spaces in post-compulsory education*. Rotterdam: Sense Publishers, 167–78.

Boshuizen, H.P.A. (2004) 'Does practice make perfect?'. In Boshuizen, H.P.A., Bromme, R. and Gruber, H. (eds) *Professional Learning: Gaps and transitions on the way from novice to expert*. Dordrecht: Kluwer Academic Publishers, 73–95.

Comunian, R., Faggian, A. and Li, Q.C. (2010) 'Unrewarded careers in the creative class: The strange case of bohemian graduates'. *Papers in Regional Science*, 89 (2), 389–410.

Gu, Q. and Day, C. (2007) 'Teachers' resilience: A necessary condition for effectiveness'. *Teaching and Teacher Education*, 23 (8), 1302–16.

Hager, P. and Hodkinson, P. (2011) 'Becoming as an appropriate metaphor for understanding professional learning'. In Scanlon, L. (ed.) *'Becoming' a Professional: An interdisciplinary analysis of professional learning*. Dordrecht: Springer, 33–56.

Illeris, K. (2007) *How We Learn: Learning and non-learning in school and beyond*. London: Routledge.

McPherson, G.E. and Zimmerman, B.J. (2002) 'Self-regulation of musical learning: A social cognitive perspective'. In Colwell, R. and Richardson, C. (eds) *The New Handbook of Research on Music Teaching and Learning*. Oxford: Oxford University Press, 327–47.

Pegg, A., Waldock, J., Hendy-Isaac, S. and Lawton, R. (2012) *Pedagogy for Employability*. York: Higher Education Academy.

Reid, A., Abrandt Dahlgren, M., Petocz, P. and Dahlgren, L.O. (2011) *From Expert Student to Novice Professional*. Dordrecht: Springer.

Ritchie, L. (2016) *Fostering Self-Efficacy in Higher Education Students*. London: Palgrave Macmillan.

Sagan, O. (2011) 'Between the lines: The transitional space of learning'. In Boddington, A. and Boys, J. (eds) *Re-Shaping Learning: A critical reader: The future of learning spaces in post-compulsory education*. Rotterdam: Sense Publishers, 69–79.

Scanlon, L. (2011) '"Becoming" a professional'. In Scanlon, L. (ed.) *'Becoming' a Professional: An interdisciplinary analysis of professional learning*. Dordrecht: Springer, 13–32.

Wenger, E. (1998) *Communities of Practice: Learning, meaning, and identity*. Cambridge: Cambridge University Press.

Winnicott, D.W. (1965) *The Maturational Processes and the Facilitating Environment: Studies in the theory of emotional development*. New York: International Universities Press.

Zimmerman, B.J. (2000) 'Self-efficacy: An essential motive to learn'. *Contemporary Educational Psychology*, 25 (1), 82–91.

Zimmerman, B.J. and Schunk, D.H. (eds) (2001) *Self-Regulated Learning and Academic Achievement: Theoretical perspectives*. Mahwah, NJ: Lawrence Erlbaum Associates.

Chapter 12
Recognizing the interior and relational spaces of workplace learning
Ruth Helyer, Philip Frame and Mary Hartog

In concluding Part 2 on space for the self, we take a look at work-based learning (WBL). However, rather than considering a perhaps conventional perspective that focuses upon the physical location of workplaces or upon work-related curricula we explore the interstices that make up the interior learning spaces (Barnett, 2011) of students who are studying and working concurrently. Barnett (2011) argues that this conception of a learning space implies an in-between space, the 'borderlands' of Chapter 7 in which unforeseen experiences might arise. In this way he contrasts learning spaces with their characteristics of freedom and self-authorship, a kind of learning 'spaciousness' (ibid.: 171), with the commonly prevailing vogue for learning outcomes, which engender control and lack of freedom.

This chapter explores how space for learning is created utilizing the workplace with a focus on developing and expanding the 'spaciousness' of student learning. It resonates with ideas around learning 'from the real' (Helyer, 2015; Hartog *et al.*, 2013), because learning from work relies upon learning from, and through, experiences (Kolb, 1984). Spaciousness is concerned with the opening up of the students' interior space, sometimes called the psychic or ontological space, in which Barnett (2011) tells us the formation of the self is implicated, and where the students can bring themselves into a new state of being (Barnett, 2007). This level of self-awareness comes from reflection and reflexivity (Schön, 1983) and deep learning (Biggs, 1989). The curriculum is the workplace and reflection on action through workplace experience and practice is the vehicle for learning. However, reflective practices can be challenging and educators need to consider their students' readiness to learn, their sense of security and their willingness to engage in reflection and self-disclosure and provide the support and guidance necessary for this type of learning.

We have selected two case studies at opposite ends of the academic spectrum to illustrate how work-based experiential learning can be supported. Both are taken from Middlesex University, which has been at the forefront of the development of WBL in the UK for many years. The first case, 'Learning from part-time work', considers how undergraduate students utilize learning from their part-time work as a vehicle for their academic studies and how that is embedded in the curriculum. Students are introduced to the cycle and process of reflecting on experience by drawing upon critical incidents they experience in the workplace. Reflection 'on and in' action (Schön, 1983) is essential in WBL, helping learners to communicate what they already know, the advantageous connections, as well as where to develop and progress: 'learning is the product of students' efforts to interpret, and translate what they experience in order to make meaning of it' (Cooper *et al.*, 2010: 62).

In the second case we explore a form of WBL where a student takes work itself as the field of study rather than simply the location for study, in which the student is immersed in their workplace or practice and learning becomes a social activity within a specific context (Workman and Garnett, 2009). The example given here is a student's learning journey through a professional doctorate, in which a new pedagogical space has been opened up to experienced practitioners who are not allied to a particular academic disciplinary field. This development is characterized by transdisciplinarity (Gibbs, 2015), where knowledge comes from a number of disciplines, as well as between and beyond the disciplinary space, creating space for learning that reflects the complex ontological position or worldviews that practitioners already hold in their world of work (see also Chapter 9 in this volume). In these circumstances the relational space of the mentor and student is a prime characteristic of learner-centred WBL.

We reflect on how these examples respond to Barnett's (2011) challenge to educators to 'open up' space for learning, increase the 'spaciousness' of students and help them make their way in the world, and adapt to the demands of a global world. But first we consider the contemporary context in which these forms of learning spaces are located.

Contemporary work-based learning spaces

> Work-based learning is what is 'learnt' by working – not reading about work, or observing work, but actually undertaking work activities. This is learning from real work and real life and accepting how inextricably linked are those activities. (Helyer, 2015: 2)

WBL takes place away from formal spaces such as classrooms and lecture theatres and situates learning within the real-life world of work, although the formalized spaces of a higher education institution (HEI) may well help the learner/worker to think about, and articulate, their learning. To formalize this learning, individuals may decide to join a work-based HE programme, or be enrolled by their employer, either individually, or as part of a company cohort. Many traditional students also work part-time and, although such jobs may not reflect their career aspirations, they still offer valuable learning opportunities, especially around skills such as problem-solving, analysis, communication, organization, management and reflection (Helyer, 2011). Thus, learning can take place in a wide range of authentic spaces and indeed the learner/worker might not recognize that learning has occurred; it is so genuinely implicit and accepted. Because of this they may well be surprised, as well as empowered, to see their existing knowledge mapped against HE-level descriptors and awarded academic credit. What these students gain credit for is their experiential learning, not their experience. The knowledge and skills gained through WBL are contextualized, rather than abstract (Collis and Margaryan, 2003). This makes the most of learning wherever it occurs, within or without a formal setting, and gives a good basis for integrating work-based activities within standard courses. However, if the learning is ad hoc, it cannot be constructively aligned to predetermined learning outcomes. Consequently accreditation systems need to be more inclusive and flexible. Barnett (2011) tells us that a tension exists between the idea of a learning space and learning outcomes.

Work-based learners are typically described as older, employed, returners to education and only able to attend the campus 'out of hours' (Helyer, 2015). But this is not the full picture. There are an increasing number of students who work alongside their studies, either from financial necessity or as planned experiential learning or to enhance employability, as HEIs pursue an agenda of 'demonstrable economic utility' (Morley, 2018: 2). Furthermore the strong UK government focus on higher and degree apprenticeships, introduced in 2014, means that students of any age are now increasingly likely to be concurrently employed and studying in HE. The government ambition of at least 3 million apprenticeships, due to start by 2020, will substantially expand the spaces for learning, places where students will spend at least 80 per cent of their working week in the workplace and 20 per cent engaged in formal learning, either face-to-face or online (Crawford-Lee, 2016). Indeed a key feature of the apprenticeship programmes is evidencing experiential learning, through portfolios and reflection on experience. The increasing number of WBL opportunities results in more curricula that are negotiated, or co-created, between the academy and the individual student, or sometimes also with their employer.

This establishes a relational space within the curriculum in which the learning is student-centred and, perhaps more significantly, where the power shifts between the student and tutor; from teacher as expert to one in which the expertise, experience and knowledge of the student is validated and recognized. This facilitator role is not unlike that of a coach or mentor, guiding the student in their thoughts and study, helping them contextualize work-related issues and supporting them to develop greater autonomy as learners. Coaching and mentoring are also features of the new apprenticeships.

The learning actually arises from practice, rather than theory, although theory will be increasingly involved as learning progresses, and indeed WBL can cause new theories to emerge. For tutors who believe that knowledge sits within the academy and is filtered to students, it is obvious that this shared approach will seem strange. WBL students often demonstrate higher levels of industry expertise than their tutors, which should be viewed as an opportunity rather than a challenge. Compared to this traditional view, WBL is more of a joint enterprise, where the academy can develop new relational spaces from what they learn from their students' placements, industries and real-life work experiences.

Learning from part-time work
Philip Frame

Space in this case study is concerned with the curriculum, and with reflective and relational spaces. *Learning from part-time work* is an undergraduate business and management module, which expands the space for learning by utilizing learning from part-time work as a mode of WBL. The challenge faced in designing this module was to create a learning framework that helped students articulate their learning. The solution provides an opportunity for reflection on experience and for the development of self, with outcomes related to the identification and articulation of transferable skills for future employment.

The articulation of experiential learning leads to academic credit, not simply the experience. Articulation is the ability to specify, describe and analyse an experience, or concept, and share the results with others. The articulation cycle (Figure 12.1) consists of four elements:

- *self-awareness*: becoming aware of your abilities
- *self-development*: becoming aware of those areas where you need to develop

- *self-actualization*: being able to identify your ambitions and set realistic goals
- *self-promotion*: being clear about who you are, what you have to offer, what you want to achieve and being able to present yourself in and to the workplace honestly and with integrity.

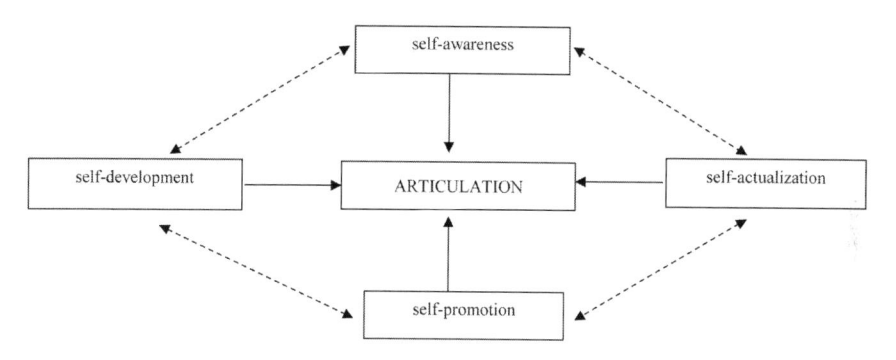

Figure 12.1: The articulation cycle (Frame, 2009)

At Middlesex University the student demographic is predominantly local London-based ethnic minority communities, and the majority of our students are first-generation participants in HE. Learning from part-time work was designed as an opportunity from which students could make the most of their existing employment experience, learn to articulate that experience and gain academic credit. Enrolment was particularly strong from students in business and management and the arts and the module attracted students who, for financial and personal reasons, could not afford to take a year out in industry, the traditional means by which undergraduates have obtained work experience.

The module introduces students to the cycle and process of reflecting on experience by drawing upon critical incidents they experience in the workplace. While many curricula concentrate on the 'what' of knowledge, here students are introduced to a heuristic ASKE (attitudes, skills, knowledge and emotions) framework to support their understanding of the 'how' of learning (Frame, 2009). This is underpinned by theories of experiential learning and reflective practice, specifically Kolb's (1984) 'experiential learning cycle', which identifies the process of learning from and through experience, Heron's (1992) 'up-hierarchy', illustrating the process of learning by working up from experience, through our feelings and emotions, and Schön's (1983) conception of reflection on and in action.

Kolb's (1984) learning cycle helped them see that they were on a learning journey beginning with experience (action), followed by reflection on that experience, then a process of sense making (theorizing) and finally a recognition of their pragmatic learning from experience. At each stage they were challenged with the reflection: 'what might I do differently?'

Heron (1989), in his model for learning facilitation, emphasizes whole-person learning, recognizing the importance of attitudes and emotions in the learning process. Linked to this, students were introduced to the concept of critical incidents, informed by Macfarlane's (2003) work on teaching business ethics, which encouraged the students to capture their 'raw' narrative accounts of critical incidents in the workplace as vignettes, from which they could later analyse their learning. Furthermore, by doing this, students can draw out their learning and 'living wisdom' (Hartog and Frame, 2004). Students sourced evidence of their learning from feedback (formal and informal), such as performance reviews and appraisals, organization rewards and recognition strategies, manager, peer and customer feedback. To help them capture their learning from experience, they were encouraged to keep learning diaries, noting events and critical incidents, such as the following incident of a student working for a West End clothing company:

> One day, my manager Shawn asked me to re-do the display. We get a general outline of what should go with what from Head Office, but then it's down to us as to how we adapt the guidelines to our particular space. I spent about two hours or more re-doing the display space; it's not big but it's complicated. I was pleased with the results and went off for my lunch. When I came back I was horrified to see the display had been dismantled and put back to where it was before I started by someone else. I was well annoyed. I'd gone to so much time and effort. The boss had told me to do it and now, along comes someone else and mucks it all up. When I tackled him about it, he said it was his job. So I talked to the boss about it the next day. It turned out that (the other employee) thought I was getting ideas above my station and he wanted to do the display job. It shows the need for effective communication, and how helpful it is to control your initial impulses before you act. And I'm glad I talked about it and came to some agreement on talking to each other about who is going to do what. It showed me the good of communication between us. And the whole thing showed me how I'd developed too.

In his reflective report, this student explained that sometimes he stands in for the manager and his ambition is to use his experience to get a job in retail management. He uses the ASKE framework to explain how he has become more aware of his attitudes and emotions in the workplace through this process of reflecting, and how he has learnt, in his words, 'to control his impulses before acting'. He goes on to say that this is an example he could use at an interview to show how reflective learning has helped the development of his skill set, making him a suitable candidate for a trainee management position.

We suggest this as a good example of how spaciousness and awareness have been expanded for this student, in that he is clearly now aware of both his attitudes and emotions and those of others, and he is able to articulate the incident and separate out his feelings about it and his learning from it. One important outcome for this student and others like him was a changed perception of the benefits of their part-time work experience, from being purely financial to encompassing their self-development, enhancement of their learning and benefiting their future employability. However, not all students immediately saw the potential benefit. Some expressed frustration at our expectations of them, complaining that their work experience was routine and lacking in opportunity for any gritty or meaningful learning. To help students see the potential for learning, tutors encouraged students to share stories of their experience in the workshops and to probe each other with questions and feedback to help them make sense of their experience, make links to the workshops and draw value from their experiential learning.

A further example comes from a student working in a call centre:

> I am a bit unsure what organisation culture is about but this is something we do at the call centre where I work ... we're all young, a lot of students and we answer calls from customers for different sorts of organizations. We answer calls about banks, insurance companies, fashion and retail outlets, transport, etc. What you say is up on the screen. You have a script. My trainer said, 'you have to stick to it, no deviations, or you will get the sack.' The atmosphere is fairly relaxed, the customers can't see you and the dress code reflects this, so people come to work in what they feel most comfortable, except when some clients are coming to check out the call centre. Then, it's a rule that we dress in a way that reflects the companies we are answering calls for. If it's a fashion company we try to look the part. If it's a bank or insurance company we come wearing a suit and tie (if we have one).

Initially this student was one who expressed doubt about what he could learn from this module, but to our delight, in his portfolio he described all that he had learnt about organization culture by reflecting on his call centre experience, including about the importance of learning to 'fit in' to an organization.

Seeing himself as an organizational member helped expand this student's self-awareness and spaciousness about the potential learning offered from his part-time work. Without the guided opportunity and support to reflect on his lived experience of the workplace, he would not have given his experience a second thought and his learning would have remained entirely tacit. A further outcome for this student was that he was able to answer an examination question on organizational culture, which he said he would not have tackled had he not been able to illustrate his learning from this experience.

Learning from part-time work has created a space for learning that utilizes the workplace as the curriculum, and supports students with tools for reflection that scaffold their experiential learning and enable them to articulate it. Given that a year in industry is beyond the grasp of many of our students, we believe that our example provides a viable alternative to improve student 'graduateness' and their prospects for employability.

Space for self-renewal and expanded awareness
Mary Hartog

Practitioner doctoral programmes typically attract working professionals keen to take the opportunity of developing their professional practice, while locating it within an academic framework, and thereby continuing their journey of lifelong learning. Barnett (2011) sees this as the need to renew oneself to meet the demands of a global learning economy. At Middlesex University the professional doctorate (DProf) programme acknowledges the 'ongoing experiential nature of developing professional capability by structuring around work-based learning' (Doncaster and Lester, 2002: 99).

Within the curriculum of these work-based doctoral programmes, space is facilitated by a pedagogy in which the 'teacher' acts as a facilitator or coach, acknowledging the student's maturity and respecting the learning they already possess from their work experiences. Armsby and Costley (2009) report the average age of a professional doctorate student as 43, because they have to be highly experienced practitioners in order to demonstrate their learning at this level. Indeed the language used in this WBL relationship refers to the student as a candidate (another marker of respect for the expertise and work-based knowledge they bring), the 'supervisor' as an advisor, and specialist advisors, as consultants. The curriculum framework is overlaid by Kolb's (1984) cycle of experiential learning and Schön's (1983) theories of reflective practice informing each stage of the curriculum. The core is the workplace and the work or practice is the curriculum (Boud and Solomon, 2001).

The professional doctorate begins with candidates undertaking a guided review of learning alongside a claim for academic credit for their professional learning and research, followed by a practice or work-based research proposal. Where candidates do not have prior experience or the understanding of carrying out a work-based research project at level 7 (postgraduate Masters level) they are required to conduct a mini-research project to demonstrate their ability before proceeding to a proposal and level 8 (doctoral level) work.

This initial work, over a period of a year to 18 months, is supported by their academic advisor and aims to draw out and articulate the professional's experiential learning, demonstrate their readiness to learn and present a rigorous practice/work-based research proposal to a doctoral panel. The review of learning requires critical reflection, which, when articulated, serves to provide an expanded account of the candidate's learning from their work or practice. We contend that this detailed and extensive groundwork expands the 'spaciousness' of student learning, preparing them to take on the doctoral journey.

Our example concerns Carole, a professional executive coach, whose doctoral research explored how managers experienced loss of resilience and how they recovered it with the help of coaching. Coaching is a relational space, where time to think is supported by a professional coach. Coincidentally, its purpose is also to expand awareness for the coachee, helping them to improve their performance and personal development goals. As a relational practice, professional coaches undertake coaching supervision to support and inform their practice and expand their awareness (spaciousness) of the dynamics involved in the coaching relationship. As part of her research, Carole invited the managers she was coaching to write narratives of their experience (losing and recovering resilience), which she used to inform the coaching conversations.

As Carole discussed her findings with me, she identified a pattern in her data where resiliency ebbed and flowed through the coaching conversations and where the coachee (like a swimmer) experiences the pull and drag of the waves, moving them sideways and backwards as they metaphorically swim towards the shore. She began to sketch a model of her theory to illustrate these nuances in how coachees made progress, were hindered and in some instances, 'put brakes on' their progress, as their stories of resiliency changed.

At this point Carole had focused on gathering data and doing research in much the same way as a traditional PhD student might carry out their research. However, practitioner research is not just about doing research 'out there', rather, it requires turning the mirror inward and exploring the interior space and self in the inquiry process. Professional practice is a form of insider research and in professional practice doctorates, there is an expectation that a student can locate themselves in their research. In this case, the practice is a relational one between the professional and a client, where they are part of the dynamic that influences the relationship. Consequently, the academic advisor asked Carole about her experience of resilience, and by doing so, she invited a reflective conversation of Carole's lived experience of resilience and how it informed her understanding of the experience her research participants had described. For Carole, this proved significant and served to expand her awareness and spaciousness of where she was in the process of this research.

Reason and Marshall (1987) tell us that research as a personal process is often neglected in traditional research. They argue that good research speaks to three audiences:

- for *them* it produces generalizable ideas of interest to others working in the field
- for *us* the research is timely and responds to concerns of practice, i.e. what works
- for *me* it speaks to the process and concerns of the researcher's 'being' in the world.

Furthermore, they suggest that researchers often, consciously or otherwise, choose research topics that have their roots in areas of unresolved anxiety or distress and this choice of research topic is intentionally or subconsciously a bid for personal development. They too see the role of the supervisor as a facilitator, paying attention to process and the here and now of the relationship.

An outcome of the doctorate for Carole was the publication of a book about resilience for coach practitioners, in which she invites her readers to assess the resilient qualities they possess. In the chapter 'You and your resilience', she states:

> When I began research on resilience, it was important that I looked at my own resilience, and that I understood how I had

dealt with life difficulties. By doing so, I came to recognise what was different between the times when I remained resilient and those when I did not. I was able to identify what I could trust would still be accessible in tough times, and what is less available. I came to understand the model I had created, and what had shaped that model. (Pemberton, 2015)

In professional practice research, space for learning includes space for research as a personal process. The candidate is supported by their advisor, who adopts a facilitative stance as the relationship and learning conversations evolve in the form of an enquiry. In this way, critical characteristics of success are through:

- a relational space – the relationship between the candidate and the advisor or, more broadly, the tutor and student
- a reflective space – the student's interior space, including *space for the self* (see also Chapters 8 and 9 in this volume)
- a developmental or transformational space, which has expanded the spaciousness for learning for the candidate or student and made a contribution to knowledge, expanding the outcomes beyond the individual to the wider community of practice.

Conclusion

Utilizing workplace experiences has the potential to 'open up' students to learning and increases their spaciousness or capacity for learning due to their exposure to real, powerful and authentic learning. It is necessary to prepare them to learn from their experiences by introducing the ideas and skills of reflection and the articulation of their experience and supporting these with careful facilitation. Creating space for learning through the workplace curriculum, in a way that enhances the spaciousness of student learning, is relevant at all levels in HE, with the opportunity for personal development and self-renewal.

References

Armsby, P. and Costley, C. (2009) 'Developing work-based learning at doctoral level'. In Garnett, J., Costley, C. and Workman, B. (eds) *Work Based Learning: Journeys to the core of higher education*. London: Middlesex University Press, 102–17.

Barnett, R. (2007) *A Will to Learn: Being a student in an age of uncertainty*. Maidenhead: Open University Press.

Barnett, R. (2011) 'Configuring learning spaces: Noticing the invisible'. In Boddington, A. and Boys, J. (eds) *Re-Shaping Learning: A critical reader: The future of learning spaces in post-compulsory education.* Rotterdam: Sense Publishers, 167–78.

Biggs, J.B. (1989) 'Approaches to the enhancement of tertiary teaching'. *Higher Education Research and Development,* 8 (1), 7–25.

Boud, D. and Solomon, N. (eds) (2001) *Work-Based Learning: A new higher education?* Buckingham: Society for Research into Higher Education and Open University Press.

Collis, B. and Margaryan, A. (2003) 'Work-based activities and the technologies that support them: A bridge between formal and informal learning in the corporate context'. Paper presented at the Learn IT: Information and Communication Technologies and the Transformation of Learning Practices Conference, Gothenburg, Sweden, 8–10 September.

Cooper, L., Orrell, J. and Bowden, M. (2010) *Work Integrated Learning: A guide to effective practice.* London: Routledge.

Crawford-Lee, M.S. (2016) 'Towards a sustainable apprenticeship system'. *Higher Education, Skills and Work-Based Learning,* 6 (4), 324–8.

Doncaster, K. and Lester, S. (2002) 'Capability and its development: Experiences from a work-based doctorate'. *Studies in Higher Education,* 27 (1), 91–101.

Frame, P. (2009) 'Articulating the learning from part time work'. In Garnett, J., Costley, C. and Workman, B. (eds) *Work Based Learning: Journeys to the core of higher education.* London: Middlesex University Press, 62–72.

Gibbs, P. (ed.) (2015) *Transdisciplinary Professional Learning and Practice.* Cham: Springer.

Hartog, M. and Frame, P. (2004) 'Business ethics in the curriculum: Integrating ethics through work experience'. *Journal of Business Ethics,* 54 (4), 399–409.

Hartog, M., Frame, P., Rigby, C. and Wilson, D. (2013) 'Learning from the real'. In Bilham, T. (ed.) *For the Love of Learning: Innovations from outstanding university teachers.* Basingstoke: Palgrave Macmillan, 204–11.

Helyer, R. (2011) 'Aligning higher education with the world of work'. *Higher Education, Skills and Work-Based Learning,* 1 (2), 95–105.

Helyer, R. (2015) 'Introduction'. In Helyer, R. (ed.) *The Work-Based Learning Student Handbook.* 2nd ed. Basingstoke: Palgrave Macmillan, 1–9.

Heron, J. (1989) *The Facilitators' Handbook.* London: Kogan Page.

Heron, J. (1992) *Feeling and Personhood: Psychology in another key.* London: SAGE Publications.

Kolb, D.A. (1984) *Experiential Learning: Experience as the source of learning and development.* Englewood Cliffs, NJ: Prentice-Hall.

Macfarlane, B. (2003) 'Tales from the front-line: Examining the potential of critical incident vignettes'. *Teaching Business Ethics,* 7 (1), 55–67.

Morley, D.A. (ed.) (2018) *Enhancing Employability in Higher Education through Work Based Learning.* Cham: Springer.

Pemberton, C. (2015) *Resilience: A practical guide for coaches.* Maidenhead: Open University Press.

Reason, P. and Marshall, J. (1987) 'Research as personal process'. In Boud, D. and Griffin, V. (eds) *Appreciating Adults Learning: From the learners' perspective.* London: Kogan Page, 112–26.

Schön, D.A. (1983) *The Reflective Practitioner: How professionals think in action.* New York: Basic Books.

Workman, B. and Garnett, J. (2009) 'The development and implementation of work based learning at Middlesex University'. In Garnett, J., Costley, C. and Workman, B. (eds) *Work Based Learning: Journeys to the core of higher education.* London: Middlesex University Press, 2–14.

Part Three

Social and collaborative spaces

Chapter 13

Live projects: Collaborative learning in and with authentic spaces

Jane Anderson

We open Part 3 on collaborative and social learning by exploring learning opportunities afforded by real projects in authentic settings. In doing so, this chapter relates back to issues discussed in Part 1 particularly in using unusual or unconventional spaces and places, for instance in Chapters 4, 5 and 19. But here, we look at how learning in these spaces and places can promote *collaborative learning* in its many forms: collaboration with clients or communities, collaboration between learners and interdisciplinary collaboration. We do this by exploring the nature and benefits of engaging in live projects.

Live projects are innovative educational practices that enable students to engage in learning outside the physical academic institution and through working collaboratively with real clients and users. As such, they involve project-based learning that takes place in 'real-world' spaces with external collaborators and have significant potential as catalysts for interdisciplinary collaboration. Elements of live project pedagogies have occurred in different disciplines in higher education (HE) over many years, in the form of service learning, extension projects, community engagement, design-build, *pro bono* provision, clinical and practice learning and 1:1 projects.

Since the 1990s live projects have become increasingly significant in architectural education. They are commonly a type of design project situated outside the studio, workshop or classroom that extends the space for learning, allowing students to gain experience of the inherent unpredictability, contingency and complexity of real design projects. As Anderson and Priest (2014: 13) explain:

> A live project comprises the negotiation of a brief, timescale, budget and product between an educational organisation and an

> external collaborator for their mutual benefit. The project must be structured to ensure that students gain learning that is relevant to their educational development.

This definition was devised to include the richness of approaches to live projects and of different disciplines adopting similar approaches.

This chapter examines space for learning from the experience of architecture and design students working collaboratively on live projects in authentic spaces. However, many of the insights are applicable across other disciplines and contexts. In our architecture and design context, learning is situated and takes place within a community of practice (Lave and Wenger, 1995) that includes social communities and other professional practitioners, along with the students and their tutors.

OB1 LIVE is a programme of live projects, directed by the author, and undertaken by first-year students as part of their curriculum at the Oxford Brookes School of Architecture. The projects involve external collaborators, normally in the local community, and range from the design and construction of prototypes for a healthcare hub, to the design and installation of an exhibition of archaeological artefacts. Only some of the projects have a permanent construction as their conclusion. Other projects involve students in the creation of design strategies, prototypes, temporary installations or events. Every project ends with a permanent outcome as a record of the student's learning and the project's conclusions, which might include books, academic publications, films, images, webpages, construction manuals, press articles, policies and design strategies. External collaborators often use these outputs to gain support, or funding, to move the project into its next phase. Since 2008, 24 projects have been completed (Anderson, 2008), with external collaborators ranging from a local family centre to the National Trust.

After describing the characteristics of live projects and the types of space in which they can be located, the chapter draws upon analysis and student feedback from all projects undertaken by OB1 LIVE and illustrated with a specific case study that shows how live project strategies and students' learning are influenced by the collaborative learning spaces in which they occur. The chapter concludes with a discussion of the lessons learnt in delivering live projects providing insights which will hopefully be useful for others considering similar initiatives.

Characteristics of live projects

The conventional Western education system has a model of learning within fixed institutions that teach learners until the academy considers them ready to join the world of work. However, their 'preparedness' for work is frequently underestimated (Eraut, 2012). In exploring the amount of learning required to transfer students' theoretical knowledge gained in an academic setting into occupational practice, Eraut (ibid.: 15) concluded that 'traditional thinking about transfer underestimates the learning involved by an order of magnitude'. Live projects seek to redress these shortcomings.

Live projects engage in some of the same activities as practice, training and apprenticeship. They take place in some of the same spaces. Their learning outcomes and real-world experiences are similar to work-based learning, but the focus is not on places of employment, but on the project itself and all that its real-world location brings with it. Students become the authors of the project and are focused on their responsibilities towards the project, its delivery, its location and its stakeholders. Although live project activity and outcomes are visible externally, significant activity such as teaching, reflection, research and support are given by the educational institution to enable live project learning to happen (Anderson, 2014). The scope of live projects can also include research-based education, as long as tutors are explicit about the application of knowledge derived from research to the project or the role of the project in creating new knowledge. In this way live projects are located, often simultaneously or reciprocally, in the normally disconnected spaces of community, education, research, practice and other disciplines. Their authentic locations vary from project to project and are a significant influence in forming different live project strategies and making them responsive and relevant to the spaces where they happen.

Our international survey of live projects found that they are often used as a device to address problems that are complex, contingent and ill-defined and consequently they tend to happen in spaces where there is a need or inequity (Anderson, 2017). These places of adversity stimulate the learning of skills and knowledge that are very difficult to gain institutionally or that are considered to be secondary to the main curriculum, for example resilience and entrepreneurialism.

The analysis in this chapter is informed by a 2017 study (ibid.) of 154 case study live projects published on the Live Projects Network (LPN)

(Anderson and Priest, 2012). LPN is an open-source online database of international live project case studies. In summary, the survey found that live projects occur in authentic spaces, are collaborative in nature and use interdisciplinary expertise that is distributed.

Spaces where live projects happen

A single live project normally occurs in several spaces, often simultaneously. This 'dialogue between normally exclusive worlds' (Rubbo, 2012: 75) manifests itself in the following ways:

- Students maintain a connection with the university during the project in terms of teaching, resources and curriculum. Attempts to describe this symbiotic relationship include 'straddling' (Anderson, 2014: 16) and being on the 'borderlands' (Harriss and Widder, 2014: 1) of the university and the world. (Borderland concepts are also explored in Chapter 7 in this volume.)
- Both students and tutors bring their own identity and networks into the space where the project will take place, strengthening the partnership where this is needed and improving the university's relationship with the local community, partner or stakeholder.
- Some live projects bring the community into the university by hosting activities on campus such as project reviews and exhibitions.
- External collaborators often bring expertise that is not available within conventional university structures.
- The authenticity and multi-headed nature of live projects enable the integration of learning, teaching, practice, research and community.

Temporal spaces

All space has a temporal quality. Some live projects happen in a space very quickly with great intensity and impact, assisting the understanding of concepts and practice; others include time for sustained research, planning, observation, immersion, dialogue and reflection (Anderson, 2017). The live project educator must reconcile the needs of the community, the students' need to learn and the structures imposed by the university. University structures normally require that learning be assessed at the end of the learning module in which it was delivered. This doesn't take into account the time needed to evaluate the impact of the project or the long-term transformative 'burn' of live project learning where learning may only become apparent in future work. Live projects also benefit from the removal of customary boundaries to enable innovation to happen 'in the present' (Tang and Mitchell, 2016).

Unfamiliar spaces

Travel between the various worlds of the live project is important in providing students with experiential learning from real-world activities. This includes learning gained from getting lost, physically or intellectually. The images and reflections produced by students from architectural live projects differ from the customary static images of polished student drawings and models (Anderson and Priest, 2012; Colwill et al., 2014). They communicate the celebration of new achievements, freedom from everyday routines, unfamiliar physically and emotionally demanding work in progress, appreciation of time spent with new people, excitement about unfamiliar places, as well as respect for the challenges that they face together.

Authentic spaces

Live project literature describes live project learning environments that could be construed as unproductive, using words like risk, failure, chaotic, messy, random, impure, compromising and uncertain – equally well-used words include flexibility, contingency, entrepreneurial, dynamic, resilient and democratic (Dodd et al., 2012; Harriss and Widder, 2014; Anderson et al., 2016). The first set of conditions needs to exist in order for a project to become necessary. Participants need to experience such authentic conditions in order to develop the highly desirable qualities of the second list that are so difficult to foster in traditional institutional learning spaces:

> The kind of random encounters and circumstances that make real projects annoying and, well, real, feature prominently in the live project and probably should in a student's educational experience too. (Raxworthy and Costello, 2012: 43)

Collaborative spaces

Real-world projects are characterized by the need to work collaboratively both within and across disciplines. In such situations where novices (students and the community) are working alongside experienced professionals, it is important to establish common ground between different interest groups and individuals. Lave and Wenger's (1995) concepts of communities of practice and of situated learning are very helpful models for establishing this as a mutually beneficial activity. Till advocates architectural live projects as one form of production termed 'spatial agency' (Till, 2012: 8) that involves collective effort in which non-experts play a vital role. Failure to engage the community effectively risks paternalism, or the creation of an illusion of consensus that sweeps unresolved issues under the carpet.

Public spaces
Public spaces are of interest to multiple disciplines. They provide live project environments rich in significant global issues. They are contested, contradictory, plural and political and they are simultaneously everyday and event spaces.

Private and commercial spaces
Live projects tend to eschew commercial work for private clients because they stimulate fewer opportunities for collaboration, innovation and learning (Anderson, 2017; Kraus, 2017). Private and commercial spaces lie more comfortably in the realm of the professional and clearly delineated disciplines. However, this can be an asset to live projects exploring professional or disciplinary expertise and aiming for high levels of resolution in project outcomes.

Places
Live projects that are distant from the university physically or culturally and projects that involve a long-term commitment to a particular place are often particularly immersive and intensely engaged with that place, its culture or its people in a way that is rarely feasible in commercial architectural practice. This expands conventional professional roles or disciplinary boundaries and extends awareness of the project to a wider audience. Deep engagement with a place can be transformative for the place, its people and its collaborators (see also Chapters 1, 3 and 7 in this volume). Revell (2012: 123) describes the benefits of intense engagement with a place as helping to 'develop a stronger educational sense of self, place and commitment to the ultimate sustainable care of our diverse communities and our land'. Sense of self and sense of place are recurrent themes across many chapters in this book.

Case study: OB1 LIVE
In 2015, OB1 LIVE collaborated with the local council and a social housing developer to design and build interactive construction site hoardings around a site in Oxford where new housing and a new community centre was being built. The build required the existing local community centre to be closed and part of the local park cordoned off for several months, to create space for the construction of the development. There was concern

about disruption to the local community during construction and a wish to encourage the integration of newcomers moving into the area post-construction.

The students' experiential learning was extensive. They began by joining local community groups such as the boxing club and bingo and volunteering at places such as the local school or interviewing shopkeepers. They made films, recording what they had learnt about the area, its people and their activities. The project architect for the local redevelopment gave a lecture on the design and construction of the new housing estate and gave the students feedback on their proposals for the construction site hoardings. The students then designed, built and installed interactive installations along the hoarding adjacent to the playing fields. Their brief was to provide a temporary replacement for the community services that were inaccessible during the construction works. These included animal habitats, a vertical garden, play structures, a lending library and a craft station. The building contractors lent their support by cutting viewing holes in the hoarding in particular locations, according to the students' designs. Construction took place over two days of torrential rain in February. After passing a safety inspection, an opening event was held for local people, the local primary school, the contractors, the developer, local councillors and county councillors.

The students fixed their contact numbers to the hoardings to enable local people or visitors to alert students to the need for repairs or replacements as a result of general use, bad weather or vandalism. They learnt valuable lessons about design in the public realm, such as its tendency to be used in ways that the designers did not anticipate and the level of durability required. It also tested the students' resilience to keep going back and fixing any problems. Some installations became beyond repair and had to be removed before the planned disassembly in May.

It might be expected that the negotiation of realities such as rain and vandalism hampered the creativity of novice designers, but an analysis of student feedback over the last six years unexpectedly reveal that the most frequent comment links the realities of a live project with creative freedom:

> Being free to design what you please. Knowing that you are designing for a live project is a nice thought to have as well as makes you want to do your best. (Student evaluation)

Jane Anderson

Figure 13.1: Hoarding installations being used by the community
Image: J. Anderson

Impacts from this project

Following this project, students used what they had learnt about the area, the people and the likely effects of the new development to undertake a theoretical project to design an alternative community centre building. The authentic learning that they gathered in the initial 'live' phase of the project had deepened their understanding of these issues.

One of the most successful aspects of this particular project was the visibility and identity that it gave to the broad range of activities happening locally, and stimulating ideas about new activities that could happen in the future.

Evaluation: The importance of space to the OB1 LIVE programme

The OB1 LIVE projects have taken place in some very different spaces. They include museums, charities, public realm and educational, healthcare, natural, cultural and commercial spaces. Fifteen projects took place

Live projects

in external spaces, 20 were in Oxford, all were accessible to the public and 15 of them were accessible for 24 hours a day. Our analysis of the programme revealed three characteristics of the space that have a significant influence on the project strategies, outcomes and on the students' learning experience. They also influence the outcomes of the project and therefore the students' learning, namely:

- accessibility
- impact
- accountability.

Accessibility

Given that authentic engagement with the place, its people and their activities is central to the pedagogical strategy of live projects, it is important that access is carefully considered at the planning stage. Students develop and apply their own local knowledge through sustained observation, research or engagement in the community. They learn by seeking out local knowledge. Participatory and collaborative design strategies thrive in these situations and students learn innovative approaches to design by engaging with them directly:

> [invaluable] to see and feel the spaces we were given to change.
>
> It helped designing for a community that you could interact with.
>
> I like that we were given a site that is near the Uni, and is a place we can visit whenever we want. (2014, 2015, student evaluations)

Ingenuity and resourcefulness tend to develop quickly in students working in such locations.

> Having to solve problems on the spot, and adapting the designs as issues arose in construction were particular areas which offered challenge and growth to the students. (Project evaluation)

In situations where this intimacy and access is not possible, strategies such as immersion and structured follow-up points of contact can work very well in making those rarer moments of engagement valuable.

Impact

The visibility of the project's location and the energetic activity of students in that space mean that participants are highly conscious of its impact. The visibility, authenticity and public accountability of these projects has a very strong effect in motivating students to test out new skills and to carry out unfamiliar actions that they would not normally undertake with such conviction. Phrases that they frequently use to describe their experience include: 'adapt very quickly', 'hands-on approach', 'fast learning curve', 'independent thinking', 'teamwork', 'challenging', 'exciting', 'communication skills', 'confidence', 'time management', 'try new things'.

> I personally feel like this module immediately plunges us into the world of architecture. As a first-year student, I was quite apprehensive and uncertain about what this degree actually consisted of and I found that the design module really allowed me to obtain a better understanding of all aspects of this profession, from analysing the site to pitching an idea to a client. (2016, student evaluation)

Vitally, it also impacted upon their perception of themselves, their abilities and on ways that they could take control of their own learning:

> I'm amazed at the strength of our student community especially with how young it is. (Perceptions of themselves.)

> Inspires me to try new things and keep going at my work until it improves. (Perceptions of their abilities.)

> Criticising my own work as well and seeing where my mistakes are. (Taking control of their learning.)

Accountability

These projects are stimulated by the mutually beneficial needs of all participants who tend to exchange expertise and resources as an alternative to the commercial transaction of professional practice. This means that through a shared goal, students and their external collaborators can develop a dialogue about appropriate ways to transform these spaces. The high levels of expectation and responsibility of the tasks creates a strong sense of accountability that is difficult to simulate in non-authentic situations. Students found fulfilment in having 'contributed to the surrounding community' and another commented that they were:

> Being taught to acknowledge that designing a building is more than just structure and cladding, etc., learning to consider the surrounding site, the local community, the movement of people and having a reason for everything you do in the process of design. (2016, student evaluation)

Lessons learnt
Ethical considerations
Live projects tend to emerge as a response to places where there is a need, conflict, injustice or crisis (Anderson, 2017; Kraus, 2017). The vulnerability of such situations places an imperative to act ethically and any intervention must be positively transformative and empowering for both the community and the students. For example, a heroic and ambitious construction project achieved against all the odds may create a financial drain on the community to maintain it if preparatory projects have not been undertaken to ensure its sustainability. In the compelling situation of the live project, issues that seemed irrelevant to students while in the university, such as health and safety, become suddenly urgent when on site. It is essential also that more privileged participants are sensitive to differences such as deprivation, destruction or ethnicity that they encounter. Charlesworth (2012: 57) recommends 'multidisciplinary design collaborations' to enable ethical working in such situations. If robust structures are created, the multi-disciplinary and ethical expertise available in a university, as well as its stability and integrity, can make universities bastions of safeguarding the ethics of live projects.

Collaborative learning and working
In live projects students work collaboratively in unfamiliar ways and places and the varied spaces alter ingrained hierarchies and structures. Local communities and students are involved in the design process and designers are involved in construction in ways that these groups rarely are normally. Tutors are no longer all-knowing; instead they must act as collaborators, coaches and role models, demonstrating discipline-specific skills. Location in the collaborative space of the project rather than in the design studio helps learners understand the potential and common discontinuities between design intent and the lived experience of design decisions. It also makes actions of design more visible to non-designers.

The altered structure of live projects breaks down barriers to the integration of learning, teaching, research and practice, altered hierarchies and new locations enabling students to perceive their own identity in relation to society in new ways. This has the potential for widening participation, internationalization of the curriculum and for developing other forms of equity in the curriculum.

Interdisciplinary collaboration

Live project collaboration can provide students with experience of working in professional multidisciplinary teams, appropriate for projects with very defined outcomes such as the design and construction of a permanent building. For projects that occur in complex and contingent situations with more fluid outcomes and roles, students can gain invaluable knowledge beyond their own discipline. As an example our architectural live projects involve collaboration with disciplines including performance, science and archaeology.

Interdisciplinarity enables different disciplines to work together to benefit from the knowledge that others bring, all members retaining and contributing the expertise of their own discipline rather than attempting to become expert in another. In this way, complex problems that cross disciplines, such as those concerned with society, nature or new technology, can be addressed more easily. These same types of complex and contingent problems tend to stimulate live projects, often tackling global issues such as urban poverty, climate change or digital innovation at a local level and connecting to applied research and interdisciplinary collaboration to enable a wide dissemination of solutions.

Greater awareness of live projects is needed across the disciplines in order to benefit from their capacity to stimulate high-quality interdisciplinary collaborative learning.

References

Anderson, J. (2008) 'OB1 LIVE'. Online. http://architecture.brookes.ac.uk/galleries/ob1 (accessed 2 July 2017).

Anderson, J. (2014) 'Undercurrent: Swimming away from the design studio'. *Charrette*, 1 (1), 3–19.

Anderson, J. (2017) 'Devising an inclusive and flexible taxonomy of international Live Projects'. *ARENA Journal of Architectural Research*, 2 (1), Article 3, 1–16. Online. https://tinyurl.com/y2hvwros (accessed 23 February 2019).

Anderson, J., Godiksen, C. and Harriss, H. (2016) 'Live Projects across the disciplines'. *Brookes eJournal of Learning and Teaching*, 8 (1–2). Online. https://tinyurl.com/yxpd9x2g (accessed 23 February 2019).

Anderson, J. and Priest, C. (2012) 'Live Projects Network'. Online. http://liveprojectsnetwork.org (accessed 30 April 2017).

Anderson, J. and Priest, C. (2014) 'Developing an inclusive definition, typological analysis and online resource for Live Projects'. In Harriss, H. and Widder, L. (eds) *Architecture Live Projects: Pedagogy into practice*. London: Routledge, 9–17.

Charlesworth, E. (2012) 'Moving beyond yellow paper dreamings: A "walking the talk" model of teaching community engagement in design'. In Dodd, M., Harrisson, F. and Charlesworth, E. (eds) *Live Projects: Designing with people.* Melbourne: RMIT University Press, 51–63.

Colwill, S., Hartig, U. and Pawlicki, P. (2014) 'Design Build Xchange'. Online. www.dbxchange.eu (accessed 30 April 2017).

Dodd, M., Harrisson, F. and Charlesworth, E. (eds) (2012) *Live Projects: Designing with people.* Melbourne: RMIT University Press.

Eraut, M. (2012) 'Transfer of knowledge between education and workplace settings'. In Daniels, H., Lauder, H. and Porter, J. (eds) *Knowledge, Values and Educational Policy: A critical perspective.* London: Routledge, 75–94.

Harriss, H. and Widder, L. (eds) (2014) 'Introduction: pedagogy into practice … or practice into pedagogy?' In Harriss, H. and Widder, L. (eds) *Architecture Live Projects: Pedagogy into practice.* Abingdon: Routledge, 1–6.

Kraus, C. (ed.) (2017) *Designbuild Education.* New York: Routledge.

Lave, J. and Wenger, E. (1995) *Situated Learning: Legitimate peripheral participation.* Cambridge: Cambridge University Press.

Raxworthy, J. and Costello, S. (2012) 'The real unreal: Lessons from the Atherton Gardens design project'. In Dodd, M., Harrisson, F. and Charlesworth, E. (eds) *Live Projects: Designing with people.* Melbourne: RMIT University Press, 38–50.

Revell, G. (2012) '"Whatchew reckon I reckon?!"'. In Dodd, M., Harrisson, F. and Charlesworth, E. (eds) *Live Projects: Designing with people.* Melbourne: RMIT University Press, 120–39.

Rubbo, A. (2012) 'Design education as engaged practice: Going "live" at home and abroad'. In Dodd, M., Harrisson, F. and Charlesworth, E. (eds) *Live Projects: Designing with people.* Melbourne: RMIT University Press, 64–77.

Tang, B. and Mitchell, M. (2016) 'Live Projects: Innovating in the present'. *Brookes eJournal of Learning and Teaching,* 8 (1–2). Online. https://tinyurl.com/y2ynvzuo (accessed 23 February 2019).

Till, J. (2012) 'Resuscitating architectural education'. In Dodd, M., Harrisson, F. and Charlesworth, E. (eds) *Live Projects: Designing with people.* Melbourne: RMIT University Press, 4–11.

Chapter 14
Collaborative and reflective spaces for developing professional practitioners
Claire Hamshire, Deborah O'Connor and Kirsten Jack

While studying in higher education (HE) students undergo a continuous process of 'becoming' (Barnett, 2007) as they develop identity, understanding and competence. For students studying vocational programmes, there is the additional transition of 'becoming a professional practitioner'. Professional learning in both university and practice spaces plays a crucial part in the education and development of such students and it is where they make the important links between academic knowledge and practical skills (Frazer *et al.*, 2014). These are social spaces where collaborative and community learning are nurtured and encouraged (Matthews *et al.*, 2011), where reflection and self-evaluation skills are developed and embedded (Jack *et al.*, 2017) and within which novice practitioners become professionals.

This chapter presents two examples of how different spaces are utilized to enhance the learning experience of students training to become healthcare professionals. Both cases utilize collaborative spaces to underline the importance of communities of practice in healthcare, the benefits of peer review and the importance of embedding reflective skills alongside practical skills within healthcare curricula.

Working within a community of practice provides opportunities for novice practitioners to reflect upon their experiences in the form of conceptual and factual knowledge, professional and skills knowledge and personal experiential knowledge (Donaghy and Morss, 2000). Green (2005) calls these 'spaces of influence', where individual learners gain insight through the support of others. She identifies five spaces within this metaspace of influence:

- spaces of 'action' in which learners take control of their own learning
- spaces of 'explicit discourse' exemplified by groups engaged in reflection in action

- spaces of 'learning' in which a tutor allows learners to move along unknown and unpredictable pathways in order to problem solve
- spaces of 'practice development' in which process occurs, often in communities of practice
- spaces of 'trust' in which learners learn from their mistakes or misjudgements without the fear of criticism.

On healthcare programmes, novice practitioners typically spend a significant proportion of their time within a practice environment and within communities of practice. As a result, they experience spaces of influence through a range of educational spaces: material and physical, curriculum and pedagogical and personal and interior (Barnett, 2011) as they progress between academic years. Transitions between these spaces demarcate a new status for the students (Henderson *et al.*, 2007), facilitating a gradual process of identity construction (Britton and Baxter, 1999) as they develop as practitioners. To achieve this, feedback and reflection become essential skills that healthcare students need to develop and embed into their practice (Kelly *et al.*, 2009). Students also need to be given opportunities and spaces to practice these skills in a supported way (King, 2002; Moon, 2013).

Such spaces take different forms. As learning is both a social and a personal experience, learners need space to become part of their community of practice and space for personal reflection. In addition, a variety of methods are required to facilitate healthcare students' ability to reflect and self-evaluate while they learn to become a professional practitioner. These techniques also aim to embed in the students a career-long commitment to professional development.

Our first case explores the challenges and benefits of using video technologies and mobile devices to promote professional skill development and reflection within a collaborative space. The second case outlines how the use of authentic clinical spaces for undergraduate students can enhance learning through communities of practice (Wenger, 1998).

Using mobile devices to promote space for reflection and skill development
Claire Hamshire and Deborah O'Connor

Reflection is fundamental to the transition to professional practice (Moon, 2013), but students often have limited time and opportunity to demonstrate sufficient depth of critical thinking in skills-based classes (Lin, 2013). Personal reflection both within their internal space and a community of practice is a complex skill that needs time to develop in the space between the taught and the learned (Sagan, 2011). It is also a deeply personal process requiring the individual to scrutinize, consider and analyse both alone and with others. These 'interior' spaces are the place of their 'being' and their own self-formation is implicated as they develop over time (Barnett, 2011). Teaching practical skills and reflection to physiotherapy students is therefore a core component of our curriculum.

Following programme evaluation, undergraduate physiotherapy students requested greater opportunities to enhance their practical skills to better prepare them for their clinical placements. Previously, although students had opportunities to view practical demonstrations of clinical procedures and received formative feedback from tutors on their practical skills, they had no permanent visual record to support ongoing learning, reflection or to aid revision. Our solution was to integrate mobile devices into practical skills sessions, specifically using the in-built video camera and with the aim of placing learning in the hands of students, promoting dialogue and changing the predominant culture of teaching and learning into a space of action (Green, 2005).

We identified a series of practical workshops that were suitable for using mobile devices. Working in small groups students created, reviewed and shared videos of their practical procedures, which allowed them to:

- review and critique their own performance and practical skills
- work collaboratively to give feedback to each other and develop peer-feedback skills
- review and critique their communication skills by recording samples of role-play interaction.

These videos were subsequently used as a starting point for dialogue, debrief and reflection with academic staff, peers and for self-reflection.

Student evaluation

Students (n = 84) within a year group were invited to participate and feedback. Fifty students gave feedback reporting several positive aspects including the ability to view tutor demonstrations and practical skill performance from different angles. The use of visual feedback offered opportunities for students to capture their practice and view it through another lens in a virtual space (Pope, 2002; Zhang et al., 2011).

Several key aspects of the reflective process such as repetition, timely feedback and clinical reasoning were reported. Students discussed reflecting both in and on action (Schön, 1987), highlighting value in terms of facilitating reflection through clarification, developing confidence and facilitating both accuracy and independence in practical skills:

> I don't always understand what I should be doing but those videos made me understand what I should be looking at.

> It just made what we were doing stay in my head. Usually I have to go over it a few times but now I remember what my main strengths and weaknesses were just from looking back at it at the time in class.

> You can actually analyse what you did to see if you did it correctly ... it's like clarification really... it helps you actually discuss and decide, is that what you're actually seeing first time round?

They noted how this created a collaborative space to reinforce changes in performance and behaviour, essentially spaces of 'practice development' in which process occurs (Green, 2005). The videos become spaces of 'action', in which students take control of their learning to develop their practice (ibid.).

For staff, one of the key benefits of using video was the creation of a collaborative space in which students reviewed videos of each other and gave feedback on their performance, promoting both self- and peer-evaluation:

> Watching each other perform a task gave the students a certain level of awareness but looking at something on the screen was something different that added to their learning ... they would pause it and rewind it and come back ... it was a very different way of looking at an activity and working together.

> What I have noticed is that, when you ask a group without iPads to comment on each other... they're less likely to critique, comment or criticise each other verbally. However, once they've videoed it, and they go back and they look at it on a screen, it's almost like they've desensitised it and they'll criticise the screen but they won't criticise one to one, face to face.

Staff noted that video desensitized the students in terms of the feedback processes within a dialogical space for debate (Savin-Baden, 2011) and the space for explicit discourse (Green, 2005). In this way collaborative learning spaces enable peers to be accepted as part of the learning process. In fact

Costello (1989) has demonstrated that learners develop many practical skills directly from their peers, even though they have supervisors.

By incorporating this peer-reviewed process, students gained multiple perspectives on their skill development, enhancing their ability to critically evaluate and provide feedback to each other. This, in turn, enabled the development of a community of practice (Kukulska-Hulme, 2012) promoting further reflection and depth of learning as well as supporting collaborative learning (Diemer et al., 2012). Staff noted that the videos enhanced the development of learners as novice practitioners on their journey to becoming experts and that the internal and collaborative learning spaces enabled students to enhance performance review and consolidate learning.

However, it was not welcomed universally. While staff felt that video did add value to the classroom, some considered it as merely an adjunct to teaching and learning and not always as a tool to replace staff input. Indeed, some staff did not feel that it had made any difference to their academic practice. This indicates that some staff are not comfortable with Green's (2005) spaces for 'learning' in which novice practitioners find their own way to solve problems, perhaps not recognizing the power of peer learning (Costello, 1989).

Using professional and clinical spaces
Claire Hamshire and Kirsten Jack

In describing communities of practice, Wenger (1998) presents a theory of learning that proposes that engagement in social practice is the fundamental process by which we learn and become who we are. This case study illustrates how nursing students use spaces for learning, practice development and creating trust. Central to these processes is the use of role modelling and joint reflection, which both support students to navigate their journey of development and growth within social communities of practice and through both clinical and academic spaces.

Currently, 50 per cent of nursing undergraduate programme hours in the UK is spent within clinical spaces, across a range of acute and community settings. Competencies required to become a qualified nurse are determined by the UK Nursing and Midwifery Council (NMC, 2018) and the requisite work-based learning is facilitated by nursing staff based within placement settings. For the duration of their clinical placements, every nursing student is assigned an educator responsible for the summative assessment of their performance. In addition to pre-training perspectives based on their own experience of being 'nursed', the clinical spaces provide many opportunities for learning. For example, peers, qualified staff from other specialities and the service users themselves all form spaces for practice development in which students can progress both their personal and professional learning.

Nursing students move through spaces of learning from the periphery to the centre of professional practice, often through unpredictable territory, as they develop their professional self. It is important, then, that the clinical space becomes one of trust as students learn from mistakes and require a supportive environment in which to trial new behaviours and ways of being. This process of developing one's professional identity is linked to the themes of belonging and becoming that are discussed elsewhere in this book, especially in Chapters 10 and 11. Their feelings of 'connectedness' to their chosen profession and hence their identities both as students and professionals also have the potential to impact on their development as learners and commitment to studying (Scanlon *et al.*, 2007; see also Chapter 1 in this volume).

The profession of nursing involves more than the learning of practical tasks, and clinical space offers multiple opportunities to learn aspects of relational care and the ability to engage with others in a therapeutic way. Indeed, the work of Carper (1978) reminds nurses, that there are several ways of knowing in nursing, namely empirical, aesthetic, ethical and personal, and each are of equal importance and require various spaces of influence as described by Green (2005). For example, through interactions with service users in the clinical space, students can begin to learn more about themselves, gaining personal knowledge of their strengths and areas for growth. The clinical space offers rich opportunities for self-development and is an important part of the professional socialization process (Ion *et al.*, 2017). This space becomes one of practice development (Green, 2005) as students progress their learning through a community of practice, which includes not only other professionals but also those who are using services directly and their relatives and carers. Experiences gained in a community with others support students' self-development on their journey to becoming a professional. These features are exemplified through the following reflection from a second-year nursing student who had concerns about dealing with dying patients and bereaved relatives:

> I was very anxious around poorly patients and felt uncomfortable around their families. I worried about what to say, or even worse, saying the wrong thing. I had learnt the theory at university, and how I was supposed to behave, but the reality is very different.

> At times, my emotions felt like they were taking over and there have been times I have wanted to cry, which would not be the right thing to do in front of patients and relatives. I then had a great placement experience with an educator called Sally. She not only knew the theory about bereavement but had a real empathy and kindness for patients. It shone through her. I emulated her style, observing her behaviour, and I tried to do the same. She was a great role model to me and I sought lots of feedback from her on my own style and way of being around others. Through reflecting together, I learnt about myself, who I was as a person, what my boundaries were, and I started to grow and felt less afraid. Now as a third year, I often imagine what Sally might do or say in certain situations. Her guidance has had a long-term effect on me and will have an effect on how I support others in the future.

This example shows the importance of collaborative spaces as places to learn. It demonstrates how students learn not only from other professionals, but also through their interaction with others within the space of practice development. Through joint reflection the student has created a space of action by taking control of her learning through emulating another person and similarly the educators learn more about themselves and how they can support students during challenging experiences.

Students can sometimes be concerned about making mistakes and causing harm to service users, particularly during the early stage of their learning (Killam and Heerschap, 2013). However, by creating a space of learning, it has been easier for the student to navigate through the uncertainty of an emotional situation and use it to problem solve and learn for the future. There are situations in nursing practice that can often be unpredictable and enabling spaces for learning is important for ongoing development. This can occur through joint reflection between educator and student, and through the sharing of experiences in the clinical and academic relational spaces (Smith and Gray, 2001). These actions create spaces for role modelling and critical reflection both in and on action, through explicit discourse about a difficult situation. The example describes a positive learning situation, although even exposure to poor role models can support students when thinking about the type of nurse they *don't* want to be (Grealish and Ranse, 2009).

Creating spaces of trust, whereby students can explore negative situations and 'trial' different ways of being without fear of being judged, can greatly influence their learning. Educators in the clinical setting have a great influence on practice learning, while lecturers model professionalism in the academic setting (Donaldson and Carter, 2005; Felstead, 2013). Both have equal importance, and developing trusting spaces wherever the student is learning is essential for development to take place and enables students to gain a range of experience on which to draw on qualification (NMC, 2018). A trusting relationship between educator and student is important, since learning experiences in practice have the greatest influence on students' motivation to complete a programme (Crombie et al., 2013). Often, watching and emulating the style of senior staff, using role-modelling techniques and reflective learning, can support students' development (Jack et al., 2017), enabling the explicit discourse required to influence positive change. Indeed, clinical educators and university lecturers are viewed by students as their main role models when learning how to care for others (Smith and Gray, 2001).

Lessons learnt

The ability to reflect both in and on action (Schön, 1987) develops as students take a critical stance when considering their practice both during and after an event. Opportunities for students to step back and review their own performance enhance their ability to become critical in a constructive and developmental manner, through the provision of a thinking space (Sagan, 2011). Reflection and review, both with peers and staff within a collaborative place that facilitates discussion and feedback, enhance students' relationships and promote their sense of belonging to a community of practice, which is essential to a space of practice development (Green, 2005).

In these two examples the opportunities for professional learning facilitated reflection. Promoting a culture of trust, respect and privacy allows students to feel comfortable exposing potential weaknesses to others, enabling emotional support and honest debate. This approach has strengthened the students' transition towards becoming professional practitioners and their internal sense of professional identity; the distinctive features of this space for learning, create opportunities for learning that involved:

- peer review and self-reflection to enhance skill development
- situated (social) learning within a community of practice
- a reflective relationship with a mentor, creating a role model, which is critical to learning.

In both examples reflection has been evident in, or on, the experience of professional practice. The students' development as professionals created, in a metaphorical sense, a bridge between the workplace and the university, constructing a space for learning that moves the student back and forth between the practice environment and the classroom in the service of professional and personal development.

References

Barnett, R. (2007) *A Will to Learn: Being a student in an age of uncertainty*. Maidenhead: Open University Press.

Barnett, R. (2011) 'Configuring learning spaces: Noticing the invisible'. In Boddington, A. and Boys, J. (eds) *Re-Shaping Learning: A critical reader: The future of learning spaces in post-compulsory education*. Rotterdam: Sense Publishers, 167–78.

Boddington, A. and Boys, J. (2011) 'Reshaping learning – an introduction'. In Boddington, A. and Boys, J. (eds) *Re-Shaping Learning: A critical reader: The future of learning spaces in post-compulsory education*. Rotterdam: Sense Publishers, xi–xxii.

Britton, C. and Baxter, A. (1999) 'Becoming a mature student: Gendered narratives of the self'. *Gender and Education*, 11 (2), 179–93.

Carper, B.A. (1978) 'Fundamental patterns of knowing in nursing'. *Advances in Nursing Science*, 1 (1), 13–23.

Costello, J. (1989) 'Learning from each other: Peer teaching and learning in student nurse training'. *Nurse Education Today*, 9 (3), 203–6.

Crombie, A., Brindley, J., Harris, D., Marks-Maran, D. and Morris Thompson, T. (2013) 'Factors that enhance rates of completion: What makes students stay?'. *Nurse Education Today*, 33 (11), 1282–7.

Diemer, T.T., Fernandez, E. and Streepey, J.W. (2012) 'Student perceptions of classroom engagement and learning using iPads'. *Journal of Teaching and Learning with Technology*, 1 (2), 13–25.

Donaghy, M.E. and Morss, K. (2000) 'Guided reflection: A framework to facilitate and assess reflective practice within the discipline of physiotherapy'. *Physiotherapy Theory and Practice*, 16 (1), 3–14.

Donaldson, J.H. and Carter, D. (2005) 'The value of role modelling: Perceptions of undergraduate and diploma nursing (adult) students'. *Nurse Education in Practice*, 5 (6), 353–9.

Felstead, I. (2013) 'Role modelling and students' professional development'. *British Journal of Nursing*, 22 (4), 223–7.

Frazer, K., Connolly, M., Naughton, C. and Kow, V. (2014) 'Identifying clinical learning needs using structured group feedback: First year evaluation of pre-registration nursing and midwifery degree programmes'. *Nurse Education Today*, 34 (7), 1104–8.

Grealish, L. and Ranse, K. (2009) 'An exploratory study of first-year nursing students' learning in the clinical workplace'. *Contemporary Nurse*, 33 (1), 80–92.

Green, P. (2005) 'Spaces of influence: A framework for analysis of an individual's contribution within communities of practice'. *Higher Education Research & Development*, 24 (4), 293–307.

Henderson, S., Holland, J., McGrellis, S., Sharpe, S. and Thomson, R. (2007) *Inventing Adulthoods: A biographical approach to youth transitions.* London: SAGE Publications.

Ion, R., Smith, K. and Dickens, G. (2017) 'Nursing and midwifery students' encounters with poor clinical practice: A systematic review'. *Nurse Education in Practice*, 23, 67–75.

Jack, K., Hamshire, C. and Chambers, A. (2017) 'The influence of role models in undergraduate nurse education'. *Journal of Clinical Nursing*, 26 (23–24), 4707–15.

Kelly, M., Lyng, C., McGrath, M. and Cannon, G. (2009) 'A multi-method study to determine the effectiveness of, and student attitudes to, online instructional videos for teaching clinical nursing skills'. *Nurse Education Today*, 29 (3), 292–300.

Killam, L.A. and Heerschap, C. (2013) 'Challenges to student learning in the clinical setting: A qualitative descriptive study'. *Nurse Education Today*, 33 (6), 684–91.

King, T. (2002) *Development of Student Skills in Reflective Writing.* Portsmouth: University of Portsmouth. In 4th World Conference of the International Consortium for Educational Development in Higher Education, Perth, Australia.

Kukulska-Hulme, A. (2012) 'How should the higher education workforce adapt to advancements in technology for teaching and learning?'. *The Internet and Higher Education*, 15 (4), 247–54.

Lin, Z.-C. (2013) 'Comparison of technology-based cooperative learning with technology-based individual learning in enhancing fundamental nursing proficiency'. *Nurse Education Today*, 33 (5), 546–51.

Matthews, K.E., Andrews, V. and Adams, P. (2011) 'Social learning spaces and student engagement'. *Higher Education Research and Development*, 30 (2), 105–20.

Moon, J.A. (2013) *Reflection in Learning and Professional Development: Theory and practice.* Abingdon: Routledge.

NMC (Nursing and Midwifery Council) (2018) *Realising Professionalism: Standards for education and training: Part 2: Standards for student supervision and assessment.* London: Nursing and Midwifery Council. Online. https://tinyurl.com/y7kfynub (accessed 24 February 2019).

Pope, P. (2002) 'Enhancing the development of effective one-to-one skills for practice'. *Practice: Social Work in Action*, 14 (3), 51–8.

Sagan, O. (2011) 'Between the lines: The transitional space of learning'. In Boddington, A. and Boys, J. (eds) *Re-Shaping Learning: A critical reader: The future of learning spaces in post-compulsory education.* Rotterdam: Sense Publishers, 69–79.

Savin-Baden, M. (2011) 'Research spaces'. In Boddington, A. and Boys, J. (eds) *Re-Shaping Learning: A critical reader: The future of learning spaces in post-compulsory education.* Rotterdam: Sense Publishers, 93–103.

Scanlon, L., Rowling, L. and Weber, Z. (2007) '"You don't have like an identity... you are just lost in a crowd": Forming a student identity in the first-year transition to university'. *Journal of Youth Studies*, 10 (2), 223–41.

Schön, D.A. (1987) *Educating the Reflective Practitioner*. San Francisco: Jossey-Bass.

Smith, P. and Gray, B. (2001) 'Reassessing the concept of emotional labour in student nurse education: Role of link lecturers and mentors in a time of change'. *Nurse Education Today*, 21 (3), 230–7.

Wenger, E. (1998) *Communities of Practice: Learning, meaning and identity*. Cambridge: Cambridge University Press.

Zhang, M., Lundeberg, M., Koehler, M.J. and Eberhardt, J. (2011) 'Understanding affordances and challenges of three types of video for teacher professional development'. *Teaching and Teacher Education*, 27 (2), 454–62.

Chapter 15
Reframing spaces for staff learning
Joy Jarvis and Rebecca Thomas

Most of the other examples of practice in this book indicate ways in which learning spaces can be interpreted, imagined and changed for student learning. However, university staff also require spaces for learning in order to identify and initiate new teaching approaches, to reflect, re-energize and develop. Staff need to be proactive in developing their practice through enquiring into their own teaching, working with colleagues and students to create innovative approaches, and engaging in scholarship in learning and teaching. This chapter explores how we can create spaces that enable all staff to have the opportunity to enquire into and develop their educational practice.

The need for dialogic space

The current 'performance measurement' culture in UK higher education and frequently in other countries and systems (Olssen and Peters, 2005), with high levels of managerial control, can lead to a 'surface view' of teaching that focuses on systems and procedures, rather than on staff exploring pedagogy and student learning more critically (Rowland, 2001). Learning and teaching initiatives are often driven by those in management roles and can result in staff 'compliance rather than reflective adoption of change' (Fanghanel, 2009: 205). Official spaces for staff to learn about teaching and learning can be reduced to contexts where they are informed of policy and given guidelines for practice. In this context there is no space for critique, for enquiry into practice or for a more distributed type of leadership. Distributed leadership accepts that expertise is widely distributed across an institution and needs to be drawn on for the good of that institution and its members (Bolden *et al.*, 2015). For this to happen, dialogic spaces for colleagues to work together, to share, challenge and develop learning and teaching practices need to be created. Dialogue is a participatory, democratic process whereby all those involved can contribute and be listened to, and through which joint decisions about actions can be made. We aimed to create collegiate spaces, drawing on the ideas of Bakhtin (Holquist, 1990) and Bohm (1996) on the importance of dialogue in developing meanings and new ways of working.

The reframing

In a school of creative arts in a large post-1992 UK university, staff with responsibility for learning and teaching identified the need to 'reframe spaces', both physically and socially, to facilitate staff learning. The authors (an academic developer and a course leader in the school), with support from the school's associate dean decided to co-create, with staff, spaces for enquiry into learning and teaching. We aimed to build staff leadership and facilitate the gathering of colleagues to explore aspects of educational practice.

Key to this initiative was the building of professional learning communities. These have been identified, for both business and educational contexts, as important for institutional as well as personal learning (Stoll and Louis, 2007; Wenger et al., 2002). The literature on staff mentoring communities (Felten et al., 2013), in which staff meet regularly with a self-chosen focus, was particularly influential as our aim was to facilitate colleagues' proactivity in leading practice change. We also used the idea of 'significant networks' of staff who, working together in small groups, talk about their practices and how these could be created and connected (Roxå and Mårtensson, 2009). We chose two approaches to reframing space for staff learning, both based on the importance of relational and social space and one that involved using outdoor space. We go on to explain these approaches, why and how they were undertaken, their impact so far and the challenges we faced.

Space one: Going out for a picnic

Our aim here was to give staff from different creative arts disciplines time to enquire into an aspect of their teaching. By connecting colleagues from different subject areas who had not worked together previously, we aimed to encourage critique and challenge assumptions. Colleagues chose their own group topic that drew on their experiences and focused on what they determined as important for their students. Initial topics chosen were: the influence of new technology on product and industrial design teaching, innovative approaches to assessment, the use of technology in teaching and facilitating student learning in galleries and other 'off-campus' sites.

A key factor influencing development as a teacher is engaging in some form of enquiry (Rowland, 2000). This generally involves reflecting upon, and subsequently evaluating, changing practice and also engaging with the scholarship of learning and teaching by sharing research literature and ultimately contributing to it. Brew and Ginns (2008: 543) suggest that 'there is a significant relationship ... between [staff] engaging in the scholarship of teaching and learning, and changes in students' course experiences.' We aimed to create such opportunities for collegiate, scholarly enquiry, to improve practice and to legitimize teaching as an academic, scholarly activity.

We chose to reframe the space, so it was as different as possible to conventional spaces for learning and teaching development in order to encourage more opportunities for thinking differently: we suggested that colleagues leave campus and go for a picnic. The idea of 'picnicking' can include emotions such as happiness and create a relaxed environment that can lead to the opening up of ideas. 'A picnic is effusively convivial, communal, and radiating good will' (Levy, 2014: 6). It involves food that can create connections and sharing between people (Thomas, 2016), and the picnic disrupts routine and can be a transgressive experience as normal dining and social conventions are changed (Levy, 2014). Quinn (2012) promotes the idea of spaces for staff learning as spaces for disruption where changing the physical and social space enables critique, challenge and innovation. A picnic is also a playful idea, with opportunities for being imaginative, which lead to more creative thinking (James and Brookfield, 2014).

Colleagues who joined in this project found the experience motivating, especially as they had ownership of what they were doing and the direction they wished this to take. Staff reported their experiences of 'going out' at a staff learning and teaching meeting and noted:

> Working outside the University ... allowed us to see the issues with fresh eyes ... and to come up with solutions.
>
> Ideas burst out when you're not here [on the campus].
>
> With no pressure to deliver anything, we actually delivered a lot.
>
> We came away feeling energised – rare at the end of term.

All staff involved in this project reported that the experience of going out and talking about teaching was different from meetings about teaching on campus. They felt more creative, less constrained by quality procedures or limited by expectations of how things were usually taught. They talked about engaging in 'rambling conversations and pooling ideas'. This may be due to the physical space itself, but it is also related to how meetings about teaching are usually conducted. In Crawford's (2010: 197) study, academics from two higher education institutions compared their teaching and their research networks: 'teaching networks were experienced as pragmatic, business and organization-led, while research-related communities were considered to be collegiate and discursive'. This relates to how teaching is often seen as compliance with central initiatives and meetings about the organization of teaching rather than the pedagogy. Additionally, the length of time given to the 'going out' projects, minimally half a day, allowed for more exploration and the sharing of ideas:

> We were so immersed in talking about it.
>
> There were endless ideas in our group.

During their time 'outside', colleagues initially talked about a wide range of issues involved in their practice, such as the constraints of modular course design and the separation of students onto narrow curricular pathways with a subsequent lack of multidisciplinary working within creative arts courses. This allowed them to challenge these constraints and produced the new assessment process developed by one group and described below:

> When I came I was worried about too much assessment then I ended up talking about something completely different – what is assessment for?

They noted that this type of discussion about teaching was very different from that they would have had on campus, which would have focused on the minutiae of practice and only resulted in minor adjustments to existing ways of working. A sense of control around where, when and how to develop practice can be lacking in contexts of compliance where planning and development activities are too systematized.

It was both the freedom of the space outside a framework and the sense that staff had agency to make changes that were important. In the learning and teaching meeting, staff members who had been on a picnic felt ownership of their 'hidden' conversation space:

> Don't tell management where we went as they will send everyone there and it's our place.

Staff in the 'going out' project saw themselves as being creative in thinking of new ideas for teaching. They noted, 'how creative we are when we are outside'. Exploring education in the UK and Australia, Burnard and White

(2008: 672) argue that 'pedagogical autonomy and professional agency' are important if teachers are to be creative in their teaching and curriculum development. The other factor that staff noticed was that going out 'takes away the pressure of coming up with immediate solutions'. Currently, there is a context of immediacy in teaching in higher education, with the expectation of quick responses to student feedback and little time to slow down and think deeply about issues. This project could be seen as contributing to the 'slow' movement in academia with a focus on time to think and to develop quality teaching and research (Berg and Seeber, 2016).

The outcome for the staff involved was significant. Each group built on this initial dialogic space. The group that had formed around product design undertook a research project on their teaching practice, subsequently producing several journal articles, and using the space project to kickstart documenting and sharing their work. They also drew on these new ideas to include them in their teaching, which gained outstanding student feedback. The 'assessment' group created a new cross-programme assessment for first-year students, which involved working in mixed-disciplinary groups and peer learning. This innovative assessment gave students from the very different disciplines of animation, music and photography an opportunity to learn experientially about how people worked in these disciplines, something that is important for professional practice. A student who took part in this assessment noted:

> [I gained] great insights into other students' ideas and how they approach a project – technically and conceptually.

The 'technology' group initiated a research project into the use of technologies on their courses that has been presented at internal and external conferences and is ongoing. The group that explored student learning in galleries and other off-campus spaces created guidelines for practice, for colleagues, and collected perspectives from students on their experiences of off-campus learning in the creative arts.

We disseminated all this learning by using a picnic-themed morning for all staff at the beginning of the next academic year. We displayed four picnic baskets containing project material. Project teams explained their specific outcomes to about 60 colleagues who recorded their feedback, ideas or interest by writing onto paper plates. Some of these ideas were subsequently incorporated into the projects by the teams.

Joy Jarvis and Rebecca Thomas

Figure 15.1: 'Going out' picnic baskets displayed in the exhibition

Image: R. Thomas

At the end of the academic year, a substantial exhibition displayed this work in a local gallery (see Figure 15.1). Entitled 'Reframing Spaces: A Pedagogic Provocation from the School of Creative Arts' (Thomas and Jarvis, 2016), it aimed to share information with staff and visitors about how learning spaces were being created and used.

The exhibition identified the positive and energizing aspects of the project and led to interest from other schools across the institution. In the School of Education several small groups of staff 'went out on a picnic' to inquire into aspects of their teaching. To share the approach more widely, ten creative arts colleagues created a short video on the value of 'going out' projects, focusing on the importance of creating spaces for staff to learn together and how creating 'different' spaces could lead to innovative outcomes. Challenges and lessons learnt are discussed towards the end of this chapter.

Space two: Staff and student dialogue about learning processes

The second approach to reframing staff learning spaces arose from a perceived need to engage staff and students together in talking about learning processes in the creative arts. Students' feedback had indicated that they didn't understand how they were supposed to be learning and wanted clearer guidelines. A similar issue is found in research studies about students transitioning into higher education who may be unclear about learning processes:

> [There] is often the unspoken requirement that students experiment, take risks, learn to assess the appropriateness of solutions according to context and engage in longer and more open-ended process of enquiry than they may previously have been used to. (Vaughan *et al.*, 2008: 132)

Talking about learning processes with students requires staff to have clear concepts of how they are expecting students to learn and a language to talk with them about learning. Discipline and professional experts, however, may hold much of their knowledge tacitly (Eraut, 2000) and so need to become aware of their own expertise in order to share approaches to learning with their students. The authors wanted to create a space that would enable collegiate dialogue about learning. The aim was for staff to become confident in talking with students about learning and to understand its importance for student engagement and attainment.

We created a space that was set in the creative arts context by focusing on illustration as a way to start the conversation. A graphic facilitator worked with about 60 staff to create a metaphor of learning and teaching by making drawings in response to staff ideas about the processes involved in learning in their discipline. Words and phrases such as 'experimenting', 'imagining', 'failing', 'gathering' and 'engaging with the world' were visually represented in the picture. A cartoon-style picture was completed (Figure 15.2), digitized and emailed to all staff in the school.

Joy Jarvis and Rebecca Thomas

Figure 15.2: The metaphor for learning processes

Image: J. Cooper

Collectively, we talked about the picture, cut out the sections of the picture showing individual processes, rearranged these into related groups and discussed how they were used in different creative arts disciplines. For example, a group of staff teaching film identified 'engaging with the world' as something that students found difficult to understand in relation to 'imagination' when they were creating innovative material that related to current concerns. Colleagues were articulating their 'pedagogical content knowledge' (Shulman, 2004: 203) whereby their disciplinary knowledge is related to teaching approaches, key concepts and the needs of learners. Conversations were documented on paper tablecloths, used as the basis for the subsequent session and later displayed in the 'Reframing Spaces' exhibition. Colleagues noted in discussions with us how this process helped them to think about the needs of their students:

> We have to make things more clear for 'Widening Participation' students.
>
> We have to be more structured, and can't rely on students picking things up unconsciously.
>
> We can develop a framework of how students develop and help them to understand their working practice. The illustration is about how we are going to develop it collectively.

The importance of creating the artefact together was important for staff engagement, as was 'owning' the work:

> This illustration does belong to the CA staff.

One outcome was making sets of illustrated playing cards as a resource to discuss learning during student transition. The aim was for students to play games with the cards, for example picking two cards and saying how these processes of learning might be linked, or putting one card on a piece of paper and writing ideas about what might be involved in the process. The use of cards was both practical, providing colleagues with a resource they could use with their students, and encouraged a playful approach. However, while we considered these cards as useful and we gave a pack to each programme leader, they were only used by a few members of staff. Modularization has created a perception that there is no time for talking about learning, as each module has its own curriculum content which takes all the time allocated. Furthermore, we see that staff are not comfortable with talking about learning and see it as something they should not be doing. For staff, focused on their discipline or industry, thinking about students as learners may be alien and could be seen as a distraction from teaching knowledge and skills.

To demonstrate how talking about learning could help students' understanding of their discipline, we undertook a number of activities focusing on exploring approaches to learning. As examples, we asked students to use photographic images to design their own cards depicting the learning processes involved in the original cards, the purpose being to bring approaches to learning to their attention. We also facilitated students to create a piece of work for an 'exchange' day, when students display their work for the rest of the school to view. One group of first-year photography students produced 'Sensorium' explained as: 'an interactive, visual and sensory installation that illustrates how first-year photography students learn individually and as a group.' Another first-year group from the same course produced the first in a series of books, which would chart their learning over the three years of their degree. Additionally, stimulated by the cards, students on this course were using their visual diaries to reflect on learning processes and gaining increased control over their own learning. These examples enabled staff to understand how the students were thinking about learning and thereby ensure their support and input was connected to their students' understanding. For example, Figure 15.3 shows how a student explores what is involved in the learning process 'breaking boundaries' and how she is going to try to do this in her own work.

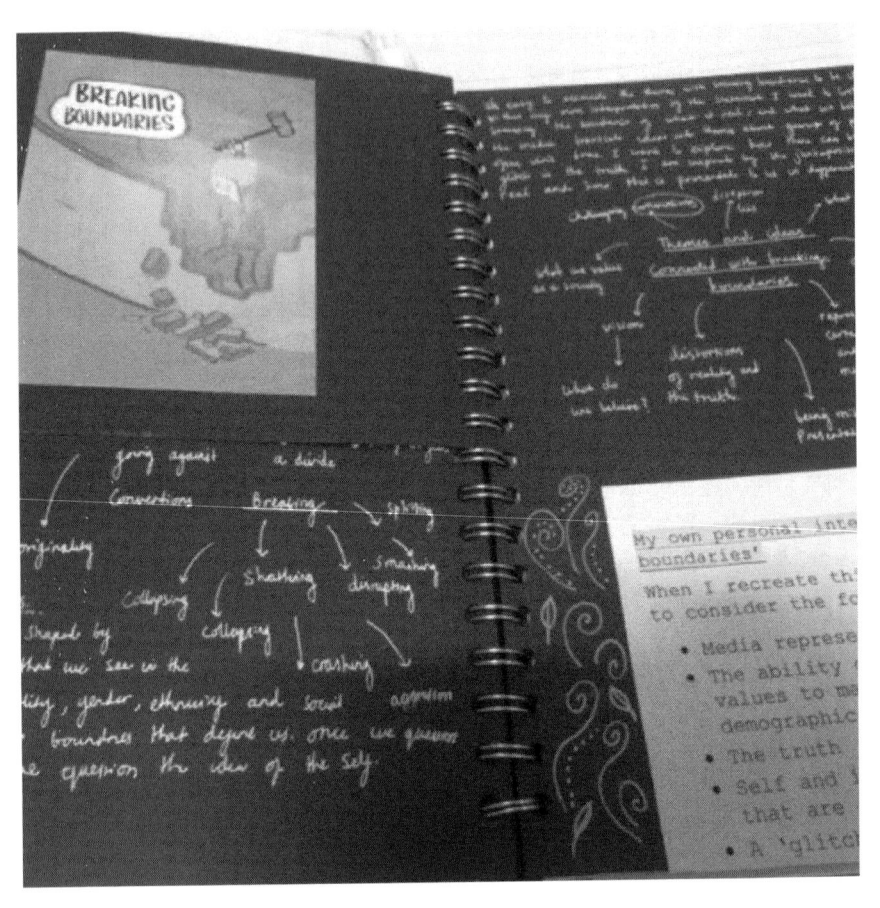

Figure 15.3: A student response in their visual diary to a learning process card
Image: R. Thomas

Evaluation and lessons learnt

Relational and social spaces for enquiry into learning and teaching are vital if disciplinary educational practice is to be a staff focus and if learning and teaching is to change and develop. As teachers and practitioners, we need the nourishment and challenge that comes from connecting with colleagues and with research around our practice.

We have been proactive in working to create these spaces, which, as Savin-Baden (2008: 65) suggests, 'seem to be marginalized and ignored across the higher education sector'. She argues that 'dialogic spaces need to be framed, delved into, argued for and prized'. We demonstrate that this can be achieved if spaces are created that are different from those that have been used previously, if there are starting points relevant to staff and students and to their discipline and if leaders provide ongoing support and encouragement so that initiatives don't get lost in a busy academic context. We have learnt that leadership needs to be both proactive and responsive and that attunement to local and national contexts helps to develop relevant ideas. Perhaps what we have learnt most from this work is that some colleagues can become highly motivated to engage in dialogue around learning and teaching and to develop their practice and their research into practice. If the space is created appropriately, some colleagues will seize the opportunity to develop their work in new and exciting ways.

Engaging in these projects was significant for some members of staff as it encouraged greater thinking about student learning and their own practice, and in some cases led to new practice. All staff joined the compulsory whole-school sessions where the initial picture about learning was created and the work displayed. They reported that they were positive about this work and appreciated a 'buzz' about teaching. However, only 12 out of 60 staff joined in the 'going out' project and fewer than that used the cards or the picture to any extent with students. The reasons for limited engagement in the learning processes project relate to factors such as what is considered appropriate module content. Unless a whole programme is thinking about learning, then it is unlikely that anyone other than a lone enthusiast will consider including it.

The limited participation in the 'going out' project can be linked to the way teaching is seen in universities and how staff time is controlled. This is exemplified by the response to presenting the 'going out' project at an external learning and teaching conference where managers expressed concern about the project, making comments such as 'How do you know they will do anything?' and 'They will just meet up to have a moan.' This lack of trust in staff, and the insinuation that they were not motivated to spend time talking about teaching, seemed shocking. It is unlikely that managers would have expressed this concern about colleagues meeting up to discuss their research projects – indeed this would be viewed as necessary. Teaching is seen in some institutions to be about compliance and not about staff taking responsibility for changing and developing practice.

Participants in the 'going out' projects, although enthusiastic – they talked about what they would like to do the following year – nevertheless considered initiating activities and exploring ideas about teaching as somehow not their role. We had anticipated that once staff saw how valuable and enjoyable these spaces could be, they would then create these without prompting. However, they seemed to feel that they needed 'permission' to do this. The project status and funding gave people this permission, although the funding itself was not particularly significant as it was not always spent. A challenge to staff leading their own learning about teaching may be that authority in teaching can be seen as lying with staff with designated roles and not with the teachers themselves.

After this project both authors worked for a year with a multi-disciplinary group of staff exploring how they could influence institutional practice in teaching. An emerging key issue was 'who is entitled to lead teaching?' One member of the group noted that in their particular context 'grass roots initiatives from experienced teachers, as opposed to researchers, do not seem to be welcomed, but are seen as a threat' (Jarvis *et al.*, 2017: 458). As we noted, 'It is highly likely that university leaders and managers would express themselves keen to engage all staff in contributing to an institution's educational practice development. In reality, hierarchical structures can limit both real and perceived opportunities to do so' (ibid.: 459).

Another challenge is that many universities define staff hours for particular tasks and as one manager said, 'all staff hours are allocated – if they want to do anything else they do it in their own time.' The time issue, while clearly fundamental, did not stop the participants in this project from 'going out', but they needed some sense that this was 'allowed'. While managers in the creative arts context were positive about the initiatives described in this chapter, once the two authors moved to other roles, these approaches were discontinued. This suggests that activities such as this are seen as optional, rather than essential, for the development of teaching.

While the projects explored in this chapter have been useful to some staff, and consequently to some students, if this type of work is to be engaged in by more colleagues, it needs to be institutionally valued and rewarded. Furthermore, for staff to lead their own learning about teaching, then time needs to be allocated for peers to work together to develop a greater understanding of practice and to create and evaluate new approaches. Without this, disciplinary teaching is unlikely to develop. And if spaces are to be used for these purposes they will need to be part of a wider reframing of the systems underpinning teaching and how it is thought about and practised in higher education.

References

Berg, M. and Seeber, B.K. (2016) *The Slow Professor: Challenging the culture of speed in the academy*. Toronto: University of Toronto Press.

Bohm, D. (1996) *On Dialogue*. London: Routledge.

Bolden, R., Jones, S., Davis, H. and Gentle, P. (2015) *Developing and Sustaining Shared Leadership in Higher Education* (Stimulus Paper). London: Leadership Foundation for Higher Education.

Brew, A. and Ginns, P. (2008) 'The relationship between engagement in the scholarship of teaching and learning and students' course experiences'. *Assessment and Evaluation in Higher Education*, 33 (5), 535–45.

Burnard, P. and White, J. (2008) 'Creativity and performativity: Counterpoints in British and Australian education'. *British Educational Research Journal*, 34 (5), 667–82.

Crawford, K. (2010) 'Influences on academics' approaches to development: Voices from below'. *International Journal for Academic Development*, 15 (3), 189–202.

Eraut, M. (2000) 'Non-formal learning and tacit knowledge in professional work'. *British Journal of Educational Psychology*, 70 (1), 113–36.

Fanghanel, J. (2009) 'Exploring teaching and learning regimes in higher education'. In Kreber, C. (ed.) *The University and Its Disciplines: Teaching and learning within and beyond disciplinary boundaries*. New York: Routledge, 196–208.

Felten, P., Bauman, H.-D.L., Kheriaty, A. and Taylor, E. (2013) *Transformative Conversations: A guide to mentoring communities among colleagues in higher education*. San Francisco: Jossey-Bass.

Holquist, M. (1990) *Dialogism: Bakhtin and his world*. London: Routledge.

James, A. and Brookfield, S.D. (2014) *Engaging Imagination: Helping students become creative and reflective thinkers*. San Francisco: Jossey-Bass.

Jarvis, J., Thomas, R., Rosella, T., Smith, J., Nimmo, S., Hodgkinson, J., Glass, L., Clark, K., Barlow, J. and Baker, T. (2017) '"Find the gap": Can a multidisciplinary group of university teachers influence learning and teaching practice?'. *Practice and Evidence of the Scholarship of Teaching and Learning in Higher Education*, 12 (3), 446–64.

Levy, W. (2014) *The Picnic: A history*. Lanham, MD: AltaMira Press.

Olssen, M. and Peters, M.A. (2005) 'Neoliberalism, higher education and the knowledge economy: From the free market to knowledge capitalism'. *Journal of Education Policy*, 20 (3), 313–45.

Quinn, L. (ed.) (2012) *Re-Imagining Academic Staff Development: Spaces for disruption*. Stellenbosch: Sun Press.

Rowland, S. (2000) *The Enquiring University Teacher*. Buckingham: Society for Research into Higher Education and Open University Press.

Rowland, S. (2001) 'Surface learning about teaching in higher education: The need for more critical conversations'. *International Journal for Academic Development*, 6 (2), 162–7.

Roxå, T. and Mårtensson, K. (2009) 'Teaching and learning regimes from within: Significant networks as a locus for the social construction of teaching and learning'. In Kreber, C. (ed.) *The University and Its Disciplines: Teaching and learning within and beyond disciplinary boundaries*. New York: Routledge, 209–18.

Savin-Baden, M. (2008) *Learning Spaces: Creating opportunities for knowledge creation in academic life*. Maidenhead: Open University Press.

Shulman, L.S. (2004) *The Wisdom of Practice: Essays on teaching, learning, and learning to teach*. San Francisco: Jossey-Bass.

Stoll, L. and Louis, K.S. (eds) (2007) *Professional Learning Communities: Divergence, depth and dilemmas*. Maidenhead: Open University Press.

Thomas, R. (2016) 'Going out on a roll: Cake, conversation and critique'. *LINK*, 2 (2). Online. https://tinyurl.com/y24atnxt (accessed 24 February 2019).

Thomas, R. and Jarvis, J. (2016) 'Reframing spaces'. *LINK*, 2 (1). Online. https://tinyurl.com/y3jk6p8g (accessed 24 February 2019).

Vaughan, S., Austerlitz, N., Blythman, M., Grove-White, A., Jones, B.A., Jones, C.A., Morgan, S.J., Orr, S. and Shreeve, A. (2008) 'Mind the gap: Expectations, ambiguity and pedagogy within art and design higher education'. In Drew, L. (ed.) *The Student Experience in Art and Design Higher Education: Drivers for change*. Cambridge: Jill Rogers Associates, 125–48.

Wenger, E., McDermott, R. and Snyder, W.M. (2002) *Cultivating Communities of Practice: A guide to managing knowledge*. Boston: Harvard Business School Press.

Chapter 16

Towards a learning landscape: The potential for technologies to create social learning spaces

Peter Klappa, Simon Lancaster, Helena Gillespie, Claire Hamshire and Tim Bilham

Technologies have the potential to extend, enhance or even replace the physical learning space, dislocating learning in terms of place and time, and allowing students to study in ways that are not bounded by their location, availability or situation. Other potential benefits include inclusivity, equity of access, increased efficiency in delivery and personalization of learning (Bilham, 2005).

The impact of the physical space on learning has been recognized and researched for many years (Cleveland and Fisher, 2014). However, as the landscape of higher education (HE) changes as technologies impact (Thomas and Morris, 2017), learning (and teaching) is no longer restricted to just physical spaces, but can easily be transferred across a range of technological spaces. This has led to new learning ecosystems that disrupt established practices and develop new pedagogies (Keegan, 2013), with enormous potential for social technologies to be used to develop new pedagogical spaces, both structured and unstructured (Barnett, 2011).

Thus, technology has the power to transform learning and teaching. However, many studies (Harasim, 2017; Henderson *et al.*, 2017; Kirkwood and Price, 2014; Conole, 2013) report a gap between potential and reality. In an extensive literature review, Kirkwood and Price (2014) concluded that the potential of technology to transform learning and teaching practices, or to establish a new paradigm, has not achieved substantial uptake in HE. They found that universities have typically focused upon the *means* in which learning and teaching occurs rather than changes in the *how*, the ways in which university teachers teach and students learn. This has resulted in most universities concentrating on using technologies to supplement or replace existing teaching rather than reconceptualizing how technology might impact upon teaching and learning and the student experience. The majority of teachers use technology to sustain existing modes of teaching rather than to innovate (Cuban, 2001). Similarly, Harasim (2017) contends that, to date, their transformative potential has been limited largely to efficiency gains, for instance in the speed of delivery or in the ability to scale up for delivery to large numbers.

There may be many reasons for this. Since the 1990s there has been considerable growth in the adoption of technology in HE with high investment, not only in infrastructure and equipment, but also the personal time of staff in learning to use technologies for teaching. This has tended to 'lock' institutions into specific systems, particularly the ubiquitous virtual learning environment (VLE), and to be risk averse (Salmon, 2005). The institutional drive to develop iconic buildings (Jamieson, 2003; see also Chapter 6 in this volume), as universities strive to attract greater numbers of students, tends to require and reinforce the large group, instructivist mode of teaching (Biggs, 1999). The pressure on academic time for other university purposes results in few opportunities for true innovation and experimentation in teaching and learning, leading to practice that lags behind the expectations and digital prowess of our current 'net generation' students. Additionally, there is an understandable reluctance to risk losing the many benefits of the traditional face-to-face mode of teaching, including among students.

For these reasons, and unsurprisingly, universities have generally adopted strategies that use technological tools to supplement and sustain traditional modes of learning. Thus, blended learning – an integration of face-to-face and online learning – becomes an effective and low-risk strategy (Garrison and Kanuka, 2004). Indeed, the evidence that it is more effective than classroom teaching alone, with both student performance and satisfaction improved (Twigg, 2003) provides further justification. Consequently the current experience of university education is already blended, with students partitioning their time between both the campus and digital spaces. Our learners, through the use of their personal devices, are both mobile and highly technologically literate (Richards, 2017). The majority of UK students have smartphones, tablets and laptops with which they easily connect to the internet and engage in learning anytime and anywhere. Thus, when considering learning spaces, it is important to recognize the contribution that the emerging and complex digital learning landscape can make to the creation of social learning, by which we mean learning with, and from, others.

Despite their familiarity with technologies and social media many students in HE see a distinction between their use for social and communication purposes and their use as fundamental to their learning. In a wide study among undergraduate students, Henderson *et al.* (2017) offer 11 affordances of technology identified by students as 'digital benefits' to their learning and university experience. Interestingly, the most highlighted benefits relate to the logistics of study, the top four being: managing and organization (46 per cent); flexibility of place and location (32.7 per cent); saving time (30.6 per cent); and review, replay and revising (27.9 per cent) (ibid.: 5). Benefits from technology explicitly related to learning were less reported but, as Henderson *et al.* (ibid.: 11) point out, this may be constrained by the bounded digital opportunities currently provided for students: 'The rather limited sets of digital practices highlighted in our data are those that best 'fit' the rather limited expectations and processes that currently constitute university teaching and learning.'

This chapter presents two case studies that demonstrate how social learning spaces have been created through the imaginative use of technologies. While ostensibly appearing to merely address the functional affordances valued by students of review and replay and flexibility of place of study (Henderson *et al.*, 2017), they subtly introduce opportunities for collaborative student learning into the pedagogic space, blurring the boundary with the physical space in extending face-to-face teaching for undergraduate students.

The first case uses a familiar social media platform to add an extra dimension to large group learning, which addressed issues valued by students. Inclusion was important for some, helping them overcome shyness, or the reluctance they felt in participating in large lecture groups. For others, convenience was most important, particularly in respect to providing flexibility and work–life balance, facilitating learning with working lives and childcare responsibilities. The second case illustrates an initiative that evolved into a space that enabled active learning and in which students became co-producers of knowledge with peers, shifting the learning space from tutor-led to student-led and thereby nurturing a social space for learning.

Learning in the digital space: Livestreaming
Peter Klappa

One method of blending the physical with the digital space is to make recorded sessions available online, so students can access them whenever is convenient. Lecture capture, by which classroom sessions are recorded using audio or video and subsequently made available via a VLE, is now commonplace. The technology allows students to catch up on missed content and access information to support revision or preparation for assessment. The downside of lecture capture is that the content is static and does not facilitate the desired interactive social space in which students can work collaboratively. An alternative is livestreaming, whereby content is simultaneously recorded and broadcast. This simultaneous streaming of conferences, lectures and workshops gives learners the opportunity to directly immerse themselves in the events; including both tutor–student and student–student interactions.

The development of livestreaming on social media platforms like Periscope, Meerkat and Facebook has the potential to expand traditional teaching and learning spaces into a new collaborative social space. The aim of this project with biosciences students at the University of Kent was to investigate the potential of Facebook livestreaming as a tool to enhance students' collaborative learning and overcome timetabling constraints. This provides additional support on topics identified by students as particularly difficult and supports student-centred learning via online question and answer sessions. In contrast to pre-recorded lectures, livestreaming allows students to be 'present' while the lecture happened, although in a virtual space and the livestreamed lectures can be easily scheduled within students' timetables. Sessions could therefore be made more accessible for students, who find it difficult to attend face-to-face sessions or who are studying remotely on placements.

Facebook was identified as the most appropriate platform as the majority of our first-year students (n = 246) are very familiar with using social media applications for communication. As such, livestreaming via Facebook was considered software and hardware 'agnostic', it could be watched on any of the plethora of devices that students already possess and no further software is needed on the user side. In addition, the chat function of Facebook allows students to directly interact with the presenter by asking questions or making comments. The presenter is able to see these questions in real time and also the name of the student, providing the opportunity to address the student personally during the livestream or in a follow-up afterwards.

To schedule a livestream lecture, an 'event' was created in a Facebook group several days in advance and all group members were invited to join. Once the livestream session started, information was received about which students had joined the stream. Students were asked to give feedback about audibility and so on by posting a 'like' or sending comments. The topic was presented developmentally, using a blank screen as a digital whiteboard on which the presenter drew with a tablet input device. At certain points, students were asked to make comments and answer questions or calculate a result. An average of 130 student comments are typical during a 60-minute session. Students work collaboratively, constructing a space for learning and developing wider learning networks as they work across the cohort, rather than just with the students with whom they share physical proximity.

Evaluation

Results from an anonymous questionnaire sent to the year cohort of 250 received a 9.3 per cent response, with 78 per cent of respondents (n = 23) indicating that they watched the livestream, and 22 per cent reporting that they watched the recorded session. Seventy-eight per cent agreed, or strongly agreed, that there should be more livestreamed sessions and more than half (59 per cent) posted comments during the live session. A thematic analysis of comments identified that one benefit of the sessions was the provision of a space for interaction and discussion, with a number of students noting a feeling of inclusion that was not apparent in the physical lecture space:

> I think the live stream is a really good idea, I'm personally quite quiet and would never contribute in front of a whole lecture theatre full of people, and I know many others are like me too, but the livestreams make it easier for everyone to participate and contribute.

> Better interaction between students and lecturer and easier to participate when asked questions.

Some students also liked the convenience of being able to access the sessions off campus, as it provided a means to participate, and engage, without travel:

> I like it as it really helps especially if I have childcare issues as I can watch it on my phone via Facebook wherever I am.

> Commuting students don't have to travel for a one-hour 9 a.m. workshop and wait somewhere for our next lecture at 2 p.m.

This case study demonstrates that the livestreaming of teaching sessions is simple to set up and is a useful addition to the digital space, a major advantage being that there are no additional costs for infrastructure. Many of the students surveyed perceived the livestreaming of sessions as a useful adjunct to the learning spaces already provided and believed that these sessions engaged students who were reluctant to share their views in larger groups or in front of their peers. It suggests that one of the potential advantages of the technology is the creation of an interactive social space and this opens up consideration of space on a number of levels, and the extent to which the 'space' itself can contribute to learning (Wenger, 1998).

Our second case study extends this discussion by exploring the potential for using digital spaces to facilitate students' development as producers of knowledge and resources.

Learning in the digital space: From lecture capture to student co-authoring
Simon Lancaster and Helena Gillespie

This project started out as a method for enhancing simple lecture capture in which a tutor shared video vignettes of sessions that ultimately led to students working collaboratively and co-authoring learning resources that were then made available to all.

Undergraduate chemistry students at the University of East Anglia (UEA) are largely taught face-to-face in a combination of lectures, seminars and laboratory sessions. These physical spaces provide a mixed learning environment in which our students work both independently and collaboratively. However, as with many disciplines, and especially science, the time available for structured reflection is considerably limited and furthermore our students did not have self-reflection skills or experience. We determined to provide a reflective space that students could make use of when working off campus to self-test their knowledge.

The original and underpinning aim was to enhance students' understanding of key concepts and to achieve this we introduced learning objects derived from lecture capture and tailored for the institutional VLE. Our initial thoughts were that this would address many of the deficiencies of lecture capture (Read and Lancaster, 2012) by paring down the recording to only the essentials necessary to explain key themes, so that students do not have to listen to the whole recording. To achieve this, we identified a fundamental idea and used video-editing tools to annotate and augment the audio narrative. The resulting short, focused videos (vignettes), typically lasting less than five minutes, included interactivity and questions that students answered before proceeding.

Feedback demonstrated that our students used these vignettes to support their understanding and as revision aids. As such, they provide a reflective space in which students evaluate their learning and identify topics that they need to explore further:

> Good revision tool because if you haven't completely understood something in the lecture or when revising then you can go to that place in the vignette and listen to the explanation again!

This prompted us to consider how we could better use the affordances of the technology to create a social learning space. Our aim was to provide a collaborative space in which the students could both control their time and direction and actively contribute learning materials. Therefore, the next step was to use the vignettes to facilitate a conceptual approach to problem-solving by providing students with opportunities to develop their own video vignettes that directly addressed their learning needs.

We worked with our students to enable them to create their own synoptic revision presentations and produce their own interactive vignettes. This process encouraged both collaborative learning and deeper understanding of the concepts they were charged with teaching, moving them away simply remembering content. Student co-authorship of these digital resources therefore represented a blurring of the boundaries between knowledge and co-production. This provides a reflective space where students can consider how the material can be presented in a format that would maximize learning for others:

> Thought about information in a different way when preparing interactive questions.

By reframing the digital space and providing an opportunity for our students to co-produce resources, a social space was created where students worked collaboratively, effectively and reflectively.

Lessons learnt

This chapter has presented two case studies that illustrate how digital spaces can be incorporated into the learning landscape to create social learning spaces and enhance student learning. In each of the examples the importance of the digital space for facilitating collaborative learning is recognized and benefits include deeper understanding and connection for students who are physically isolated. Many academics have found digital spaces and social media an invaluable means to engender effective engagement with their students (Doolan, 2011; Stoller, 2017) and Laurillard (2012) has called for educators to regard teaching as a 'design science' to build effective learning in digital spaces. Through consideration of the potential of digital spaces we need to ensure that we blend the physical with the digital to maximize the potential of the learning landscape that is created (Thody, 2011). To maximize the benefits for our students, Boys (2009) advocates the need to engage with space at a number of different 'levels', including socio-spatial relationships and conceptual spaces of learning, and Thody (2011) stresses the importance of aligning the physical and digital spaces and embedding this into a learning landscape. In truth, however, many traditional learning spaces within UK higher education institutions are not well configured to support new methodologies of learning activities and the potential of technology in teaching and learning is yet to be fully realized. There are constraints of both estate and timetabling and, consequently, pragmatic design solutions might utilize the digital space to enhance students' learning via the creation of a social learning space.

Such social spaces enable more open-ended learning in which students can participate in an unstructured, interactive environment and peer-to-peer learning is encouraged (Wenger, 1998). Blending the structured elements of the curriculum in both the physical spaces and the digital space facilitates online networks and collaboration with the potential to blur boundaries and develop new learning cultures (Keegan, 2013), a paradigm shift that is badly needed in higher education.

References

Barnett, R. (2011) 'Configuring learning spaces: Noticing the invisible'. In Boddington, A. and Boys, J. (eds) *Re-Shaping Learning: A critical reader: The future of learning spaces in post-compulsory education*. Rotterdam: Sense Publishers, 167–78.

Biggs, J. (1999) *Teaching for Quality Learning at University*. Buckingham: Society for Research into Higher Education and Open University Press.

Bilham, T. (2005) 'Online learning: Can communities of practice deliver personalization in learning?'. In de Freitas, S. and Yapp, C. (eds) *Personalizing Learning in the 21st Century*. Stafford: Network Educational Press, 73–7.

Boys, J. (2009) 'Beyond the beanbag? Towards new ways of thinking about learning spaces'. *Networks*, 8, 16–19.

Cleveland, B. and Fisher, K. (2014) 'The evaluation of physical learning environments: A critical review of the literature'. *Learning Environments Research*, 17 (1), 1–28.

Conole, G. (2013) *Designing for Learning in an Open World*. New York: Springer.

Cuban, L. (2001) *Oversold and Underused: Computers in the classroom*. Cambridge, MA: Harvard University Press.

Doolan, M.A. (2011) 'Using Technology to Support Collaborative Learning through Assessment Design'. Unpublished EdD thesis, University of Hertfordshire. Online. https://tinyurl.com/y6eqq2ym (accessed 25 February 2019).

Garrison, D.R. and Kanuka, H. (2004) 'Blended learning: Uncovering its transformative potential in higher education'. *The Internet and Higher Education*, 7 (2), 95–105.

Harasim, L. (2017) *Learning Theory and Online Technologies*. 2nd ed. New York: Routledge.

Henderson, M., Selwyn, N. and Aston, R. (2017) 'What works and why? Student perceptions of "useful" digital technology in university teaching and learning'. *Studies in Higher Education*, 42 (8), 1567–79.

Jamieson, P. (2003) 'Designing more effective on-campus teaching and learning spaces: A role for academic developers'. *International Journal for Academic Development*, 8 (1–2), 119–33.

Keegan, H. (2013) 'New learning ecosystems: Blurring boundaries, changing minds'. In Bilham, T. (ed.) *For the Love of Learning: Innovations from outstanding university teachers*. Basingstoke: Palgrave Macmillan, 36–9.

Kirkwood, A. and Price, L. (2014) 'Technology-enhanced learning and teaching in higher education: What is "enhanced" and how do we know? A critical literature review'. *Learning, Media and Technology*, 39 (1), 6–36.

Laurillard, D. (2012) *Teaching as a Design Science: Building pedagogical patterns for learning and technology*. New York: Routledge.

Read, D. and Lancaster, S. (2012) 'Unlocking video: 24/7 learning for the iPod generation'. *Education in Chemistry*, 49 (4), 13–16. Online. https://tinyurl.com/mlnmtdo (accessed 25 February 2019).

Richards, R. (2017) 'Theory of mobile learning'. Constructivist Toolkit. Online. www.constructivisttoolkit.com/vault/theory-of-mobile-learning (accessed 9 October 2017).

Salmon, G. (2005) 'Flying not flapping: A strategic framework for e-learning and pedagogical innovation in higher education institutions'. *ALT-J: Research in Learning Technology*, 13 (3), 201–18.

Stoller, E. (2017) 'How digital engagement enhances the student experience'. *Getting Digital: Social Media and Higher Education*, 4 December. Online. https://tinyurl.com/y3da5r6y (accessed 25 February 2019).

Thody, A. (2011) '"Learning landscapes" as a shared vocabulary for learning spaces'. In Boddington, A. and Boys, J. (eds) *Re-Shaping Learning: A critical reader: The future of learning spaces in post-compulsory education*. Rotterdam: Sense Publishers, 121–35.

Thomas, A. and Morris, N. (2017) 'Is digital technology changing learning and teaching? The big debate from Digifest 2017'. JISC News, 15 March. Online. www.jisc.ac.uk/news/is-digital-technology-changing-learning-and-teaching-15-mar-2017 (accessed 9 October 2017).

Twigg, C.A. (2003) *Improving Learning and Reducing Costs: Lessons learned from Round I of the PEW Grant Program in Course Redesign.* Troy, NY: Center for Academic Transformation.

Wenger, E. (1998) *Communities of Practice: Learning, meaning, and identity.* Cambridge: Cambridge University Press.

Chapter 17

Expanding the cross-cultural space: Providing international experiences in the digital global classroom

Natascha Radclyffe-Thomas, Catherine McDermott and Rachel Forsyth

In this chapter, we explore the possibilities in using novel teaching spaces to embed aspects of internationalization into higher education practice. In this context, we will use the working definition of internationalization proposed by Knight (2003: 1):

> Internationalization at the national, sector, and institutional levels is defined as the process of integrating an international, intercultural, or global dimension into the purpose, functions or delivery of post-secondary education.

The contested concept of internationalization in higher education

A recurrent argument for internationalization in higher education (HE) points to the need for graduates to be able to demonstrate global citizenship (see, for instance, Stearns, 2009). Global citizenship education, according to UNESCO (2014: 9), 'is a framing paradigm which encapsulates how education can develop the knowledge, skills, values and attitudes learners need for securing a world which is more just, peaceful, tolerant, inclusive, secure and sustainable'. This definition represents what Stier (2004) has called the 'idealistic' approach to internationalization, but there is no doubt that it is a strong motivator for many educators. Stier identifies two further characteristics: an 'educational' ideology of internationalization, which essentially situates international experiences as a key part of the development of critical thinking and lifelong learning, and in contrast, an 'instrumental' ideology, which sees internationalization as an opportunity to expand markets, prepare students more adequately for the globalized workforce and to transmit received ideologies to other parts of the world. This last approach is often rejected by teachers, but may subtly underpin institutional policies.

There is much critique of the potential problems of a neoliberal or instrumental interpretation of internationalization, and the emphasis in some institutions on its use to increase student numbers amid calls to refocus attention on the 'higher order' values that should be associated with internationalization (Jiang, 2008; Knight, 2013; Yemini, 2015). The case studies in this chapter adopt the educational approach, to use Stier's (2004) characterization, to illustrate the value of developing an international space for teaching and learning.

Reframing spaces for internationalization

Barnett (2011) introduces the idea of intentional educational spaces in which students are invited to make a journey, and considers the kind of constraints that might be placed on such a space and where its boundaries may lie. The idea of a cross-cultural space can be very challenging in terms of designing teaching. Knight's (2003) definition of internationalization clearly covers a very wide range of potential activities that might be carried out in universities. Stearns (2009), for instance, lists study abroad programmes, language learning, volunteering and engagement with theoretical aspects of internationalization and reflective engagement as ways to internationalize within a university. Each of these possibilities risks becoming a standalone activity without true integration within a student's curriculum. As such, while they remain valuable activities in terms of individual development, they may not be accessible to all students – students may not have the funding to travel, language training may not fit into an already-crowded professional curriculum, there may be little opportunity to interact with international students on their particular programme, and so on. Integration into the curriculum may also be challenging for another reason: teaching staff may find this kind of development to be 'one obligation to many', as Stearns (ibid.: 9) points out. The challenge seems to be finding ways of including internationalization in the intentional educational space. While Barnett (2011) is being metaphorical in his conceptualization of a student journey, it is useful to consider how a cross-cultural space can provide students and teachers with a real sense of travel by working with colleagues from other organizations across the world.

A cross-cultural space is intended to achieve what both Halliday (1999) and De Vita and Case (2003) describe as being 'open to the other' as part of the curriculum. This kind of openness is particularly important for education in creative subject areas, although the case can be made across all disciplines. Cross-cultural understanding is important for developing creative techniques and also for developing a global approach to the creative industries. The UK Creative Industries Federation has reported (Easton, 2015) that the number of people of ethnic minority origin working in the sector is low, and that design curricula can demonstrate an unconscious bias about creative work in other countries. For example, there may be misconceptions that Africa is about need and not talent, or that China is about copying and not creating: cross-cultural working helps to dispel some of these myths. The three case studies here focus particularly on creative industries, but they illustrate neatly how internationalization of any kind rests on the development of cross-cultural competencies and the challenges that may be faced in this work.

Digital global classroom: Social media as a third space for co-creation of learning

For this project Natascha Radclyffe-Thomas worked with Anne Peirson-Smith, City University Hong Kong, Ana Roncha, London College of Fashion, London, Adrian Huang LASALLE College of the Arts, Singapore, and Anais Lacouture, RMIT Vietnam

The development of widespread access to communications technologies has generated many interesting opportunities to collaborate internationally using digital spaces. Since 2013, a group of international scholars has been facilitating an annual global classroom project between the UK and Asia. This collaborative project, which facilitated student interaction and co-creation of learning and was originally initiated between students at University of the Arts London (UAL) and City University Hong Kong, has extended to include students from LASALLE School of the Arts Singapore and, most recently, students from RMIT Vietnam. Over 450 students have taken part in the global classroom, which has become an international community of practice. A more detailed version can be found in Radclyffe-Thomas *et al.* (2016).

How the partnership began

The original partnership was incubated during a conference held in Hong Kong where international educators explored the impact and pedagogic potentials for harnessing the energy and enthusiasm that students display regarding popular culture. Both tutors involved in the initial scoping conversation use social media in their teaching practice to build learning communities through sharing resources, which enhance digital literacies and expand students' discipline networks. Although our backgrounds were in different discipline areas (English and management respectively), we discovered that our teaching shared commonalities in the areas of media and communications and our personal research interests also aligned with a shared interest in pedagogy and cross-cultural communication.

UAL has a high proportion of non-UK students and internationalizing the curriculum is a key attainment strategy that we believed could be promoted through our students working together globally. Furthermore, as many of UAL's international students are from Asia, we wanted to enhance their self-efficacy by focusing our studies on a non-UK region with which they would likely be more familiar than their UK classmates.

The intercultural literature emphasizes the importance of a mindful approach where engagement with other cultures and reflection on one's own are facilitated by educators (Byram, 2008). The pedagogical underpinning of our first collaboration between London and Hong Kong was to internationalize the curriculum and inculcate cross-cultural communication competences. Technology offered the opportunity to 'internationalise at home' (Killick, 2016; Nilsson, 2003), and tutors from both institutions were motivated to use our collaborative, online international learning space as a place to foster deep and meaningful international connections and to support agency of international students, particularly the large number of students from East Asia studying at UAL.

Key actions

Tutors in both universities shared course outlines to find synergies between their teaching, and discovered common learning outcomes in relation to researching and analysing marketing communications. We set about designing ways in which our students, who were located thousands of miles away from each other, could meet to discuss their perceptions and critiques of marketing communications. It was decided that due to the time difference, we would work asynchronously to undertake seminar activities separately, but share the outcomes.

By naming our global classroom 'The International Fashion Panel', our aim was to flatten hierarchies between teacher and student, between 'home' and 'international' students and to situate our students as experts in their discipline and local spheres. Students were given research tasks to collate information about their local markets and specific brand strategies, which are then presented through posts in the Facebook group. As well as seeking information from their online classmates which inform their own work, students share draft assignments for which they received international peer review through online comments – comments that were universally constructive and often suggested explicit improvements which were subsequently incorporated into final drafts. Modern creative industry practices foster open-source and knowledge co-creation, which aligns closely with the constructivist pedagogies we employ and which suggest that such peer interaction both engages and empowers students. This aspect of international peer critique was observed by the tutors and commented on by many participants.

Having decided in principle to host teaching materials in an online space, we considered using one or more of our institutional VLEs. However, that option was rejected due to accessibility prohibitions. Needing a space that could be accessed by groups of both teachers and learners that enabled image and text sharing and that could capture class discussions, we found that Facebook offered a good solution and we set up a private Facebook group. The first global classroom project ran during autumn 2013 as a means for students in Hong Kong and London to come together to co-create learning outcomes. Participation in the project was voluntary.

The initial collaboration was treated as a pilot for international collaborative projects and we recorded student evaluations and surveyed activity on the panel, as well as asking for written responses on the interaction. Students responded so positively to the intercultural communication that it gave us confidence to expand the interaction – which had always been one of the project's aims – to other partner colleges. A Hong Kong student reflected:

> What I really understood from the panel was intercultural communication and support. ... I discovered the beauty of people from two cultures working together voluntarily.

In order to contextualize the discussion around to what extent businesses operating internationally do, or should, localize content, the first Facebook exercise asked students to introduce themselves by stating their career aspirations and where in the world they would like to live and work in the future. It was interesting for students to see they shared similar aspirations. One student said:

> It was interesting to see what brands they aspired to work for, some instantly recognisable and some not. ... It has also helped me understand my peers.

Subsequently, we created cross-cultural dialogues around such questions as 'to what extent do you think there is global fashion, i.e. people wearing the same fashions around the world?' and 'which fashion items do you associate with your home country?'

We deliberately designed student interactions as global classroom touch points where students would learn about each other through exploring their shared subject discipline. For one of the core activities we developed online resources that featured marketing from international brands aimed at the young millennial customer (our students) to discover the degree to which students in each location shared similar understandings of brand image, advertising and visual merchandising in the fashion sector. We started by designing a range of visuals representing several fashion brands, posting these into the Facebook group together with a series of question prompts for use during seminars. Students worked in small groups, collating their responses and posting them as comments below each brand visual.

A Hong Kong student commented:

> Things that have been learnt through the fashion panel are the differences in the brands. The culture of different brands can be seen through the use of imagery on the websites. It has shown me the differences between UK and Asian brands and the different way they use media channels.

A London student posted:

> It has definitely made me more aware of the global nature of fashion and how differently brands can be perceived in different markets, which only reiterates how challenging it is to market an international brand in so many different markets simultaneously.

Extending the partnership

Following this successful London–Hong Kong pilot, we identified the shared commitment to the underlying philosophy of internationalizing the curriculum as a key success factor, and through sharing our work at international conferences we found our next two collaborators, in Singapore and Vietnam. From this we have found that students across different disciplines, and year cohorts, can successfully and productively work together on common issues as long as we are able to match curriculum content. At UAL, this project has been primarily aligned with a first-year 'branding' unit, whereas in Hong Kong the students are attending options in the English department at any stage of their studies.

Each partner's assessments centred on ways in which fashion brands might operate successfully internationally. For example, the students based in London were required to research and develop a brand extension into a non-homogeneous market. The current iteration of the project imagines a brand extension to Hong Kong, Singapore or Vietnam, representing each of our partners' locations. Several features of social media platforms make them efficacious for pedagogic ends. Their accessibility, the common interest community building and the ability to easily share information are all available in one space, which we came to consider as a third space for learning, sitting as it does between the social and academic spheres of both students and teachers.

Considerations

One issue we came across when working with students in Singapore is that many did not use Facebook, and so had to be encouraged to use it to join the project. This was not a huge hurdle, however, and when surveyed 84 per cent of the Singapore students preferred using Facebook for collaboration, compared to their institutional platform used on a previous collaborative project.

Vietnam is an emerging international fashion industry, and consequently there were some initial reservations about students' confidence or willingness to interact with collaborators abroad. This was entirely misplaced with students reporting their pride in 'representing' Vietnam.

> Students may take inspiration from each other's posts and potentially incorporate it into their work. It is a form of research very similar to word of mouth. (London student)

> The International Fashion Panel Facebook is a clever idea to gather creative ideas between students. The exchange of ideas between Hong Kong students and foreign students makes this idea even better. It is because we have different culture background and we may have very different views on the same issue. (Hong Kong student)

Outcomes

Although conceived with multiple tangible and intangible outcomes, the collaboration has exceeded our expectations in terms of engagement, self-efficacy as well as global citizenship. What started as a ten-week project-specific collaboration has become a community of practice with a significant afterlife. Each iteration has expanded its reach by not only bringing in new institutional partners, but also adding additional contact points and, importantly, bringing the online and offline spaces together by using the student groups to host seminar activities. Although the Facebook group is administered by teachers, students demonstrate their agency in this online space by continuing to keep their membership of it, and by seeking its members' expertise, requesting information to support their subsequent coursework, including data gathering for final-year projects.

Despite some practical challenges, including time differences and academic calendars, it has proved an accessible platform with immense potential for international collaborations. Students found the Facebook platform accessible, and its status as a social network meant that informality, such as the use of emoticons to give feedback on each other's work and acceptance of less formal English language, facilitated engagement. Reviewing the global classroom project over its several iterations has identified some common emergent themes. First, the ease with which social media platforms can be utilized for educational activities. Second, that internationalizing the curriculum can be as simple as asking students to explore non-homogeneous cultures and that their own curiosity is a great motivator. Third, that students are happy to share knowledge about their own culture and subject practices and are often very generous doing so. One of the Hong Kong students summed up how working collaboratively created a common bond, not as citizens of any particular place, or even institution, but in an international partnership of students:

> Having the same identity of a student, I understand that people will be grateful to be helped on their researches and I am glad to do so. Students can help each other and create co-operation between universities and countries.

Our next two case studies similarly demonstrate the innovative use of digital cultural spaces and represented through the emerging discipline of contemporary curation and by projects in two very different countries, China and Zimbabwe. These projects also support the need for UK design education to become more culturally diverse and international. The British Council provided both projects with ongoing funding over six years.

Dream Lab: An online design science project in China
Catherine McDermott

Dream Lab was a five-year, £1.5 million design science competition funded by the British Council to showcase and promote UK educational expertise in interdisciplinary practice. The funding supported an online teaching platform for Chinese teams to connect with British design education and British scientists. The deliverables included three online competitions involving over 400 Chinese teams in 150 Chinese universities alongside UK students and researchers. The same project was offered to UK science and design teams with outcomes including a curated exhibition and event at the Science Museum in London.

How the partnership began
Since the early 2010s the role of the contemporary curator has experienced an important shift from a focus on museum collections to a different definition of what constitutes programmed space. Nowadays, curators are just as likely to work in spaces like social media platforms, retail and public environments as they are in traditional galleries. These changing spaces for creative practice were also part of significant changes in twenty-first-century design and design education, most visible in the shift from 'object' to 'process' and the use of interdisciplinary methodologies. The interdisciplinary approach underpinning the new curated briefs and spaces also opened up opportunities to address challenges around internationalization.

This project explored a range of spaces that delivered content for innovative and interdisciplinary subject learning sets in which the learning was placed explicitly within the context of practice and curriculum. These spaces, of course, were not in themselves 'new', but bringing them together in the context of contemporary curating practice helped to pioneer sector change, melding existing education design practices to deliver impact on real-world learning.

Key actions
A UK team drawn from universities and museums produced a science design brief that was given to nearly 600 Chinese undergraduates. They interacted with the team via a specially designed online platform, which allowed students feedback and contact with Chinese tutors. The six teams and tutors selected as finalists attended a live presentation ceremony in Beijing.

Extending the partnership
Dream Lab offers a teaching space to colleagues in different universities and industry sectors across science and design and, in 2014, it was extended

to design and electronic engineering, with the additional objectives of addressing concerns about falling recruitment in science and engineering and the low recruitment of women. Since then we have delivered three Dream Lab briefs:

- *the Science of Sleeping* (2009), involving Bournemouth and Kingston universities with the Science Museum
- *the Future of Eating* (2012): Royal College of Art, Kingston University and the Science Museum
- *Creative Challenge* (2014), which combines electronic engineering (universities of Coventry, Central Lancashire and Huddersfield) and design (universities of Kingston, Sheffield Hallam and the Royal College of Art).

Outcomes

Dream Lab has pioneered a pedagogy that links practitioners to real-world practice and with a focus on employability. The three briefs have enabled over 50 UK academics and IT staff to work together and experience a groundbreaking opportunity to teach Chinese students as an online team. Over 400 competing teams from 150 leading Chinese universities and high schools experienced, for the first time, UK teaching in the field of collaborative practice. It offered the team a shared learning experience, as we addressed problems of online feedback, through sharing different approaches, exploring how to assess the creative elements of student work and, as designers, trying to evaluate the science underpinning an idea. It was an insightful learning curve.

These teaching spaces brought about important curricula and pedagogic change by offering Kingston staff and students, often for the first time, engagement in collaborative interdisciplinary teaching practice and strategy. One colleague reflected on the challenge not only to change the perceptions of diverse disciplines, but also different teaching cultures in China and the UK.

> Coming from a science background I did not think I could work with design but I realised the barrier was getting over familiar patterns of thinking. (Faculty of Science, Kingston University)

UK staff found that their perceptions of Chinese teaching practice were significantly altered and have used their experience to change the curriculum space for UK students, thereby internationalizing the curriculum across the two countries:

The challenge was changing my own mindset. Dream Lab was a timely reminder to include contemporary China in the curriculum and build stronger teaching partnerships with my Chinese students.

These imaginative teaching spaces, both virtual and real, also made a significant contribution by building confidence in the practice of interdisciplinary teaching, which in turn inspired an impressive range of outcomes. For example, Huddersfield University used the project as a best-practice case study in electronic and electrical engineering; the Royal College of Art integrated their experience into their MA Global Innovation Design; the Science Museum presented the project at a sell-out public event alongside staff and students from Hongik University Seoul. These outcomes are more than a list. They have made a significant contribution to the emerging practice of science design, making a strong claim that creating learning spaces to deliver such global teaching is not marginal but central to future curricula.

Making Baskets: Kingston University and the Lupane Women's Centre
For this project Catherine McDermott worked with the British Council Zimbabwe and Raphael Chikukwa from Harare National Gallery

This project addressed the serious lack in UK design education and visual programming of content exploring contemporary African creativity. In London, there are few galleries programming twenty-first-century African creativity, the October Gallery in Holborn being an exception. African creativity felt invisible, and in spite of the fact that London is one of the most culturally diverse cities in the world, its record of showcasing contemporary African creativity is limited. In response, and over a period of five years, Project Kingston Africa developed a multi-site initiative set across South Africa and Zimbabwe.

Making Baskets was the first attempt at Kingston to rebalance an understanding of African design. In 2012–13 the project brief on African creative basket making was offered to more than 300 students across the Kingston schools of design and business. The brief was to connect the designing and making skills at Kingston with the craft making experience of African weavers. The teaching spaces used were many and varied: a digital platform, studio space, fieldwork in the Lupane Women's Centre, gallery spaces in Bulawayo and leading design festivals in Cape Town and London.

The experience of these 'spaces' changed the perception of students that, for different reasons and cultures, was limited, and they offered confidence to African students and those of African ethnicity, whose cultural background had not previously been included.

UK students learnt about the materials and techniques used directly from the African makers and, from their work, ideas were developed in Lupane, which were then used in the London and African exhibitions. The African makers benefited from a one-week workshop, introducing them to new processes and ideas, for example engaging for the first time in drawing. We funded a Kingston/Zimbabwean team to work in Lupane, including a photographer, designers, the Women's Centre director and the founder of Design Afrika, Binky Newman, who also visited and connected with students in London. Based in Cape Town, Design Afrika was established in 1995 and is committed to nurturing the creative and entrepreneurial skills of rural communities, marketing and promoting fine basketry and fabrics in a sustainable and ethical manner (Design Afrika, 1995).

The presentation of the project at Design Indaba and at the London Design Festival resulted in opportunities for Lupane makers' work to sell in high-end UK retailers like The Conran Shop. The project gave students engagement with the African creative economies predicted for expansion in the next decade and offered future collaborative exchange and work opportunities.

The impact on the learning experience of both Kingston and African designers and students has had a far-reaching and permanent influence:

> Teaching about Africa focuses on need, not creativity, and if UK designers want to practise in the future world they need to start thinking differently. (Raphael Chikukwa, Kingston graduate, Chief Curator, National Gallery of Zimbabwe)

Students experiencing the project 'reset' their career perspectives away from the West to a more global perspective. An informal poll of students, before and after, the Africa project saw an increase of 60 per cent in students now interested in working with Africa. One UK graduate is now a curator in Cape Town's Drawing Room Gallery and another is Head of the Southern Guild in South Africa.

To deliver national and international impact we supported participating students in placing their work in exhibitions to attract media and public interest. This strategy has been very successful, resulting in several influential sector awards. Making Baskets was funded and selected for the British Council's prestigious international showcase, named by the

UK's *Craft* magazine as best show and in 2013 it was selected by one of the world's leading curators, South African Li Edelkoort, for inclusion in her touring exhibition 'Memphis Meets Africa'. In 2013, Edelkoort and Kingston alumnus Candice Allison installed the student work in the National Galleries of Harare and Bulawayo. Through this Africa project four students went on to employment with the British Council and in the museum sector, with an additional two enrolling in research degrees in the area of contemporary African creativity. The collaborative impact continued with the Bulawayo gallery director selected for Arts Council training in 2017. Africa now remains part of the Design School's view of global design.

Extending the reach

Both the Chinese and African projects utilized virtual spaces, collaborative spaces and museum and galleries and, through shared curating briefs, offered best-practice methods in blending online spaces with face-to-face learning and community spaces. In both projects, small numbers of staff experienced global fieldwork, which was documented online for the benefit of the wider African, Chinese and UK communities of practice alongside the online, and home communities who participated in the learning experience. Fieldwork for the projects enabled three Kingston staff and three African team members to work in Lupane, Matabeleland and China and enabled a series of three annual projects with up to 20 academic partners.

Developing the cross-cultural space

In these international spaces, both students and teachers have had the opportunity to experience cross-cultural activities that exemplify Stier's (2004) educational approach to internationalization. From an idealistic point of view, the projects have helped to develop global networks of practice, pioneering and championing new ways of defining the boundaries of educational spaces for the benefit of UK and overseas students. Equally important, there has been practical benefit as well: these teaching spaces provided students from very different educational and cultural backgrounds with new opportunities in the creative sector. Working in these different spaces has helped to change the UK student experience from a focus on a single Western discipline approach to communicating complex ideas through collaborative, professional briefs with partnerships across countries and sectors. This creative and pioneering pedagogy is about a generation of practitioners who will be inextricably linked to 'real-world' practice with an intense focus on employability:

> The lesson we learnt is that by investing in the spaces to explore internationalisation, perceptions are changed. (Dream Lab participant)

Finally, the international space also powerfully demonstrated the importance of belonging to place, reminding us that seeking to teach globally is also about understanding our own, and our partners', sense of national identity.

References

Barnett, R. (2011) 'Configuring learning spaces: Noticing the invisible'. In Boddington, A. and Boys, J. (eds) *Re-Shaping Learning: A critical reader: The future of learning spaces in post-compulsory education*. Rotterdam: Sense Publishers, 167–78.

Byram, M. (2008) *From Foreign Language Education to Education for Intercultural Citizenship: Essays and reflections*. Clevedon: Multilingual Matters.

Design Afrika (1995) 'Revitalizing the ancient craft of African basket weaving'. Online. http://designafrika.co.za (accessed 26 October 2018).

De Vita, G. and Case, P. (2003) 'Rethinking the internationalisation agenda in UK higher education'. *Journal of Further and Higher Education*, 27 (4), 383–98.

Easton, E. (2015) *Creative Diversity: The state of diversity in the UK's creative industries, and what we can do about it*. London: Creative Industries Federation. Online. https://tinyurl.com/y2hkufrz (accessed 25 February 2019).

Halliday, F. (1999) 'The chimera of the "International University"'. *International Affairs*, 75 (1), 99–120.

Jiang, X. (2008) 'Towards the internationalisation of higher education from a critical perspective'. *Journal of Further and Higher Education*, 32 (4), 347–58.

Killick, D. (2016) *Internationalization and Diversity in Higher Education: Implications for teaching, learning and assessment*. London: Palgrave Macmillan.

Knight, J. (2003) 'Updating the definition of internationalization'. *International Higher Education*, 33, 2–3.

Knight, J. (2013) 'The changing landscape of higher education internationalisation – for better or worse?'. *Perspectives: Policy and Practice in Higher Education*, 17 (3), 84–90.

Nilsson, B. (2003) 'Internationalisation at home from a Swedish perspective: The case of Malmö'. *Journal of Studies in International Education*, 7 (1), 27–40.

Radclyffe-Thomas, N., Peirson-Smith, A., Roncha, A. and Huang, A. (2016) 'Creative cross-cultural connections: Facebook as a third space for international collaborations'. In Blessinger, P. and Cozza, B. (eds) *University Partnerships for Academic Programs and Professional Development*. Bingley: Emerald Group Publishing, 243–66.

Stearns, P.N. (2009) *Educating Global Citizens in Colleges and Universities: Challenges and opportunities*. New York: Routledge.

Stier, J. (2004) 'Taking a critical stance toward internationalization ideologies in higher education: Idealism, instrumentalism and educationalism'. *Globalisation, Societies and Education*, 2 (1), 83–97.

UNESCO (United Nations Educational, Scientific and Cultural Organization) (2014) *Global Citizenship Education: Preparing learners for the challenges of the 21st century*. Paris: United Nations Educational, Scientific and Cultural Organization. Online. https://tinyurl.com/y2u7y5qq (accessed 25 February 2019).

Yemini, M. (2015) 'Internationalisation discourse hits the tipping point: A new definition is needed'. *Perspectives: Policy and Practice in Higher Education*, 19 (1), 19–22.

Chapter 18

Without walls: Using massive open online courses to extend collaborative learning spaces

Momna Hejmadi and Tim Bilham

We conclude our discussion on collaborative learning with an example of a disruptive innovation that provides access to higher education (HE) for learners previously excluded from traditional provision, while also promoting collaboration between both learners and developers. A disruptive innovation is seen as process, rather than an end-point, which adopts a novel business model and invariably appeals initially to previously unserved consumers before migrating to the mainstream (Christensen *et al.*, 2015). In HE, the main disruptive innovation identified by Clayton Christensen is online education (ibid.: 11).

The previous two chapters have looked at how online education extends the collaborative space for learning for campus students (Chapter 16) and for defined and closed communities of global learners (Chapter 17). This chapter considers the use and development of massive open online courses (MOOCs) to reach learners far beyond the confines of the campus or the virtual learning environment (VLE). The idea of learning 'without walls' is potent and alluring, technology providing the modern-day equivalent of the nineteenth-century University Extension Movement in which the great universities took extra-mural provision to communities without access to academic institutions.

This study describes a free online course, Inside Cancer, that extends learning spaces to a global community of learners, including school pupils, healthcare professionals familiar with biological concepts and cancer survivors with no background in biology, but a strong motivation to learn about cancer and their treatments. The course was also used to complement Cancer Biology, a second-year undergraduate course based on campus at the University of Bath, with assessments as one of the drivers for enrolment from this student group. Both communities of learners shared the online discussion forum. Despite the fact that our learners presented with a diverse range of motivations to learn and had never met each other, the course developed a powerful community of mutually supportive learners.

The large student population – over 40,000 learners enrolled upon this MOOC – provides a rich, large source of data, allowing quantitative and mixed-methods analysis. This provided a unique perspective upon impact and participation and led to some unexpected and intriguing benefits, which we report in this chapter.

Why MOOCs?

MOOCs are global platforms that generally offer free courses online, with the content developed collaboratively between academic institutes and professional and commercial organizations. Their great advantages are in reaching large numbers of globally dispersed learners often at relatively low cost. The first MOOCs were introduced in the United States and arrived in the UK in 2012–13, when the Open University introduced 'FutureLearn' (FL), a MOOC platform. Since then, FL has offered hundreds of courses developed by UK and overseas institutions.

However, the development of MOOCs has not been without political and academic criticism. MOOCs challenge both the established status quo and, as is to be expected from a disruptive innovation, traditional university business models (Conole, 2016). Critics highlight significantly lower completion rates relative to more formal modes of learning (Daniel, 2012), while proponents argue that examining completion rates is misleading because MOOC learners select only what they need from the course without formally completing (LeBar, 2014).

As they have evolved, MOOCs have bifurcated into two types, cMOOCs and xMOOCs, terms coined by Stephen Downes (2012) to differentiate their underpinning educational pedagogies. cMOOCs are based upon a connectivist paradigm, establishing a 'many-to-many' networked learning community, and creating a learning space that is open to all. xMOOCs adopt a cognitive behaviourist pedagogical model that takes a more traditional instructivist approach, with high-quality predetermined content. The primary innovation of xMOOCs is their scalability (Rodriguez, 2013), whereas in cMOOCs learning and knowledge are said to 'rest in diversity of opinions' (Siemens, 2005) and maintaining connections is critical to effective learning (Ravenscroft, 2011). Both types of MOOC extend learning spaces to global learners, particularly those who are otherwise unable to access traditional education, creating learning spaces that blur hierarchies and the traditional notions of who are our 'students'. cMOOCs demonstrate the power of collaborative learning in creating space for the co-creation of knowledge and mutual support in a community of learners, connecting students otherwise working alone, isolated by distance, time or place. The Inside Cancer MOOC is most clearly identified as a cMOOC and the choice of a platform that supported this pedagogy was crucial to its eventual outcomes.

The Inside Cancer MOOC
Momna Hejmadi
The University of Bath was an early adopter of the FL virtual learning space, and Inside Cancer was the first of two MOOCs launched by Bath in 2014. I jumped at the chance to develop this first MOOC because it was an opportunity to discover how to teach a class of thousands and to test-drive this educational innovation. My course, Inside Cancer, was designed to be 'a beginner's guide to cancer genetics', open to anyone interested in understanding the biology of cancer without having studied biology at school or university.

How the course design and content was developed?
The content, based on my second-year undergraduate course on cancer genetics, was significantly and deliberately adapted to meet the needs of diverse learners, which included cancer patients or survivors, with little knowledge of biology, healthcare professionals wishing to enhance their professional development and supporting school pupils' content enrichment and transition to university. The collaborative design team brought together academics and clinical oncologists alongside digital learning technologists. The course began with genetic fundamentals and progressed, over a six-week period, to the detailed cancer genetic hallmarks, culminating in a discussion of current and emerging treatments. The design incorporated a partial blended learning approach, which proved to be invaluable for learner engagement. Each week consisted of three hours of study, including three to five short, interactive videos, supporting text and articles with links for further reading. Tutors engaged in the online forum and produced brief, end-of-week podcasts that discussed interesting questions and comments to cement the content. The podcast and online discussion was designed to create a social and interactive learning community, and participants were encouraged to post questions and weblinks, answer questions and take a more open-ended approach to their learning.

Without walls

Learner demographics

Since 2014, Inside Cancer has run eight times, attracting 41,543 diverse learners from 147 countries. Figure 18.1 shows the average number of comments posted by the learner types, including school pupils, university students, healthcare professionals (for instance, GPs and pharmacists) and also cancer patients or survivors and the general public. An analysis of the demographics of learners showed that Inside Cancer typically attracted older, female learners from Organisation for Economic Co-operation and Development (OECD) countries, whereas learners from non-OECD countries tended to be younger males. The retention rate was 36 per cent (compared to average rates of 17 per cent on other FL courses) and over 98 per cent of learners would recommend the course to friends.

72 — School pupil

189 — University student

261 — Healthcare professional

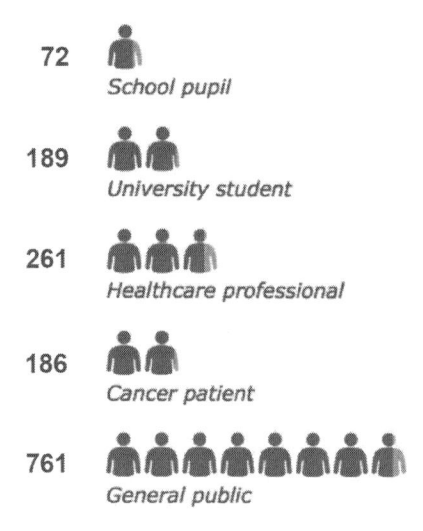

186 — Cancer patient

761 — General public

Figure 18.1: Average number of course comments posted per cohort by active learner type

Image: G. Upton

By FL definitions, a learner is someone who has viewed at least one part of the course, an active learner will have completed at least one step and a social learner made at least one comment. Over the eight cohorts 49 per cent of all enrolments became learners and of those 81 per cent were active learners and 29 per cent social learners. Interestingly, the proportion of social learners between different runs varied between 11 per cent and 39 per cent, but the large number of learners overall meant that this still represented a large collaborative community.

All social learners identified the weekly podcasts and the power of the community in addressing questions or comments from participants as outstanding features. In terms of dropout, our post-course survey showed that 98 per cent of learners who posted two or more comments completed the course, a result aligned with studies that showed that the number of comments posted is an indicator of attrition for cMOOC courses (Cobos *et al.*, 2017), whereas time spent studying was the best indicator in xMOOCs. The breakdown of social learners across each sub-category shows the general public to be the largest group of social learners (41 per cent), whereas school pupils were the least social learners (7 per cent), suggesting that the latter may be the group most likely to prefer, or be more used to, a passive, instructivist approach to learning (Figure 18.2). A majority of the general public identified themselves as either cancer patients or survivors or having a close friend or family member affected by the disease, and that their main motivation in taking the course was to understand the disease better. In the post-course survey, 98 per cent of respondents indicated that the course had either met or exceeded their expectations in 'learning new things'.

Social learners by category (%)

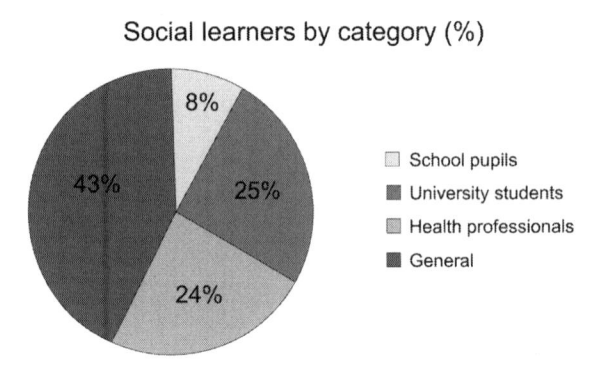

- School pupils: 8%
- University students: 25%
- Health professionals: 24%
- General: 43%

Figure 18.2: Profile of social learner categories (self-identification, based on comment posts)

Image: G. Upton

Did the learning spaces work?

We did not anticipate the success of peer-to-peer learning created by Inside Cancer. Participants were highly motivated and engaged learners, who were having numerous 'virtual' conversations. One of the most refreshing aspects was that knowledgeable peers, often students, were actively involved in giving detailed and clear answers to those with less knowledge, often providing additional links to reading materials.

Without walls

I'm almost feeling a little sad now that it's drawing to a close. ... Thanks also to all the students – your contributions have greatly enriched the course.

The personal response at the end of each week has changed this course into a truly interactive and participatory one.

Global perspectives and new, free-flowing ideas were part of the dialogue. It was rare for the academic team to intervene to address misconceptions because these were quickly picked up and addressed by peer learners.

Evaluation of impact on learners

Further analysis of the impact of the course based on the four learner profiles was done using 'wordclouds' of comments and qualitative comments posted online (Figure 18.3).

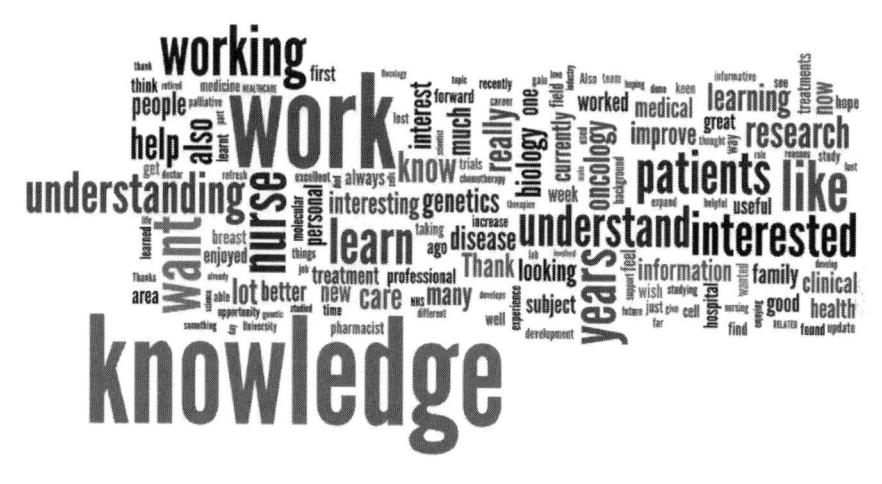

Figure 18.3: Example of a wordcloud for cancer sufferers

Image: G. Upton

General Public: The most social learners on the course, the 'general public' (which includes cancer patients or survivors) identified 'UNDERSTAND' as the keyword when asked about the impact of the course on their learning. Compared to other types of learners they valued the personal development aspects more highly. Cancer patients commonly identified increased confidence, improving their understanding of the development of their own cancer and reducing fear:

I have really enjoyed this course (much to the amusement of my Oncologist) and he was a little taken aback when I asked how the treatments I am to have work!

> The course has helped me understand my late husband's fight against chronic myeloid leukaemia. He was diagnosed in the blast phase and was treated with chemotherapy, monoclonal therapy and stem cell transplant which had no effect. I now understand why.

Others identified a genuine curiosity to learn and also appreciated the social aspects of engaging with a community:

> I have not experienced cancer as yet and feel very humbled by the number of participants who are in the middle of treatment. This course has made Monday morning a pleasure.

Healthcare Professionals: The second of the most social learners explicitly identified 'KNOWLEDGE' as the main impact of the MOOC on their learning.

> I am a stomal therapy nurse and wound care specialist working in an oncology hospital. One of my clients was diagnosed with biliary tract cancer 12 weeks ago, he was scheduled for surgery but sadly the surgeon was unable to progress due to metastasis spreading. My client was able to return home where he passed away peacefully this week, and because of this course I could explain to his family how metastasis spreads; for this I am incredibly grateful.

University Students: Two-thirds of university students, who were either currently in study or had completed study at Bath or elsewhere, identified 'KNOWLEDGE' and 'WORK' as key to their learning. Many identified other educational benefits, for instance using the course as a refresher, as supplementary to their studies or as a revision tool:

> I am a second-year Radiotherapy and Oncology undergraduate and I wanted to try and understand the fundamentals regarding cancer development and progression more fully.

> It's been a really fantastic course and has made me realize that although I've been out of science for a long time, it still holds a real fascination for me.

School Pupils: This group identified 'KNOWLEDGE' and 'UNIVERSITY' as key to their learning. They posted fewer comments or questions to the online discussions, the reasons perhaps being due to either age or motivation. Many students identified understanding cancer within an educational context (A Levels or secondary education) as the reason they registered. Despite their competence with social media, the younger demographic may be more comfortable with traditional classroom modes of learning, or may lack confidence and experience in social interaction explicitly linked to science and consequently tended to post fewer comments online:

> This is really helping with my school work and giving me the additional understanding I need.
>
> I'm studying A Levels at the moment and am really interested in molecular biology, and this course has been really interesting.

A summary of the analysis of this qualitative data reveals a very broad range of positive impacts that the MOOC has had on learners, from supporting academic work, informing practice, prompting behavioural changes in the workplace, increased confidence among those suffering from cancer, knowledge sharing with others outside the course and the enthusiasm to complete more MOOCs.

Impact upon the educators?

The content and structure of the course provided some unexpected positive and additional outcomes that enabled it to be used in multiple ways as extended learning spaces.

1. Comments from cancer patients undergoing treatment allowed undergraduate students on my courses to receive an invaluable, authentic and 'real-world' perspective, away from the textbook, on how research impacts lives. They actively engaged in posting answers and links to science-related questions from other learners on the discussion forum:

    > Thank you. As a cancer survivor, I feel so lucky to have come across this course. It has developed my sense of empowerment and my feeling of confidence about the future.
    >
    > I have learnt so much and have a much greater understanding of my own cancer, removing some of the fear, blame and guilt, now that I understand some of the science. This has been a worthwhile and cathartic course for me.

2. I embedded the course in my 'flipped' classroom environment, drawing on the content to extend critical thinking discussions in class. A flipped classroom is a pedagogical approach that inverts the traditional notion of classroom teaching. Learners are offered the learning content in

advance of the class, and often online, so that the classroom time can be used to focus upon common misunderstandings, encourage peer discussion and provide facilitated problem-solving. Forsey *et al.* (2013) show that, in flipped classroom activities, inclusion of MOOCs as part of the extended space improve face-to-face collaboration and group dynamics in the physical learning spaces. 'Flipped' classrooms are one form of blended learning, although where blended learning suggests a continuum; flipped learning implies a distinct separation into two separate, but mutually supportive, learning spaces.

3. I have used the course to support outreach work in schools, ranging from enrichment talks on cancer genetics to extended DNA-based activities. School pupils have used the course content as part of their Extended Project Qualifications (EPQ) to enhance their Universities and Colleges Admissions Service (UCAS) applications for a place at university:

> I have been inspired to base my Extended Project Qualification on a related topic.
>
> I'm really enjoying the course, and looking forward to starting A Level Biology at school on Thursday.
>
> I am taking this course because I want to find out more about genetics. I hope this course will help me narrow down my choices for study options after my A Levels this year.

Undergraduate students were also inspired to pursue further studies and research in the field.

4. Data from the course analytics was used by colleagues to disseminate the impact of cancer research to general audiences (public engagement talks, research networks) and to external agencies as part of a Research Excellence Framework (REF2020) impact case study.

Limitations of the analysis

One of the limitations in this analysis is the incomplete data posted in the online forum. Comments along the lines of 'I found the course helpful', without contextualization, had to be discarded because of difficulties in measuring impact on professional practice, personal development or academic study.

A second limitation is the self-identification of positive impact by the learners. As MOOCs are free, most learners were incredibly grateful for the opportunity to learn and were not aiming to meet a specific academic or professional goal. Inside Cancer, in particular, was designed to engage audiences with the science underlying cancer, and therefore learners tended to be less critical compared to fee-paying students concerned about qualifications and with professional attainment goals.

Lessons learnt

For colleagues considering developing a MOOC as a virtual learning space, we offer the following advice:

- *Have a shared vision:* ensuring the course team all have a clear and shared vision across the course team is vital. Questions to consider are: Who is the course for? Why do we want to do this course? The rationale also underpins how you measure success. For instance, is your course designed to engage the public in your research? Is the course a 'taster' or an additional resource for a campus-based programme of study? Answers will help you not only in designing your course but also in how you measure successful outcomes.
- *Take care in choosing your collaborators:* the shared vision will help you put together the right group of people with whom to work, which might include external experts, governmental policymakers or professional practitioners. Involving institutional professional services (such as marketing, and the university press office) from the start will help maximize the impact of your MOOC.
- *Tell a story:* the most successful MOOCs tell an interesting story that keeps the learners intrigued and motivated.
- *Keep it short:* research supports our experience that courses lasting longer than three to four weeks have higher dropout rates and lower learner engagement.
- *Have an open and flexible approach*: an open, flexible and participative approach between tutors and developers and with the technical team is important. Our self-acknowledged lack of experience in distance learning meant that we were more open and willing to adopt or adapt our approach, based on expert advice and evidence-based research on distance learning, which served us well.
- *Be clear on your budget:* high-quality MOOCs can be expensive, but cheaper MOOCs can be equally successful, if designed correctly. You may be able to budget for a MOOC in a research grant or as part of dissemination or public engagement exercise.

Conclusion

Overall, the success of the course was humbling, unexpected and exhilarating. The development of a worldwide classroom, without walls or barriers to access, open to global learners and one that values the experiences and expertise of all learners can be potentially transformational:

> I'm studying biochemistry ... when I finish my degree I would like to study biomedicine and dedicate my future working life to research against cancer.

In learning environments such as these, the notion of material space disappears and collaborative learning and knowledge generation is facilitated. Or, as Anne Boddington (2011: 190) puts it, when calling for a more vital co-operative model for learning and teaching:

> We can reconstruct discovery as our craft and the world ... as our classroom, and as a truly public sphere within which to reshape and invigorate our future learning.

Acknowledgements

We would like to thank Gemma Upton and Flora Casson, final-year students at the University of Bath, for their analysis of the data arising from the MOOC, which was used in compiling this case study.

References

Boddington, A. (2011) 'Designing education and reshaping learning'. In Boddington, A. and Boys, J. (eds) *Re-Shaping Learning: A critical reader: The future of learning spaces in post-compulsory education*. Rotterdam: Sense Publishers, 179–91.

Christensen, C.M., Raynor, M. and McDonald, R. (2015) 'What is disruptive innovation?'. *Harvard Business Review*, 93 (12), 44–53.

Cobos, R., Wilde, A. and Zaluska, E. (2017) 'Predicting attrition from Massive Open Online Courses in FutureLearn and edX'. In *Proceedings of the 7th International Learning Analytics and Knowledge Conference, Simon Fraser University, Vancouver, BC, Canada*, 13–17 March. Online. https://eprints.soton.ac.uk/405268/2/FL_LAK_rc_agw_ejz2.pdf (accessed 12 April 2018).

Conole, G. (2016) 'MOOCs as disruptive technologies: Strategies for enhancing the learner experience and quality of MOOCs'. *RED: Revista de Educación a Distancia*, 50, Article 2, 1–18. Online. www.um.es/ead/red/50/conole.pdf (accessed 25 February 2019).

Daniel, J. (2012) 'Making sense of MOOCs: Musings in a maze of myth, paradox and possibility'. *Journal of Interactive Media in Education*, 3, Article 18, 1–20. Online. https://tinyurl.com/yypu8ghw (accessed 25 February 2019).

Downes, S. (2012) 'Massively Open Online Courses are "here to stay"'. Online. www.downes.ca/post/58676 (accessed 18 April 2018).

Forsey, M., Low, M. and Glance, D. (2013) 'Flipping the sociology classroom: Towards a practice of online pedagogy'. *Journal of Sociology*, 49 (4), 471–85.

LeBar, M. (2014) 'MOOCs – completion is not important'. Forbes, 16 September. Online. https://tinyurl.com/y2j5lf9q (accessed 25 February 2019).

Ravenscroft, A. (2011) 'Dialogue and connectivism: A new approach to understanding and promoting dialogue-rich networked learning'. *International Review of Research in Open and Distance Learning*, 12 (3), 139–60.

Rodriguez, O. (2013) 'The concept of openness behind c and x-MOOCs (Massive Open Online Courses)'. *Open Praxis*, 5 (1), 67–73.

Siemens, G. (2005) 'Connectivism: A learning theory for the digital age'. *International Journal of Instructional Technology and Distance Learning*, 2 (1), 3–10.

Part Four

Integrating spaces

4

Chapter 19

Thinking outside the box: Utilizing real-world space in teaching and learning

Clive Holtham and Angela Dove

Our final chapter presents a case study that deftly links the major themes of the book and the previous three parts, namely physical and authentic learning places, space for the self and collaborative and social learning, reflecting Barnett's (2011) taxonomy that has been foundational to many previous chapters. Of course, many other chapters span these same themes but here we provide an example that explicitly integrates these spaces, challenging us to think outside the restrictive architecture of conventional teaching spaces and also serving as an effective summary for the entire book.

The chapter explores an innovative undergraduate teaching module created to meet the rapidly changing needs of employers for 'intuitive' qualities in students in the aftermath of the 2007–8 business and financial failures (Brown *et al.*, 2011). The module utilized several diverse and unconventional spaces for authentic and collaborative learning, including spaces within and external to the campus.

Context

City, University of London's (2016) strategy places a great emphasis on meeting the needs of business and the professions. This new module arose following discussions with major employers in which they identified that two particularly underemphasized components in UK graduates were self-awareness and reflective skills. These employers were placing less emphasis on rational, functional skills, with surprisingly little emphasis on analytical skills and knowledge acquired from conventional business-school disciplinary modules. This suggested that the rational-analytical base of undergraduate management education needed to be augmented, as a matter of urgency, with much more intuitive approaches (McGilchrist, 2009; Sadler-Smith and Burke, 2009). A particularly influential critique came from the Carnegie Foundation Study (Colby *et al.*, 2011), which advocated analytical thinking, the classic heart of rational and scientific education, being paralleled by themes such as multiple framing and reflective exploration of meaning, which are much more characteristic of education in the arts and humanities, but nevertheless vital in addressing the widespread ambiguities faced in managerial tasks.

In our terminology, we represent analytical thinking as involving six 'rational' qualities, to be contrasted with six 'intuitive' qualities. Combined together, these represent two interlocking dimensions of the successful manager as shown in our hexagon framework model (Figure 19.1). The inner part of the hexagon represents the intuitive qualities, the outer part the rational. They are paired across six spectra. For example, communication is a spectrum, with its rational pole focusing on being articulate, while its intuitive pole is in being persuasive.

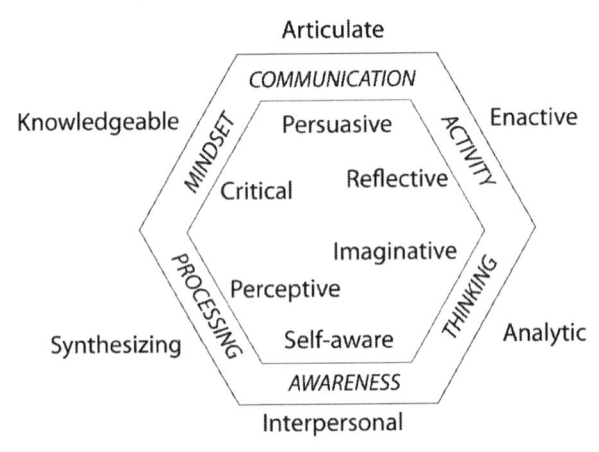

Figure 19.1: Rational and intuitive qualities of management (Holtham, 2011)

Table 19.1: Six spectra relating to the intuitive and rational qualities needed by twenty-first-century managers

RATIONAL	SPECTRUM	INTUITIVE
Interpersonal	⟵⟶	Self-Aware
Able to engage and converse with diverse range of people; this is unrelated to whether the individual is introvert or extrovert	AWARENESS	Able to consider and continually review reflectively one's own characteristics, qualities, strengths and weaknesses, including their impact on relationships with other people

Thinking outside the box

RATIONAL	SPECTRUM	INTUITIVE
Knowledgeable ⟵⟶		**Perceptive**
Having developed a body of personal knowledge which can be drawn on, but also being able to augment that through learning, search, conversation or engagement with experts	PROCESSING	It is vital in leadership to develop instincts for close observations, not only of the important but also for curiosity about the everyday. Sometimes even tiny anomalies may provide a clue to something much more profound
Analytical ⟵⟶		**Imaginative**
Able to design and organize the collation of information, weigh up its reliability and value, then apply that information through structured frameworks to produce evidence	THINKING	This is a key component of creativity, which avoids some of the baggage associated with the more heavily used word 'creative'
Synthesizing ⟵⟶		**Critical**
Not only being able to uncover information from one perspective, but to be able to do so from several perspectives and then relate them together	MINDSET	Corporate failures often arise because key individuals or whole groups fail to challenge even basic assumptions or data. To counter this, leaders need to develop a sceptical approach
Enactive ⟵⟶		**Reflective**
The ability to get things in the physical or digital worlds, which will typically involve 'making' artefacts, broadly defined, by one or more people	ACTIVITY	It is important for managers and professionals not only being able to act and to do, but also to reflect on and learn from action, including for double-loop learning
Articulate ⟵⟶		**Persuasive**
It is important to be able to express relational ideas in a clear, confident and straightforward fashion using a wide variety of media	COMMUNICATION	Persuasive communication is the modern translation of the ancient word 'rhetoric', one of the core subjects in the medieval university

Each paired quality is defined briefly in Table 19.1. To be successful leaders, students will need to be able to move vertically and horizontally across and between the intuitive and rational qualities shown in these six spectra.

Design and implementation of the module

We used these analyses to design a new module that addresses these qualities and aimed to promote self-awareness and reflective practice for first-year business students, who primarily came from rationalist education systems and who typically self-identified as personally rationalist.

Entitled 'The Reflective Practitioner', the module first ran in January 2011, its design building upon nearly a decade of work at MBA and MSc level. The curriculum design draws on constructivist pedagogies (Wenger, 1998) that are distinctively different from the more transmissive pedagogies used to teach most other first-year modules in our business school. We created a reflective educational approach coupled with physical spaces that would reinforce the importance of their intuitive qualities to students. Physical space is used in ways unusual in a business school, namely studio space, external visits and an exhibition. Indeed there is a conscious aim to seek out unfamiliar spaces that may be intellectually uncomfortable.

The module is grounded in a number of key principles related to managerial qualities, space, collaboration and reflection (Holtham, 2011). (Reflective practice originated, in part, from the management discipline (Argyris and Schön, 1978) but through practice has been extended and developed very substantially (Grey and Fitzgibbon, 2003).) The module runs with two streams of 20–25 students over 11 weeks. There are almost no lectures apart from short briefings and some external speakers. Each study week involves activities and explicit reflection time, leading up to a major exhibition in week 11 on which the two streams work collaboratively. There are four specific and distinctive student-learning outputs, namely reflective journals, physical artefacts, the public exhibition of student work and external visits. We describe these here and in each case provide a table summarizing how the element relates to the three themes of the book.

Reflective journal

This 80-page, partly pre-printed, journal was developed to provide explicit scaffolding for reflection by business students. This is the practical spine of the module, and most students evolve their distinctive written and visual 'voice' through the activities that take place over many weeks. Reflective journaling is positioned as a key leadership quality (Reynolds and Vince, 2017), and the module aims to encourage the habit of lifelong journalling. The journal represents a major part of the coursework marks. The journal is entirely private, except to faculty. However, students are asked to select one page to be curated into a single composite artefact in the exhibition.

Table 19.2: Summary of how element delivers to the book themes: reflective journal

	Authentic Learning	Spaces for the Self	Collaborative and Social Learning
Reflective Journal	Reflective journalling is positioned as a key leadership quality, and the module aims to encourage the habit of lifelong journalling	This 80-page partly pre-printed private journal is a major part of the coursework	Entirely private, except to faculty. One page is selected though for a composite artefact in the exhibition

Artefact

'Making' can be an important part of reflection. Students create an 'identity box', currently a medium-size (unused) pizza box, which enables them to visualize and publicly communicate their identity. Figure 19.2 shows the artefacts awaiting review by the external examiner. The artefact is, in itself, a designed and constructed 3D physical space, and students need to uncover and then exploit its affordances; the inside of a box is shown in Figure 19.3.

> The enthusiasm and the opportunity to create something were the best things about the module. (Student evaluation)

Many approaches are possible to explore self and identity for business professionals. Our decision was to use the 'Brand You' concept (Purkiss and Royston-Lee, 2012), not only because of its theoretical excellence, but also because there was a good range of material to support it. The concept is that the individuals must consider themselves as a brand, and then draw explicitly on the tools of branding to develop, protect and extend their brand. Use of a marketing concept like 'brand' makes an approach like this comprehensible to business students. Further experimentation has also proved it to be usable in practice by first-year students.

Figure 19.2: Pizza box artefacts awaiting external examiner

Image: C. Holtham

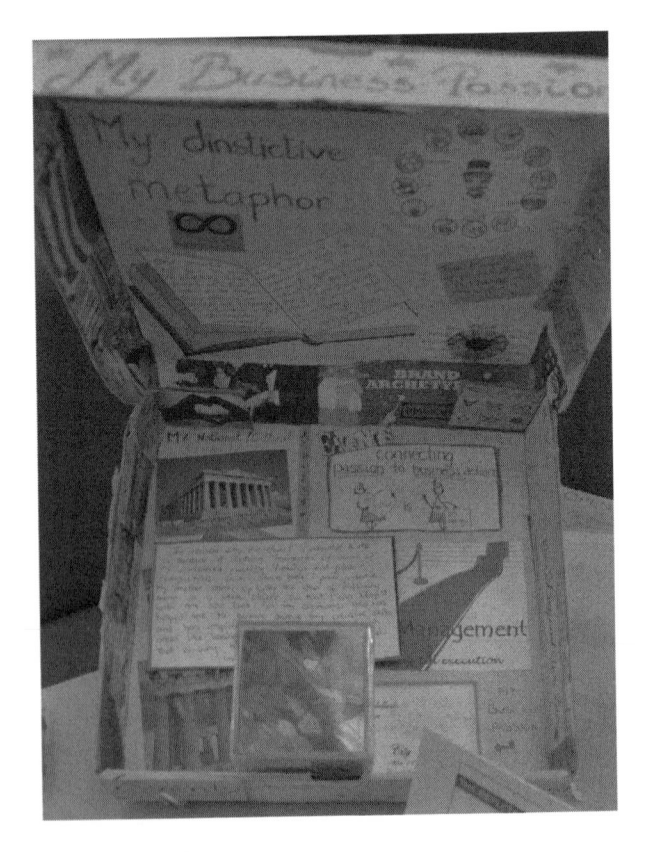

Figure 19.3: Inside a pizza box

Image: C. Holtham

Table 19.3: Summary of how element delivers to the book themes: artefact

	Authentic Learning	Spaces for the Self	Collaborative and Social Learning
Artefact	Although we don't expect this exact task to be reproduced in the workplace, the question of articulating and communicating personal identity is fundamental	The reflective journal is partly used to plan the design of the artefact, as well as to reflect on the final output	Because the artefacts are exhibited, students gain insights into each other very rapidly

Public exhibition

The final phase of the module is in planning a public exhibition and making the exhibits, plus the hectic work needed on the day itself. The design thinking here is that the activities involved in managing the exhibition, directly involve Fayol's (1949) classic definition of management: planning, controlling, organizing and leading. Consequently, students face real management tasks and the very physical exhibition context provides a rich stimulus for reflection. This is unquestionably authentic learning about the practice of management. A final reflection, which is crucial to the process, is completed shortly after the event, reinforcing the connection between the abstract task of reflection and the everyday reality of being an effective manager. The benefits of the exhibition as a final summative and collective collaborative event was reflected in student feedback:

> I found the exhibition a very successful and rewarding experience in terms of gaining invaluable management skills of planning and organising, guiding and sharing with several guests the many lessons this course had taught us all.

> The final exhibition was a great opportunity not only to show visitors the work we have done during these eleven weeks, but also an enjoyable way of networking with guest speakers, lecturers and students in the management group.

Invitations are sent to faculty and professional staff across the university, to visiting lecturers and business colleagues and to friends and relatives of students. The interaction with the visitors is central to the student experience because they themselves are the hosts, and will be asked to explain not only their own work, but that of other students as well.

Visitors to the exhibition are asked for detailed feedback, for example that provided by Professor Susannah Quinsee, NTF (2001) and an NTF Ambassador:

> The Reflective Practitioner exhibition was one of the best events I have attended in the university this year. The energy and enthusiasm emanating from the students was palpable. It was brilliant to hear them talking about their work and their personal journey through the module. I loved the artefact boxes, the diaries, the photos, so much creativity. What struck me as well was how proud they were, not only of their own achievements, but in the achievements of their classmates, demonstrating a true learning community.

Table 19.4: Summary of how element delivers to the book themes: public exhibition

	Authentic Learning	Spaces for the Self	Collaborative and Social Learning
Public Exhibition	This enables all phases of planning, organizing, leading and controlling to be put into practice by all students	The exhibition is a rich stimulus to the final section and holistic conclusions to the reflective journal	Each stage of the preparation and delivery involves working in ad hoc and latterly formal groups, not least in critique of options in the planning stage

External visits

Our review of teaching and learning, when moving to a new building in 2003, considered that insufficient advantage was taken from drawing upon the hinterland of the Business School in inner London. A subsequent initiative led to an examination of different ways to bring this about, through visits, walks or other approaches. The lessons from the review directly impacted our curriculum as the module was designed to include sessions that took place in external spaces. We explore these in some depth, because we believe this approach could be applied across diverse academic disciplines, using relevant local spaces, particularly museums and archives.

These locations were important as an explicit signal to students of different expectations and opportunities than those possible on campus. Some students were apprehensive about events off campus, both from a logistical viewpoint and more significantly because of the uncertainty, and even fear, that it would be a waste of time. These general concerns were possibly accentuated by the three locations that have been used, two museums and an archive, that are not obviously about business management. Some students asked why they could not visit 'real' workplaces. Our first response was that visits to real workplaces are most typically simply guided tours for both confidentiality and logistical reasons. The more fundamental response lay in the fact that these non-office environments enabled us to develop learning experiences that would help them cope with going to unfamiliar business locations, such as an audit or consulting client, contractor, subsidiary or regional office. Students would have to identify, through their own initiative and observation skills, what was actually going on, and develop the skill of asking good questions in a very short period of time. The learning remains authentic to the key business qualities being developed, even though the physical location is not itself authentic of most business workplaces.

The Churchill War Rooms

At the time, one of the authors was researching decision-making under crisis and had visited the Churchill War Rooms near Downing Street. The idea emerged of organizing a teaching session at the museum, with specially designed activities. The organization of an external visit, even for a group of 20–30 students, turned out to be non-trivial in terms of lecturer effort, financial costs and logistics. There is also the culture of museums and galleries, which may see students as passive learners, the opposite of our intention. However, education is an important function of most British museums and galleries, and there is interest in attracting new students from courses (such as management) who would not normally visit cultural spaces. Nevertheless, at times, some robust negotiation was needed to tailor the visit to the exact needs of the student group.

The Churchill War Rooms have an excellent education room and staff, and a brief historic introduction was all that was needed. Students worked collaboratively in pairs, and each was allocated a topic related to intuitive skills in management such as 'collaboration', 'risk' and 'humour'. Our aim was to develop intuitive skills in collecting evidence and organize into a convincing presentation. The student task was to locate and investigate information relating to their topic, and then to present it to their peers with a particular emphasis on using evidence. On the first visit, the teaching team were anxious as to how the group of first-years, including many for whom English was not their first language, would deal with such an overtly British location as the War Rooms. In the event, any fears were misplaced. The response of students was quite independent of nationality and English skills. What we observed was incredibly close attention paid to fine details in exhibits and almost obsessive preoccupation with building up a persuasive story to share at the end. When asked about this, one student said that their pair had treated the work as if it was a computer game where each room possibly contained clues that would help them assemble the final deliverable.

> It was a great opportunity to touch the unknown past and to feel for a moment like being there for real. Browsing through old documents and photos gave me unimaginable feeling of the time elapsing as well as evolution of human thinking ... I had no idea how important it is to keep records of what we do, so that the next generations can learn from us. ... Our team was able to work in a very dynamic and creative way even under the big time pressure.

The Hunterian Museum

Our next location was the Hunterian Museum, a niche museum at the Royal College of Surgeons, which celebrates the foundation of modern medicine over 200 years ago. The challenge there was quite different. We suggested to our students that management science is currently in a similar position to medicine at the time the museum was founded. Their task was to examine the lessons that arose from that evolution, from the craft of surgery and from the emerging medical sciences, to explore how could these be made relevant to the future enhancement of management. An unfamiliar task was tackled in a very unfamiliar physical space. Once again, careful observation and imaginative and colourful storytelling were achieved as part of collaborative team learning:

> Overall, this module not only helped us to improve our employability skills but also our personal skills. For instance, we have been working towards the enhancement of our own self-awareness, our ability to work within a team and our communication skills. Without forgetting the main aspect of the

module: everything had to be innovative, creative and visually attractive.

The only problem we faced was that some of the exhibits were unsuitable for those of a nervous disposition, and this upset a small number of students in some years.

The London Metropolitan Archive

Our third and current location is the London Metropolitan Archive. This is less than five minutes' walk from the university, and unusually has a major specialism in business history, including the donated archives of a number of major organizations. The business archivist selects about eight historic artefacts for each of four or five organizations. Students are required to deliver a 'sales pitch' to the producer of a television programme as to why 'their' organization should be the subject of a 30-minute programme on business history. Most students have never been to an archive, much less engaged with historic objects. Yet once again, their curiosity and imagination seemed to be released. The group work leads on to presentations in *Dragon's Den* format. (*Dragon's Den* is a British TV programme, based upon an original Japanese idea, in which aspiring entrepreneurs 'pitch' a business proposition to a group of wealthy investors to seek a financial investment in their business in return for a stake in their company.) The archivist selects the 'winning' group:

> The non-conventional learning has been extremely interesting.
> I learnt a lot about intuitive skills and developing managerial qualities.

The session concludes by bringing out the wider business relevance of needing to interrogate static and ambiguous information. Students from all backgrounds engaged with the material, one of the most impressive was an international student who was faced with an enormous yellowed ledger, with ancient handwriting. Her close audit uncovered that the brewery had a major deficit in the early 1800s.

These visits have become a unique selling point for our module, providing invaluable experience in terms of confronting the unknown. But there are considerable logistical overheads in juggling dates and times – often they cannot be organized during the regular timetable slot. There are routine anxieties over whether students will get lost or be significantly late. Costs are also rising faster than inflation.

Table 19.5: Summary of how element delivers to the book themes: external visits

	Authentic Learning	Spaces for the Self	Collaborative and Social Learning
External Visit	This does not attempt to replicate a visit to a real workplace. But it does emulate visiting an unfamiliar location and needing to observe closely and reach credible conclusions based on limited information	Reflections on the group processes are as important as on the intellectual content	The tasks are assigned to randomly created groups who have to develop solutions and make presentations within tight time constraints

Reflections upon a reflective module

Exploiting a diversity of spaces represents, perhaps surprisingly, an effective means to also explore and articulate deeper thoughts about self and identity, and to develop in students their skills in reflective practice. We summarize this in a simple framework (Figure 19.4), comprising three dimensions that mirror Barnett's (2011) taxonomy of learning spaces, namely self, collaboration and physical space, the area within the triangle containing the practical tasks facing the students. The artefact and journal are orientated towards self; the visit and exhibition involve both collaboration and space. The importance of these tasks lies much more in the way that they help to develop underlying intuitive qualities, than in their apparent practical purpose. The journal aims to stimulate deep reflection, the exhibited artefact to encourage students to understand their own identity and then to be able to represent that in public. The dramatic use of unusual physical space is to unfreeze students from passive mindsets that can become entrenched when in conventional lecture rooms.

Thinking outside the box

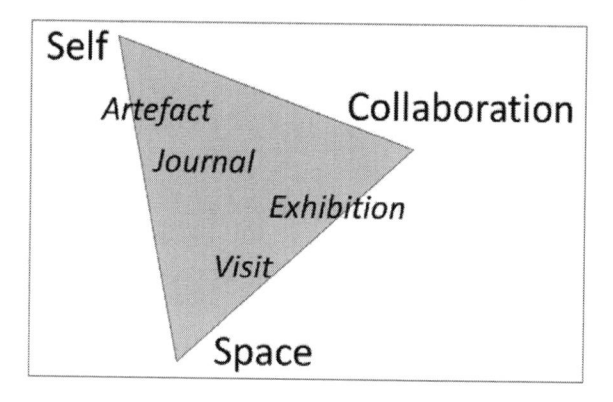

Figure 19.4: Components of the learning approach showing the four learning activities

Image: C. Holtham and A. Dove, 2019

It is illuminating to note that, in a context where most of the school's management teaching adopts a rational approach, the external examiner's review of the Reflective Practitioner concluded:

> It is interesting to see how students are challenged in visualising deep thinking and differentiate themselves from others by reflecting on their individuality. I find the feedback provided back to students precise, guiding and consistent although within the context of this unorthodox module.

We summarize each of the four elements in terms of contribution to the six intuitive qualities (Table 19.6). Creating this matrix was important at the design stage of the module to ensure that the curriculum would actually address the expressed needs of employers.

Table 19.6: Demonstration of how far each student output element contributes to the six intuitive qualities

	Reflective Journal	Artefact	Public Exhibition	External Visit
Self-aware	*	*		
Perceptive	*		*	*
Imaginative	*	*	*	*
Critical	*		*	*
Reflective	*	*		
Persuasive		*	*	*

Given the emphasis on creating slightly uncomfortable environments, it is perhaps not surprising that, when they wrote their final reflections, a significant minority of students expressed how doubtful they were about their choice of elective in the early weeks of the module. But as the module proceeded, they found they overcame those doubts through the cumulative increase of confidence. There is little doubt that atypical physical spaces, combined with design of constructivist activities played a key part in both the unsettling and also its resolution.

Recommendations

Our experiences allow us to suggest some key recommendations for institutions in relation to physical teaching and learning spaces and related policies:

- The strategic design process for space needs to be strongly informed by diverse perspectives from front-line teachers
- When planning to introduce innovative learning approaches, gaining significant support from prospective employers may be valuable in dealing with the potential concerns of both academic colleagues and of students
- The public exhibition of student work can be a powerful motivator and provide a valuable vehicle for engagement with employers and indeed colleagues from across the university. Restrictions on the use of walls and furniture can be detrimental to the effective exhibition of work, so policies need to be developed to create or permit the more flexible use of space to support exhibitions
- External visits increasingly involve fees, and if module design is to connect learners with authentic or relevant external visits, budgetary provision needs to be explicitly made for this, and for the additional faculty workload
- Where developing innovative methods or using unusual spaces, which can cause student anxiety, it is always useful to make explicit precisely how this contributes to their professional learning
- Universities should increase the percentage of their learning spaces that are versatile across radically different teaching modes, and ensure room allocation policies enable active-learning classes to be allocated to the studio type of spaces they need.

References

Argyris, C. and Schön, D.A. (1978) *Organizational Learning: A theory of action perspective*. Reading, MA: Addison-Wesley.

Barnett, R. (2011) 'Configuring learning spaces: Noticing the invisible'. In Boddington, A. and Boys, J. (eds) *Re-Shaping Learning: A critical reader: The future of learning spaces in post-compulsory education*. Rotterdam: Sense Publishers, 167–78.

Brown, A., Holtham, C., Rich, M. and Dove, A. (2011) 'After the financial crisis: Preparing graduates for a dramatic change in employers' expectations'. BMAF Conference 2011, Bournemouth.

City, University of London, (2016) *City University Vision*, London: City, University of London.

Colby, A., Ehrlich, T., Sullivan, W.M. and Dolle, J.R. (2011) *Rethinking Undergraduate Business Education: Liberal learning for the profession*. San Francisco: Jossey-Bass.

Fayol, H. (1949) *General and Industrial Management*. Trans. Storrs, C. London: Sir Isaac Pitman and Sons.

Grey, A. and Fitzgibbon, K. (2003) 'Reflection-in-action and business undergraduates: What learning curve?'. *Reflective Practice*, 4 (1), 11–18.

Holtham, C. (2011) 'Creating an innovative first year module on reflective practice'. Association of National Teaching Fellows' Symposium, Leicester, 9–10 May.

McGilchrist, I. (2009) *The Master and His Emissary: The divided brain and the making of the Western world*. New Haven, CT: Yale University Press.

Purkiss, J. and Royston-Lee, D. (2012) *Brand You: Turn your unique talents into a winning formula*. 2nd ed. Harlow: Pearson.

Reynolds, M. and Vince, R. (eds) (2017) *Organizing Reflection*. Abingdon: Routledge.

Sadler-Smith, E. and Burke, L.A. (2009) 'Fostering intuition in management education: Activities and resources'. *Journal of Management Education*, 33 (2), 239–62.

Wenger, E. (1998) *Communities of Practice: Learning, meaning, and identity*. Cambridge: Cambridge University Press.

Postscript: Teaching excellence and the NTFS

Sally Brown

Chair of the Association of National Teaching Fellows, 2015–18

National Teaching Fellowships are awarded to higher education (HE) teachers in the UK who have been recognized at a national level as excellent university teachers through a competitive process organized through the Higher Education Academy (HEA, now Advance HE). Only around 55 Fellowships are awarded each year. All National Teaching Fellows (NTFs) then become members of the Association of National Teaching Fellows (ANTF) and currently the association includes over 750 members.

The National Teaching Fellowship Scheme (NTFS), which began in 2000, reflects the characteristics of parallel schemes in Australia, Canada, New Zealand and the USA in recognition of outstanding university teachers. NTFS criteria have been refined over the lifetime of the awards and now focus on a judgement based on each applicant demonstrating:

> Evidence of enhancing and transforming student outcomes and/or the teaching profession: demonstrating impact commensurate with the individual's context and the opportunities afforded by it.

> Evidence of supporting colleagues and influencing support for student learning and/or the teaching profession; demonstrating impact and engagement beyond the nominee's immediate academic or professional role.

> Evidence of the nominee's commitment to and impact of ongoing professional development with regard to teaching and learning and/or learning support. (HEA, 2018)

The fellowship of fellowship-holders

The innovative work of NTFs has created a field of practice-based research that has reframed space for learning and challenged the orthodoxies of traditional teaching, learning and assessment practice in HE. This has had high impact, not just in the United Kingdom, but also globally. Fellows have opportunities to meet at annual NTF symposia and to network with

Postscript

colleagues via the ANTF, specifically to share good practice, seek advice, try out partially formed plans for teaching innovations, develop research partnerships, seek guidance and request (and offer) support. This is a really positive aspect of the scheme. NTFs call on one another when, for example, wishing to apply for professorships or other senior appointments and when thinking about changing roles or institutions. NTFs also write and publish together (for example, Bilham, 2013, and indeed in this volume).

It is clear from reviewing applications and meeting NTFs that excellent teaching does not happen by accident. Typically, NTFs are people who:

- are great energizers of student learning
- are experts not just in their originating disciplines, but also have a strong grounding in the scholarship that underpins pedagogic excellence
- work hard to achieve seemingly effortless excellence while at the same time being unafraid to take risks and push the boundaries of teaching.

There is no single model of excellence: while many NTFs are highly innovative, awards are also given to those who, through conventional modes of delivery, bring to the process passion, commitment and a strong orientation towards engendering student learning. The disciplinary spread of NTFs is broad, and the community includes learning support staff, librarians, educational developers and educational technologists, as well as academics.

Meeting the challenges of twenty-first-century HE pedagogy

HE practitioners internationally work in a complex and ever-changing environment and it is the premise of this book that NTFs are well placed to rise and respond positively to these challenges. Elsewhere, Brown (2015) and I have identified four issues that face HE pedagogy, which are relevant when proactively creating spaces for learning:

1. No university or indeed national HE system can behave as if it is not working in a global environment.
2. Education is transformative and can be either a locus for redressing disadvantage or conversely for reinforcing elitism.
3. Education in universities needs to be a joint endeavour in which learners and teachers work in partnership.

4. No sensible university teacher can behave as if we do not live in a digital age and no sensible university should fail to help teaching and learning support staff to continuously upgrade their skills.

To these, I would add a further two:

5. To ensure that in assessment of our students we are assessing the right thing.
6. The imperative to adopt a truly analytic and critically reflective approach to our own practice and exploring ways to contribute to the community of practice around teaching excellence.

These are not isolated, abstract ideas: it is clear that the editors and authors within this volume share these preoccupations and strive to address them throughout their professional practice.

A global space for learning

A rapidly changing political and social environment requires HE practitioners to be quick on their feet and globally responsible. Notwithstanding some curtailing of the mobility of students and staff, there can be no retreat from an internationalized learning environment, particularly since face-to-face and virtual approaches to teaching rely heavily on the availability of international curricula, learning resources and models of pedagogy. Students expect case studies, examples and texts to transcend national boundaries and we have a responsibility to foster among our students, our colleagues and ourselves cross-cultural capability and the capacity to live and work as global citizens (Killick, 2013, 2016; Ryan, 2012). Our personal responses to the global HE agenda might include:

- informing ourselves about the great diversity of pedagogic practices our students and colleagues may have experienced outside the nation and context in which we teach (see, for example, Carroll and Ryan, 2005 and Killick, 2016, the seminal work by another NTF)
- regularly interrogating the curricula we deliver to ensure that we are culturally inclusive, particularly in relation to going beyond our own national contexts
- engaging widely with international pedagogic experts (NTFs, for example) particularly gain benefits from working with similarly recognized scholars in Australia, New Zealand, Canada, the United States and India. The International Federation of National Teaching Fellows (IFNTF; see also www.ifntf.org), launched in 2016, provides further opportunities.

The work of other NTFs has made major contributions to pedagogic thought in the twenty-first century (including Grainne Conole, 2013; Rachel McCrindle in Adams and McCrindle, 2008; Gilly Salmon, 2004, 2013; Helen Beetham and Rhona Sharpe, 2013; Chrissi Nerantzi, 2013; and Simon Thomson, 2016, to mention an invidiously small sample from a very rich constituency).

Transformative learning

If students entering HE are not changed by the experience, we have to ask what is the purpose of it? NTFs are in the vanguard of fostering transformative learning as the examples provided in Bilham (2013) demonstrate – of using laughter to demystify statistics, scaffolding problem-based learning, working across boundaries with interdisciplinary cultures, promoting inclusivity, blending traditional and digital approaches, using games to promote engagement, fostering employability and developing students' skills and competences, *inter alia*.

The importance of building, imagining and reframing authentic and enabling environments for learning is the focus of this book and it comes at a most opportune moment, as universities seek to expand their teaching spaces in many directions – extramurally, internationally and virtually.

Transformative approaches to teaching and learning have long been championed by NTFs, including perhaps its best-known pioneer Graham Gibbs (his publications are too numerous to list here, but perhaps one of the most relevant here is Gibbs and Coffey (2004), which discusses training for university teachers). Through the Oxford Brookes staff and Learning Development unit, he led a number of national programmes (including Teaching More Students, when the UK moved from elite to mass education) and nurtured the development of a number of subsequent NFTs, including Chris Rust, Gina Wisker, Rhona Sharpe and myself.

If we want to make learning transformative, we can usefully aim, like Graham, to:

- keep a watchful eye on current pedagogic developments in HE and devise ways of supporting staff and students to make the best of arising opportunities
- focus on making teaching and assessment practical, manageable and achievable, recognizing that teachers in the live and virtual classroom have limited time and energy to engage with untested innovations
- recognize the importance of both qualitative and quantitative research to back up arguments for pedagogic change management programmes

(Graham particularly recognized the importance of convincing policymakers and senior managers of the value of doing things differently and was very effective at making a business case for the changes he proposed)
- be unafraid of being considered quirky in your thinking, because transformation sometimes involves mould-breaking
- retain students at the centre of transformative initiatives: if a change does not bring about improvements in the student experience, its value must be questionable.

Working in partnership to co-create learning

As traditional top-down models of teaching are progressively replaced with more interactive approaches, the place of the student within HE is being re-evaluated. In the UK, the Quality Assurance Agency (QAA, 2018) has for some years required student representatives to be included in all stages of quality assurance and enhancement processes and this has led to an exploration of creative ways of working in partnership with students. In the classroom, too, it is increasingly recognized that learning happens best when students are active partners in the learning process, facilitating learning rather than focusing on output models as NTF Phil Race (2014) argues. NTF Colin Bryson (2013, in Bilham, 2013) similarly makes a good case for opening up dialogues with students to help to make space for learning. In assessment, similarly, the importance of dialogue is recognized (Sambell *et al.*, 2017), particularly the value of making feedback a dialogic rather than a monologic process, so students can better engage with the formative advice they receive.

As practitioners, we can advance partnerships in learning by:

- consulting regularly with learners about how we can best support their learning. For example, university estate managers regularly discuss with users how best to allocate space for formal and informal learning
- familiarizing ourselves with the diverse range of learners we encounter in our teaching so we can ensure inclusivity
- working closely with course representatives in all aspects of programme design, delivery, assessment, evaluation and enhancement.

Self-renewal

As part of the application process all NTFs must demonstrate a commitment to ongoing personal and professional development in relation to teaching and learning by keeping up to date both within their subject specialisms and within pedagogic developments. This aspect of professional practice is also emphasized within all four levels of the HEA's (2012) teaching fellowship professional recognition scheme, as mapped onto the UK Professional Standards Framework. HE practitioners urgently need to review our own ways of working if we are not to become stale and repetitive. Two other NTFs, Jan Sellars and Bernard Moss (2016), have produced an eloquent edited collection emphasizing the value of creative powerful physical spaces to promote reflective learning using labyrinths.

Continuous and focused professional development requires a range of additional activities to sustain our teaching practices. These include contributing to the 'community of practice' (Wenger, 1998) that is especially relevant: the community of higher education pedagogy practitioners. We can refresh ourselves regularly by:

- *reading* a selection from the plethora of informal and formal publications produced annually around teaching
- *writing* about the innovations we have introduced and the research we have undertaken on our own practice, so we can ourselves contribute to the discourse
- *sharing* what we have learnt by encouraging others to read and discuss current pedagogic thinking. This could include both helping those new to teaching in universities to develop a research-informed approach as well as upwardly briefing our managers on topics of current relevance
- *networking* through the many live and virtual opportunities available to help us keep up to date. These include not just internal, national and international conferences on pedagogy (for example, the Staff and Educational Developers Association (SEDA) annual conference), but also webinars and tweetchats (see for example, #lthechat: a weekly Wednesday night conversation via Twitter at 8 p.m. GMT).

Conclusion: Recognizing excellent teaching

In the UK in 2015 a national initiative to recognize and reward teaching excellence in British universities was proposed. The Teaching Excellence Framework set out to use publicly available metrics to rate teaching excellence in British universities, with Gold, Silver and Bronze awards given to institutions in relation to their benchmarked HEIs. From the outset, the ambition to find relevant, meaningful and more nuanced metrics, rather than proxies that measure only what is easy to measure has been hugely contentious. The NTF community has been highly prominent in national discussions and eager to see the peer-reviewed NTFS considered among the metrics, but this sadly has not been the case. Instead, other metrics that do not directly relate to teaching are being used, such as salaries on graduation, which clearly reflect existing advantage of university entrants, rather than any evident value added by the higher education institutions. Other controversial metrics under current consideration include contact hours and age/experience of those who teach students.

Other nations, for example Ireland, are similarly seeking to find ways how best to recognize the professionalism of their staff, but the task is not easy. Excellent university teaching is multifaceted, highly diverse, inevitably hard to describe and arguably easy to recognize, which is why blunt systems to evaluate it rarely capture the reality that students and colleagues are delighted to experience. A key purpose in the establishment of a community of NTFs was to provide diverse and inspiring exemplars of outstanding university teaching, and it is encouraging that this aim has been taken forward by successive cohorts of NTFs who have been eager to share with and learn from one another. This book manifestly delivers on our commitment to engage with the wider community of HE practitioners, university leaders, employers, quality assurers and students for, and I have no doubt, our mutual benefit.

References

Adams, A.A. and McCrindle, R.J. (2008) *Pandora's Box: Social and professional issues of the information age.* Chichester: John Wiley and Sons.

Beetham, H. and Sharpe, R. (2013) *Rethinking Pedagogy for a Digital Age: Designing for 21st century learning.* 2nd ed. New York: Routledge.

Bilham, T. (ed.) (2013) *For the Love of Learning: Innovations from outstanding university teachers.* Basingstoke: Palgrave Macmillan.

Brown, S. (2015) *Learning, Teaching and Assessment in Higher Education: Global perspectives.* London: Palgrave Macmillan.

Bryson, C. (2013) 'Creating space for student autonomy and engagement through partnership and letting go'. In Bilham, T. (ed.) *For the Love of Learning: Innovations from outstanding university teachers.* Basingstoke: Palgrave Macmillan, 180–4.

Carroll, J. and Ryan, J. (eds) (2005) *Teaching International Students: Improving learning for all.* London: Routledge.

Conole, G. (2013) *Designing for Learning in an Open World.* New York: Springer.

Gibbs, G. and Coffey, M. (2004) 'The impact of training of university teachers on their teaching skills, their approach to teaching and the approach to learning of their students'. *Active Learning in Higher Education*, 5 (1), 87–100.

HEA (Higher Education Academy) (2012) 'UK Professional Standards Framework'. Advance HE. Online. www.heacademy.ac.uk/ukpsf (accessed 4 April 2018).

HEA (Higher Education Academy) (2018) 'National Teaching Fellowship Scheme'. Advance HE. Online. www.heacademy.ac.uk/individuals/national-teaching-fellowship-scheme/NTF (accessed 4 April 2018).

Killick, D. (2013) 'Building curriculum internationalisation from the bottom up'. In Bilham, T. (ed.) *For the Love of Learning: Innovations from outstanding university teachers.* Basingstoke: Palgrave Macmillan, 142–8.

Killick, D. (2016) *Internationalization and Diversity in Higher Education: Implications for teaching, learning and assessment.* London: Palgrave Macmillan.

Nerantzi, C. (2013) 'OER? What OER? Integrating video OER in a teacher education programme'. *Journal of Perspectives in Applied Academic Practice,* 1 (2), 61–5.

QAA (Quality Assurance Agency) (2018) Quality Assurance Agency. Online. www.qaa.ac.uk/quality-code (accessed 6 April 2018).

Race, P. (2014) *Making Learning Happen: A guide for post-compulsory education.* 3rd ed. London: SAGE Publications.

Ryan, J. (ed.) (2012) *Cross-Cultural Teaching and Learning for Home and International Students: Internationalisation of pedagogy and curriculum in higher education.* London: Routledge.

Salmon, G. (2004) *E-moderating: The key to teaching and learning online.* 2nd ed. London: RoutledgeFalmer.

Salmon, G. (2013) *E-tivities: The key to active online learning.* 2nd ed. New York: Routledge.

Sambell, K., Brown, S. and Graham, L. (2017) *Professionalism in Practice: Key directions in higher education learning, teaching and assessment.* Cham: Palgrave Macmillan.

Sellers, J. and Moss, B. (eds) (2016) *Learning with the Labyrinth: Creating reflective space in higher education.* London: Palgrave Macmillan.

Thomson, S. (2016) 'To what extent do academic staff see an e-learning framework as being effective in supporting technology enhanced learning (TEL) discussions and activities?'. *Journal of Perspectives in Applied Academic Practice,* 4 (2), 2–11.

Wenger, E. (1998) *Communities of Practice: Learning, meaning, and identity.* Cambridge: Cambridge University Press.

Index

3D construction space 81; -making space 71; physical space 241; printing 71, 76

academic citizenship 8; identity xxxviii, 102, 125, 126; self-concept 126; success 124, 132
academic identity xxxviii, 125, 126; place 6, 29; professional xxxiv, 137, 179, 181; student xxxi, 54, 124
academic writing 113, 115, 118
action learning 103, 106, 128; sets 128, 131, 133
action research 73, 103, 104
active learning xxxvi, 7, 12, 14, 45, 67, 81, 130, 133, 201, 250; space 67
adaptive systems 17, 18, 22
adult learners 134; community of xxxi, 224, 226; global 224, 234; passive 245; reflective 7; social 227, 228
adult learning 30, 126
aesthetic xxxiii, 53, 61, 68, 74, 179
agency 96, 98, 99, 113, 188, 212, 216
alchemy 54
ambiguity 88, 89
anxiety xxxiv, xxxiii, xxxv, xxxvii, 97, 108, 114, 117, 127, 132, 140, 247, 156, 250
anxious 104, 179, 246
arts-based approaches 31, 37
attachment 2, 4, 29, 44
audition space 138, 139
augmented reality 74
authentic clinical spaces 175
authentic experience 145; learning 3, 12, 13, 25, 48, 63, 157, 168, 237, 241, 243, 244, 248
authentic locations 7, 163; places xxxviii, 2, 3; spaces 149, 162, 164, 165
authority in teaching 196
autonomy in learning xxxv, 53, 54, 64, 189; student autonomy 94, 138, 140, 150

Barnett, Ron xxxiv, xxxv, 41, 210
Be My ... Valentine 60
becoming xxxv, xxxviii, 46, 89, 97, 137, 139, 174, 179, 181
being, sense of 62
belonging xxxi, xxxii, 2, 4, 5, 31, 41, 54, 62, 98, 124, 127, 131, 181, 222; space xxxi, xxxiv
blended learning 67, 200, 226, 232
Boddington, Anne xxxiv, 234
border crossers 35, 89
borderland spaces 88, 90, 97, 98, 99

boundaries of space 21, 41, 57, 137, 210, 221; disciplinary 165, 166, 205, 255
Boys, Jos xxxiv
'Brand You' 241
breaking boundaries 193
British Council 74, 216, 217, 219, 221
built pedagogy xxxi

café 15, 45, 47, 53, 64, 72, 92
caravan conference xxxvii, 42, 44
Care-O-bot 18
China xxxix, 74, 211, 216, 217, 219
Christensen, Clayton 224
citizenship 8; conference 98; global 209, 216
cMOOCs 225, 228
coaching 23, 106, 143, 150, 155, 156, 171
co-creating, co-creation 74; learning xxxix, 109, 211; knowledge 13, 22, 24, 213, 226
co-curricular spaces 89
co-design 69, 76, 78, 81
Co.lab 81, 82
cognitive authenticity 14; control 117, 121; dissonance 99, 128
co-inquiry 90
collaborative learning xxxviii, xl, 21, 30, 60, 64, 77, 121, 161, 171, 177, 205, 224, 234, 237; space xxxix, 121, 162, 177, 224
collaborative projects 37, 73; international 213
collective learning 54
collegiate spaces 185
communities of learners xxxii, 13, 24, 224; of practice 5, 12, 13, 25, 68, 73, 132, 165, 174, 175, 178, 221
community -based participatory research 34; places 29; spaces xxxviii, 67, 221
Companion Humanoid Autonomous Robot for Living with You (CHARLY) 18
competencies 2, 14, 15, 77, 178; technical 145; cross-cultural 211
conceptual spaces 206
connected teaching 108
constructivist learning xli, 5, 25
constructivist paradigm 8, 113; pedagogies 213, 240
contact zones 90
contemplative pedagogies 50
conversation space 188
co-producers of knowledge 201, 205
creativity xxxv, 48, 53, 68, 113, 115, 126, 138, 167, 239
creative spaces xxxvii, 53, 72, 77
creative writing 49, 50, 115
critical incidents 106, 148, 151, 152
critical pedagogies xli
cross-cultural communication 212; dialogues 214; spaces xxxix; working 211
cross-disciplinary 3, 60; learning xxxvii, 64

260

Index

cultural differences 127, 130, 133; heritage 55; norms 88, 97, 130, 134
curating 60, 62, 217, 221
curriculum space xxxiv, 15, 18, 46, 128, 141, 145, 219

Dautenhahn, Kersten 21
deep engagement with place 166
deep learning 147
'Design for Campus' toolkit 72
Dewey, John 12
dialogical space xxxv, xxxix, 91, 177, 185, 189, 194; pedagogies 98, 256
digital spaces xxxv, 200, 204, 206, 211; digital cultural spaces 216
digital studio 71
disciplinary boundaries 166
discipline networks 212
discourse xxxvi, 18, 115, 177, 181, 257; educational 88, 174
dislocation 6, 7, 35, 199
disruption 32, 53, 56, 59, 61, 77, 89, 93, 99, 145, 167, 187, 199
disruptive innovation 53, 224, 225
distance education 6, 233
distinctive spaces for learning 145
distributed expertise 164, 185; leadership 185; learners 4; learning 13; spaces 2
diversity 64, 89, 124, 132, 133; of opinions 127, 225; of practice 254; of spaces 248
domestic service robot 18
Downes, Stephen 225
Dream Lab 217, 218, 219
Dryburgh, John 69

e-learning 22
educational practice 69, 125, 161, 185, 194; development 196
educative values 102, 107, 111
emoticons 216
enquiry-based learning 14, 15
entrepreneurial 143, 163, 247; flair 45; skills 139, 220; space 138, 143
e-tivities 24
evaluation 20, 22, 24, 53, 59, 79, 99, 111, 168, 194, 203, 229; peer 177; self- 174; student 176, 213
excessive cognitive control 117
experiential learning 2, 3, 29, 37, 63, 91, 103, 126, 129, 145, 147, 149, 165, 167; cycle 151, 155
extra-curricula activities 60, 125
extra-mural space 8, 29, 67, 224

Facebook 92, 202, 212, 213, 215
facilitator 90, 150, 154, 156, 191
feedback from student 16, 105, 125, 162, 167, 189; negative 83, 99

feed-forward 58
felt-sense 54, 115, 119
field teaching 73
fieldwork xxxvi, 14, 15, 22, 220, 221
filmmaking xxxvii, 30, 31, 32, 37, 162, 167, 192
flexible pedagogies 68
flipped classroom 91, 231, 232
formal spaces for learning 68, 121, 149
formative feedback 134, 176
freedom to learn xxxiv, 109, 110
freewriting 115, 119, 121
FutureLearn (FL) 225, 226, 227

galleries xxxiv, 8, 53, 55, 63, 92, 186, 189, 217, 221, 245
'going out' projects 186, 187, 188, 195
'good enough' mother or teacher 114, 117
global classroom xxxix, 209, 211, 212, 216
global space for learning 254

habitus 127, 132
haptic tools 76
Higher education Funding Council for England (HEFCE) 5; pedagogy 253; practitioners 253, 254, 257
heterotopia 56
holding 107, 111, 116; open the space for learning 117
Hong Kong xxxiii, 211, 212, 215
human–computer interaction (HCI) 18
human–robot interaction 17
hybrid learning environment 114; space 114

Iceland xxxiii, xxxvi, 15
'identity box' 241
identity construction 175
imaginative usage 43, 65, 201; teaching spaces 41, 219
inclusion 29, 126, 129, 201, 203
induction of student xxxviii, 46, 124, 126, 131, 133
informal spaces for learning 68, 92
innovation xxxv, 51, 138, 165, 172, 187, 200, 225, 226, 253, 257
intense engagement 166
intentional educational spaces 210
intercultural communication 213
interdisciplinary 13, 69, 164; collaboration 161, 172; culture 255; groups 73; practice 76, 217, 218
interior space xxxiv, xxxviii, 45, 48, 102, 137, 138, 147, 156, 176
international collaboration 14, 213, 216; partnership of students 216; students 18, 126, 130, 210, 212
international space for teaching and learning 210, 221

261

Index

internationalization xxxix, 171, 209, 210, 217, 221
intra muros learning spaces 31
ipsative assessment 58

landscape, campus 7; learning 2, 199, 206; urban 42
learner voice 32; identity 89
learning cycle 142, 151, 152
learning environment 56, 83, 113, 117, 124, 127, 143, 165, 254; virtual 92, 200, 224
learning journey 98, 103, 127, 131, 137, 148, 152; styles 37, 130
legitimate peripheral participation 13
lifelong learning xxx, 2, 30, 137, 154, 209
liminal space (in-between spaces) xxxi, xxxv, 41, 55, 58, 72, 89, 97, 137, 147
live projects 8, 81, 161, 163, 164, 171
Live Projects Network (LPN) 163, 164
livestreaming 202, 204
living theory 107, 108

maker space xxxvii, 68, 71, 74
Maslow, Abraham hierarchy of needs 124
mastery 137, 138
mental space 118, 120, 121
mentorship xi, 13, 54, 92, 138, 143, 148, 150, 181, 186
'messy' research 35, 37
'messy' spaces 89, 99
metaphor of learning 191
mobile devices 175, 176
MOOC 224, 225, 226; space xxxix
museums xxxiii, 53, 56, 64, 92, 168, 217, 245

National Teaching Fellows (NTFs) xxviii, xxx, xxxiii, xl, 252; community xxxii, 48, 257; symposia xxxii, 253
non-traditional learning spaces 37, 53, 142
Northern Ireland 29, 31, 32
novel teaching spaces xxxvii, 51, 88, 89, 209
novelty 53, 88, 94, 97
novice 70, 75, 128, 165, 167; practitioners 174, 175, 178; professional 137, 174
NVivo 93

online courses xxx, 224; design 217; learning space 21, 212
ontological 42, 90, 148; drivers 45; risk 144; space xxxiv, 147
open learning 31, 79
outdoor space 186
outward bound (OB) 129, 131

participatory action research 31, 34; design 68, 169; learners 13

partnership collaborative 31, 37, 60, 82, 164; international 211, 214, 216, 218; learning 97, 106, 107; research 253; student–staff 64, 98, 253, 256
passive learning 132, 228, 245, 248
pedagogical space xxxi, xxxiv, 18, 148, 199
pedagogies xxxii, 32, 88, 98, 102, 142, 154, 161, 185, 199, 218, 226, 253; built xxxi; constructivist 98, 213, 225, 240; contemplative 50; critical xii, 98; dialogic 98; flexible 68; place-based 3, 12; situated 4
peer learning 73, 130, 178, 189, 206, 228; peer-led study 57
peer networks 7, 57
performance space 138, 139, 142
personal development 99, 103, 106, 143, 155, 156, 182, 229, 232
personal space xxxvi, 72
physical space xxx, xxxiv, xl, 41, 53, 63, 69, 76, 93, 102, 188, 199, 201, 204, 240, 246, 248, 257
physical teaching and learning spaces 67, 68, 199, 232, 250
picnic xxxix, 186, 187, 189, 190
place-based education xxxvi, 3, 4, 12, 14, 29, 31
places of adversity 163
play xxxiii, 48, 49, 50, 72, 167, 193; role- 13, 91, 176; -space 114, 121
power dynamics 108
practice-based research xli, 102, 252
practice development 178, 196; space 175, 177, 179, 180
practice environment 175, 182
practice space 174
problem-based learning 13, 22, 255
professional development xxx, xxxv, 41, 46, 102, 175, 226, 252, 256, 257; learning 137, 155, 174, 179, 181, 186, 250
project-based learning 77, 161
psychic space 127
public space 56, 65, 142, 166

Quality Assurance Agency (QAA) 256

rationalist education systems 240
readiness to learn 54, 108, 143, 147, 155
real projects 161, 165
real-world activities 12, 13, 18, 142, 163, 165; learning 3, 23, 217, 218, 231; projects 165; space 17, 94, 161, 237
reflection 2, 30, 47, 72, 77, 89, 102, 116, 127, 132, 141, 147, 175, 212, 240, 243; on and in action 148, 151, 163, 174; on practice 105, 108, 109; self- 121, 124, 176, 181, 204

262

Index

reflective educational approach 240; essays 109, 113, 122; journals 240; mode 114; practice xli, 102, 106, 107, 142, 147, 151, 155, 240, 248; practitioner 106, 109, 240, 244, 249; space xxx, xxxv, xxxix, 157, 174, 204, 205
reflexive 102, 118, 121; self- 138
reflexivity 118, 147
relational spaces xxxiv, xxxix, 18, 20, 147, 150, 180
Republic of Ireland xxxiii, 259
Research Excellence Framework (REF) 232
research-informed learning 21
research-related communities 188
restorative environment 29
risk xxxi, xxxiv, 7, 13, 98, 126, 131, 138, 143, 144, 165, 200, 245, 253; at- 29, 32; averse 200
robotic systems 17
role model 180, 181; -play 13, 91, 176

safe spaces 36, 114, 115, 141, 144
Savin-Baden, Maggi xxxiv, xxxix
scaffold learning 15, 24, 75, 105, 128, 131, 132, 133, 154, 255; reflection 127, 240
scholarship xxxiv, xxxv, 2, 102, 185, 187, 253
science, technology, engineering, mathematics (STEM) 93
self- authorship 88, 90, 96, 97, 147; actualization 124, 143, 151; awareness 51, 147, 150, 154, 240, 246; efficacy 7, 89, 126, 139, 140, 212, 216; esteem 34, 124, 133; renewal 154, 157, 256; study 103, 104, 106, 107; validation 141
sense of place xxxvi, xli, 3, 4, 6, 76, 166
sense of self xxxviii, 54, 102, 104, 113, 126, 145, 166
Singapore xxxiii, 211, 214, 215
situated environment xxxi, 30
social capital 6, 29, 30, 34, 37
social construction of knowledge 3, 5
social learning 161, 181, 200, 237; design 46; spaces 83, 128, 145, 199, 201, 205
social media xxxix, 7, 59, 92, 201, 211, 231; platforms 201, 202, 215, 217
social spaces xxxvi, 2, 68, 127, 174, 186, 187, 194, 201, 202, 204, 205
socio-spatial xxxvi, 3, 206; perspectives 88
soft structures 116
space for performance 137; for practice development 179; for staff learning 185, 187; for the self xxxviii, 102, 104, 110, 113, 147, 157, 237; of action 176, 180; of influence 174, 175, 179; of learning 99, 179, 206; of practice 97, 180, 181; of trust 180

spaciousness 147, 153, 155, 157
spatial agency 165
staff development xxxix, 42 50; learning xxxix, 185, 186, 191; mentoring communities 186
Staff and Educational Developers Association (SEDA) 257
Stanier, Phil 50
storyboarding 19
student engagement 5, 25, 48, 68, 82, 99, 127, 145; and attainment 191
student identity xxxi, 54, 124; journey 137, 210; participation 68, 104; retention 5; voice 109, 125
student-centred xxxviii, 68, 77, 126; learning 8, 53, 150, 202
subject-directed competencies 15

tablet technology 17, 203
taxonomy of learning spaces xxxiv, 41, 137, 237, 248
teacher-centric 67
Teaching Excellence Framework (TEF) xxxii, xl, 257
teaching practice xxx, xl, 103, 105, 107, 164, 189, 211, 218
temporal spaces 164
territory 41, 42, 58, 83, 116, 179
thinking space 181
third space 211, 215
threshold 6, 90, 96, 138; conceptual 98; -space 56
transdisciplinarity 148
transformational 132, 234 impact 124 space 157
transformative 'burn' 164; impact 36, 98, 166, 171, 256; learning 29, 33, 253, 255; potential 90, 200; space 99
transition xxxiii, 6, 56, 89, 124, 125, 133, 137, 140, 174, 181, 191, 226
transitional spaces xxxiv, xxxvii, 55, 103, 111, 140
transmissive pedagogies 91, 240

unconventional spaces and places xxxvii, 141, 144, 161, 237
unfamiliar culture xxxiii, 23; pedagogy 89; space 54, 97, 165, 240, 246; surroundings xxxiii, xl, 23, 60, 93, 88, 127, 171, 245, 248
unusual spaces 47, 250

Vietnam xxxiii, 211, 214, 215
virtual clinics xxxiii, 21, 22; communities of practice 13; networks 3; proximity 24; worlds 4, 89, 92
virtual learning environment (VLE) xxxiv, 8, 25, 92, 200; spaces xxx, xxxiii, xxxviii, 4, 14, 25, 41, 46, 67, 90, 93, 176, 202, 219, 221, 224, 226, 233
virtual reality (VR) 76
visual diary 194; feedback 176

263

Index

visual 'voice' 240
voice xxxiii, 30, 34, 54, 76, 108, 114; learners' 30, 32, 111, 129, 240

Winnicott, D.W. 103, 116
work-based learning xxxv, 147, 148, 154, 178

workplace learning 109, 147
writing block 117; identity 115; voice xxxv, 102, 115, 120

xMOOCs 225, 228

Zimbabwe xxxiii, 216, 219, 220